Marnie Perverzoff

(604) 988-2578

them!

DOGS

An Owner's Guide

DOGS
An Owner's Guide

 Helen Stillwell

Saraband

Published by Saraband (Scotland) Limited
The Arthouse, 752–756 Argyle Street,
Glasgow G3 8UJ, Scotland
hermes@saraband.net

Copyright © 2003 Saraband (Scotland) Ltd.

ISBN 1-887354-33-6

Printed in China

10 9 8 7 6 5 4 3 2 1

Acknowledgments and Photo Credits
The publisher would like to thank the following people for their help in the preparation of this book: Kerry Ryan, editorial assistant and indexer; Phoebe Tak-Yin Wong, graphic design assistant; George Berger and Kathryn Klanderman of the AKC; Mary Bloom. Special thanks are also due to the children who appear with their dogs in the training and behavior photographs in this book, especially: Chloe and Lottie van Grieken, Orlaith and Naoimh Hughes, and Seonaid Weightman.

All photographs in the book are © Nikki L. Fesak unless otherwise listed by page number below:

© **2002 Arttoday.com, Inc**: 8 (both), 9 (all), 10, 56b, 62b, 63b, 64b, 87b, 92t, 121b, 164br, 169bl, 170t, 173b, 193br, 216r (all), 218br, 239 (both); © **Mary Bloom:** 16b, 30 (both), 41t, 55b, 70t, 75t, 100t, 112b, 113t, 115t, 124b, 138l (2nd row), 139tr, 196l (3rd row), 212l (3rd row), 242c (2nd row); © **Comstock, Inc.:** 1, 2, 5, 7bc, 82t, 103b, 118t, 120b, 148t&br, 152r (2nd bottom), 154b, 163bc, 164tl, 166br, 167 (tr, cl, & br), 168t, 169tl, 170bl, 171tl, 183t, 184c, 187br, 202tr, 203tc&bl, 204, 212bc, 214br, 215b, 218bl, 220cl, 221b, 224tc, 232tl, 236bl, 237b, 243tl&tr, 258tl, 249tr; © **Corbis Corporation:** 227t, 240br; **Saraband Image Library:** 148c.

Photographer's Acknowledgments
I would like to acknowledge the kind cooperation of all those who participated in the photography for this book. Many owners and handlers allowed me to photograph their dogs for this volume, and, although space does not permit each person or dog to be listed by name, I am grateful to all—human and canine—for their assistance. Special thanks are also due to those listed below:

The Pet Centre, Dundalk, Co. Louth; Irish Kennel Club; Westminster Kennel Club; American Kennel Club; The Kennel Club and Crufts 2003; Tracy Carlisle and ANCU Veterinary Hospital; Mary Bloom; Le Chien Pet Store, New York; Sara Hunt and Daisy; Orlaith Hughes and Pepsi; Naoimh Hughes and Honey; Roisin Hughes and Sasha; Fearghal Hughes; Maggie Murphy; Helen, Conor, and Megan Hewett and Ellie, Biko, and Tia; Carrick Boarding Kennels; Ronan and Aundrine Milton and Fred and Snowball; Carol and Ronald Brown and Thornton; Lucky the Rescue Dog; Kim Planert and Bruce; Alison Orr and Angus; Daniel Murray; Richard McGivern and Taff; Bega and Knuckles, the Rhodesian Ridgebacks; Anthony Ligorelli; Harriet Kamps and Kamps I've Got a Secret; Rosemary Larkin, Elaine Johnston, and Jubin; Sheri Clark and Jake; Lee Grunewald and Andy; Patricia Martello and Cowboy; Bonnie Yurga and Solomon; Megan Everswick, Diva, and Scooter; Connie Blanken and Sam; Cheri Sullo and Kage; Joan Morningstar and Koj; Jody Alhers, Donald Robinder, and Viv; Tina Toohey and Jack; Lorelei Bacchus and Elle; David and Lari Goldsmith and Jasper; Marilyn Currey and Houston; Barbara O'Maille and Pip; Patricia Huey, Lismoyle Fennel, and Lismoyle Flaxen; Simon Jon and Janet Elizabeth Rudbach and Bailey; Anita Foley Duggan and Tia, Clay, and Elly; John and Noreen Murray and Sly and Misty; C. and G. Matthews and McKenzie and Carie; Norman McDade and Ardlyns Darby O'Gill; Brenda Doyle and Sevenoaks Star Belle; Harry Nelson and Byeways Murphy Himself JW; M. Presland and M. Vincent and Humphrey; Sharon Rainey and Angels Sparkle at Khanthav; Mary Deegan and Terrijay Clermont Ferrand at Tomeilis; John Walsh and Helmlake Blue Gunner at Yandamar; Jackie Hand and Bealinstown Little Lad; Fred and Ruby Brown, Roseyard Seven Towers, Roseyard Mr. Jingles, and Aralders Baskerville at Roseyard; Jane Gostynska and Bubas Soldier Bear; Heather Timmins and Sh Ch Tirsellig McManus; Peter & Belinda Mellor, Celia Hughes, Abbi, Saffron, and Phoenix; Fiona Hurley, Ch Rasara Syma, Kydro Dreamy Maker, Augsberg Holly of Lahume, and Owengarve Royal Rufus of Lahume; Michael Clancy and Ch Milbethan Toddie; Sean Carroll and James Newman and Shadow; Frank Barry, IRCH Baszer Magic Moment and Baszer Celtic Storm; Michelle and Leo Beattie and Jack; Trudy Walsh and Ardbraccan Setters; Natasha Carragher and McGuigan; Casey, Gemma, and most importantly, Sasha, who took care of me and taught me all about dogs even though she never knew she was one.

—*Nikki L. Fesak, 2003*

EDITOR: Sara Hunt
MANAGING EDITOR: Karen Fitzpatrick
ART AND PRODUCTION EDITOR: Deborah Hayes
PHOTOGRAPHY: Nikki L. Fesak
ASSOCIATE EDITOR: M. Jane Taylor

CONTENTS

Introduction

The relationship between humankind and dogs goes back some 40,000 years, to Paleolithic times, when stone-age peoples first tamed wolves to exploit their hunting skills, their love of companionship, and, more practically, their bodily warmth. Both humans and dogs have changed a great deal since that time, but we do share with our ancestors an appreciation of the unquestioning devotion demonstrated by pet dogs for their owners, as well as a great respect for these animals' innate talents as guards, hunters, or simply as friendly companions.

Many people love their dogs devotedly, but the first canine-human relationships were, in all likelihood, more practical than sentimental. Dogs worked to serve their human masters, surviving on any scraps of food they could scavenge, and if they did not please their masters—that is, if they were fearful or aggressive— they were killed. Today, we have the luxury of being able to provide for and protect our animals, and we realize that owning a dog is both a privilege and a responsibility. We do everything we can to ensure that our dogs lead happy and fulfilled lives. Given the ancient relationship between humans and dogs, it is nothing less than they deserve.

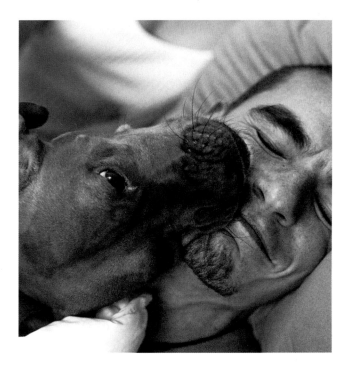

🐾 *The companionship dogs provide is appreciated universally. The photo at left is a 1940s image of the childhood household of Queen Elizabeth II of England, complete with the family pets.*

In return for security, shelter, and food, dogs provide us with companionship and unquestioning loyalty, as well as protection and, thus, comfort, a valuable combination of assets. Anthropologists and behavioral scientists report that dog ownership makes us more rounded and healthy individuals: dogs really are "man's best friend," all across the globe, with more one-third of households owning dogs in the United States, Australia, and France, and a quarter of households owning dogs in Britain. With more than 40 percent of South African and Zimbabwean households also owning dogs, these statistics show that dog ownership is not simply the preserve of the affluent developed world.

There is strong evidence to suggest that stroking a dog lowers blood pressure and diminishes stress and anxiety. Furthermore, one British study found that dog owners are healthier than non-owners, being less prone to headaches, colds, stomach complaints, and back pain. This good health may be the result of taking more exercise with the family pet, and it is probably reinforced by the fact that people who have something to care for enjoy a better quality of life than those who do not.

A Brief History of Dogs

The domestic dog species, *Canis familiaris*, encompasses an extremely diverse range of animals in terms of variety of physical characteristics. Dogs are native to every part of the planet and they have adapted to every geographical area and climate—from the icy Arctic tundra to the searing hot deserts. More than 400 different breeds of dog are recognized around the world, and it is hard to believe that such a wide variety of animals are descended from one common ancestor.

The great nineteenth-century naturalist Charles Darwin found the sheer number of dog breeds so overwhelming that he believed dogs were descended from two wild species, the wolf (*Canis lupus*) and the golden jackal (*Canis aureus*). More recently, however, by analyzing behavior patterns and genetic evidence, experts have decided that domestic dogs are descended exclusively from the wolf. However, wolves themselves vary tremendously in size throughout the world, and this is one factor that explains the diversified appearance of modern-day dogs. For example, the European Gray Wolf (now extant only in parts of Scandinavia, Central Europe, and the Iberian Peninsula) is a close cousin of the North American wolf, but both are far larger than the small Red Wolf, the Mexican Wolf, or the Asiatic or Arab Wolf. Dogs descended from these very different wolves have diverse physical characteristics, not surprisingly.

Wolves are the most widespread and sociable predators on earth, after humans. Some 40,000 years ago, wolf cubs may have been adopted by humans as pets. Paleolithic people were probably as susceptible as their modern descendants are to these small, furry, and (more importantly) warm animals. Like puppies, wolf cubs can be trained, if they are adopted by humans at around three to seven weeks, and they will demonstrate as much affection as dogs do toward their human masters.

Good Breeding

Over time, wolves and humans learned to coexist quite closely. Selective breeding began very early in dogs' association with humans, by the rather crude method of pushing away the small cubs that, for whatever reason, did not please their human companions. Over many generations, local varieties of dogs emerged, their appearance partly governed by climatic and geographical factors. For example, Nordic and mountain dogs have dense, insulating coats, while many African and Asian dogs have short fur. Dogs became valued for their particular skills, such as their speed in pursuit of prey, their abilities as guard dogs, or their reliable herding talents. As early humans settled in permanent villages and their survival became more secure, they could even afford to keep dogs simply for their good looks and companionship. Untroubled by the science of genetics, dog breeders simply understood that mating two large dogs would probably result in another large dog, and that the progeny of two long-legged hunting dogs would produce similar pups.

Over many hundreds of years, the appearance of dogs changed tremendously, with each type of dog being valued for a particular skill. Pointers, retrievers, water dogs, herders, and terriers were bred to assist human hunters, while the very wealthy members of society (such as nobility and royalty) could afford to breed small dogs, simply for their looks and temperament, rather than any utilitarian skills they might possess. Nevertheless, working dogs became the most numerous members of the canine world and were employed as pack animals, watchdogs, herders, hunters of small game, rescue animals, for sport, and even as domestic help (for example, small terriers were sometimes trained as "turnspits," to propel spits of meat hung over a fire).

🐾 *From wild wolf to lap dog, the evolution of dogs over time has led to remarkable diversity in the species.*

Working Dogs

As long ago as 10 B.C., the Roman writer Marcus Terentius Varro noted in *De Re Rustica* that: "There are two kinds [of dog] one for hunting connected with the wild beasts of the woods, the other trained for purposes of defense, and used by shepherds." Canine work has not altered radically over the centuries, although dogs' skills have been adapted to match new inventions and technology. Sight and scent hounds accustomed to hunting were trained as gun dogs from the seventeenth century, and were taught to retrieve shot game or to flush out birds for the huntsmen. Today, tracking dogs, including spaniels, Beagles, German Shepherds, and Labrador Retrievers, are employed both to sniff out illicit drugs or explosives and to help locate injured people at the scene of a disaster, often with great success. Other breeds, such as the Doberman Pinscher, are highly efficient watchdogs and can be trained to restrain rather than injure intruders. Newfoundlands are employed by the air-sea rescue service in France for their great strength and for their ability to rescue swimmers in distress, while St. Bernards are still used in the Alps in mountain search-and-rescue operations. And, even as the world of agriculture becomes more and more technical, Border Collies and other selectively bred sheep- and cattle dogs are still highly valued for their skills in herding livestock.

One of the most valuable areas of canine work is as seeing-eye dogs for the blind or hearing dogs for the deaf. Dogs for the blind were first trained in Germany after World War I, to respond to the needs of soldiers blinded in battle and, by the 1930s, similar schemes had been adopted around Europe, Britain, and in the United States. Golden or black Labrador Retrievers are most commonly used, although German Shepherds are also excellent in this role. Training is rigorous and begins at the age of six weeks, when carefully selected puppies are housed, socialized, and walked by trainers before being assigned, at the age of about two, to act as the eyes of a blind or partially sighted person. Other organizations provide "hearing dogs" for the deaf, training dogs to assist their deaf owners (for example, by alerting them when the telephone or doorbell rings). Dogs are also trained to assist disabled people, with each dog being specially tutored to assist one individual. Finally, Pets As Therapy is an admirable organization that takes specially chosen dogs to visit long-term residents of care homes, hospices, or hospitals, enabling the patients to build up friendships with the animals and to take an active interest in their lives and activities.

Kennel Clubs

At the end of the nineteenth century, various kennel clubs and organizations sought to impose some order on, and to establish definitive standards for, the very many dog breeds already in existence. Dogs had become valued for their good looks as well as for their practical skills, and the very first dog show was held in Birmingham, England, in 1860.

In 1873, the Kennel Club of Great Britain was established and quickly compiled a stud book to document and track the parentage of all purebred dogs. It began with a record of forty breeds and, today, it recognizes 189. It continues to publish the *Breeds Record Supplement*, an invaluable record of registered breeders, their litters,

🐾 *This period illustration depicts a farm dog awaiting his master's command.*

and the transfer of ownership. The Kennel Club's influence over selective breeding began with the announcement that no dog could be exhibited at a show unless it was registered with the Kennel Club; quite simply, it meant that a dog breed was defined as a group of dogs recognized by a kennel club.

Kennel clubs sprang up throughout the world: the French *Société Centrale Canine* was founded in 1882, and the following year, the American Kennel Club opened its offices in New York City.

In the wild, features that interfere with an animal's natural ability to survive would be eliminated by natural selection. But many of the breed standards established by kennel clubs accentuate features that are purely aesthetic (features that have been emphasized by human interference). A prime example is the large heads of bulldogs, a factor emphasized by the breed standard. However, bulldogs' heads have become so large that many bulldog puppies now have to be delivered by cesarean section.

Today, reputable breeders are more aware of hereditary problems, such as deafness or hip dysplasia, and work to remove such unhealthy strains from breeds. Specialist breeders produce healthy dogs for one specific purpose, such as winning on the racetrack (in the case of Greyhounds) or being able to "eye" sheep (in the case of Border Collies). They are constantly working to improve a breed by concentrating the gene pool to emphasize and accentuate the particular talents of their dogs.

Pedigree Dogs

Most countries now have a national canine authority, which has established breed standards for recognized breeds. They also provide support and guidance for breeders and dog owners, as well as running national championship shows for purebred dogs. A dog is defined as a pedigree animal if it can claim purebred parents and can prove an inheritance of purebred forebears. Unless the parentage of a dog is certain, it cannot be registered with national kennel clubs.

Dog breeds are divided into a number of groups, which vary slightly from country to country. The groups are somewhat arbitrary, but have some reference to the work the breed originally carried out. The *Fédération Cynologique Internationale* (FCI) was formed to impose international standards on the var-

Two popular small breeds: the Skye Terrier and Smooth Fox Terrier.

ious national systems of organization. This book has used the American Kennel Club's system of organizing the many breeds into groups.

How to Use This Book

This book is intended for all dog lovers, regardless of their experience of dogs, and it will also prove useful to those contemplating the great leap into the world of dog ownership. The first section profiles the breeds recognized by the American Kennel Club, noting the size and characteristics of each type, with icons (see below) symbolizing key features of each breed. Packed with useful facts and photographs, it will help prospective owners choose a dog that is right for their lifestyle and family circumstances.

The remaining chapters address all the issues associated with dog owning; among them: what sort of dog to choose, how to prepare your home, how to care for a puppy, the pros and cons of neutering, as well as information on obedience training, health, and first aid. Practical subjects, such as training, are illustrated in a series of simple step-by-step routines. There are suggestions for dealing with behavioral problems that may arise, as well as an explanation of the origins of canine habits. Finally, there is a brief introduction to the world of dog shows and competitions.

Key to Icons

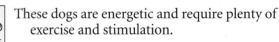 Breeds featuring this symbol tend to make good watchdogs.

 These dogs are energetic and require plenty of exercise and stimulation.

Considerable grooming will be necessary to maintain the coat condition.

 Well socialized dogs of this breed are usually (though not necessarily) good with children.

 These dogs usually respond well to obedience training.

I
The Breeds

Toy Dogs

The miniature size and the cute expressions of toy breeds have always exerted a certain fascination and lent them an enduring appeal. These dogs were once highly prized by royalty and the wealthy, in times past when it was fashionable to have a "lap dog"—partly as a fashion accessory and partly for their warmth. (As a matter of fact, all the dogs in the toy group today are small enough to curl up in one's lap.) Toy dogs appear in court portraits from the sixteenth century onwards, and some painters (such as Hogarth, who painted his own pet Pug) included them in their own self-portraits.

Some toy breeds, like the Affenpinscher, are naturally small dogs, while others, such as Pugs and Italian Greyhounds, are descended from working dogs whose size has been bred down over generations of selective miniaturization. They all make excellent pets for owners with limited space and, in general, they are easier to take care of than larger dogs: they eat less, require less exercise, and their size makes them easier to control in many respects than larger dogs.

Size can be deceptive, however, as many toy breeds have larger-than-life characters—and it is not uncommon to find a toy fearlessly defending its home and human family against much larger opponents (either real or perceived), often with persistent barking.

Affenpinscher

Playful and mischievous, Affenpinschers are among the oldest of the toy breeds. They originated in central Europe, and their name translates (from the German) as "Monkey-terrier," while the French refer to them as "mustachioed little devils." Both names are highly suitable for this wiry-haired, energetic dog. Active, tough, and agile enough to catch mice and rats—as they were bred to do in kitchens, granaries, and stables—this breed's moderate exercise needs can be met by playing indoors and by short walks on a leash.

Temperament Due to its sense of humor and desire to entertain, the Affenpinscher makes a fun member of the family. Members of this breed show great loyalty and affection to master and friends alike.

Appearance Square-proportioned and compact, Affenpinschers are small and terrierlike. The rough, short coat is neat but shaggy, and longer and harsher on the head, neck, chest, stomach, and legs; the face is covered in coarse hair with a beard and moustache. Various colors are seen, but black, silver, gray, red, and black and tan predominate. Widely spaced, prominent eyes and a round face with a short muzzle give this dog its monkeylike appearance.

Size & weight Height at withers 9–11 in. (23–28 cm); 7–9 lb. (3–4 kg)

Exercise needs Moderate   **Grooming** Moderate   **Life expectancy** 12–14 years

Points to consider Affenpinschers like to bark and climb; they can be irritable and difficult to train.

Brussels Griffon (Griffon Bruxelles)

The Brussels Griffon is the product of European interbreeding over many generations. In Belgium they were used by the coachmen of Brussels as ratters to kill stable vermin. The breed was crossed with a Pug in the 1800s, which led to the smooth-coated version, and later crosses may have included Yorkshire Terriers and spaniels.

Temperament This is a good family pet that is entertaining and sensitive, but also full of self-importance.

Appearance With a small, puglike face, which is covered in harsh hair, the Brussels Griffon's dark eyes peer out with a determined glint. The jaw is naturally undershot and the forehead is domed. Thickset, compact, well balanced, and well boned for its size, the breed has a purposeful trot and moderate reach. The rough coat is wiry, with longer hair on the head and around the eyes, nose, cheeks, and chin to form a fringe; or smooth with short, glossy hair all over. Colors seen are red, belge (mixed red-brown and black), black and tan, or black.

Size & weight Height at withers 7–10 in. (18–25 cm); 8–12 lb. (3.5–5.5 kg)

Exercise needs Moderate   **Grooming** Minimal

Life expectancy 12–15 years

Points to consider Brussels Griffons have a tendency to bark and climb.

Papillon

Well known as companions to the noble ladies of Europe and subjects of famous paintings, Papillons are charming and vivacious, but have also retained a certain degree of toughness (a remnant from their gun-dog ancestors). This breed is easily distinguished from other dogs by its butterfly ears, for which it is named.

Temperament The Papillon can be trained to a high level of obedience and relishes mental stimulation. It is responsive, playful, affectionate, and usually good with children, although some can be timid.

Appearance The abundant coat is long, silky, straight, flowing, and principally white; it is decorated with patches of color on the ears, head, and torso. Traditional markings on the head and ears emphasize the butterfly illusion.

Size & weight Height at withers 8–11 in. (20–28 cm); 9–10 lb. (4–4.5 kg)

Exercise needs Low to moderate   **Grooming** Moderate   **Life expectancy** 12–15 years

Points to consider These dogs are a good choice for people in small apartments.

(Australian) Silky Terrier

Bred in Australia from Australian Terriers and Yorkshire Terriers, these blue-and-tan terriers were established as a separate breed at the beginning of the twentieth century.

Temperament Silkies are bold, inquisitive, and full of character. They can be aggressive toward other dogs and pets and are inclined to be yappy. Intelligent with a mischievous streak, these dogs enjoy brisk play and exercise.

Appearance Silky Terriers have a piercing, inquisitive expression. They are longer than they are tall, with a refined bone structure, but they retain the strength to kill small rodents. The Silky Terrier's straight, single coat is its crowning glory, and it follows the body outline. This dog is virtually odorless and nonshedding, but its coat needs to be brushed for about ten minutes every day to keep it shining and free of mats.

Size & weight Height at withers 9–10 in. (23–25 cm); 8–11 lb. (3.5–5 kg)

Exercise needs Moderate   **Grooming** Considerable

Life expectancy 11–14 years

Points to consider This dog barks a lot.

Yorkshire Terrier

Yorkshire Terriers were originally bred in England by Yorkshire miners who wanted dogs small enough to carry in their pockets to chase rats underground in the mines. These tough, industrial origins rather belie the pampered appearance of many Yorkies today, but they remain tough dogs at heart. They do not require a great deal of exercise, but they love playing and interacting with their family.

Temperament The breed seems oblivious to its small stature and can be aggressive with strange dogs and small animals. Inquisitive and adventurous, Yorkies have a tendency to bark a lot, but they can be trained not to. Unsurprisingly, they make good watchdogs.

Appearance Dark, steel-blue, and tan colors are trademark characteristics of this breed. The coat is parted along the back and hangs evenly straight down the sides of the body. It should be brushed or combed every day. Their tails are usually docked to medium length and held high. Heads are small and the ears V-shaped, while the rest of the body is compact.

Size & weight Height at withers 8–9 in. (20–23 cm); 7 lb. (3.2 kg)

Exercise needs Low

Grooming Considerable

Life expectancy 14–16 years

Points to consider This breed is prone to several hereditary health problems. Yorkies are not reliable with young children and often show aggression toward other dogs. They should be thoroughly trained and socialized early.

Despite their small size, Yorkies are feisty and very assertive and are rarely seen sitting still. This dog is groomed for showing; the hair can be parted at the top of the head rather than tied with a bow.

Shih Tzu

"Shih Tzu" translated means "lion dog," and these gentle lapdogs were favorites of the royal family in China during the Ming Dynasty, who put considerable effort into their breeding. They were originally exhibited as Lhasa Terriers or Tibetan Poodles, and only after 1934 were they given separate breed status—being dubbed with their colloquial Chinese name Shih Tzu.

Temperament Shih Tzus make lively companions and love to play and romp around, but they can be surprisingly stubborn. They need daily exercise of some sort, either a short walk or vigorous games. They do not do well in humid and hot environments.

🐾 *It is easy to see why Shih Tzus have become known as fashionable accessories, but it takes work to maintain the coat in this condition.*

Appearance The Shih Tzu has a proud bearing and an aristocratic carriage, with the head held high and the tail elegantly curved over its back. Their luxurious coat hides a sturdy body and smooth, effortless stride. The long, dense double coat is mostly straight and comes in any color. Grooming needs are considerable; the coat needs brushing or combing every day and clipping occasionally.

Size & weight Height at withers 8–11 in. (20–28 cm); 9–16 lb. (4–7 kg)

Exercise needs Low to moderate

Grooming Considerable

Life expectancy 11–14 years

Points to consider This dog does not tolerate extremes of temperature.

Havanese

Related to the Bichon (Barbichon) family of small dogs, which originated in the Mediterranean (possibly on the island of Malta), today's Havanese is descended from the dogs that were brought to Cuba, where they served as pampered pets of the wealthy. These dogs are also known as Habeneros and as "White Cubans." The breed eventually declined, but was revived when three Havanese-owning families moved to the United States, where the breed has grown steadily in popularity.

Temperament The Havanese is an affectionate, equable dog that is friendly with children.

Appearance This is a small, sturdy, short-legged dog with a unique gait that is lively and springy. The profuse double coat is wavy or slightly curled, and can be any color or combination of colors. The head is slightly pointed, and the large, dark eyes are covered by a long fringe of hair.

Size & weight Height at withers 8–11 in. (20–28 cm); 7–13 lb. (3–6 kg)

Exercise needs Low to moderate

Grooming Moderate

Life expectancy 12–14 years

Points to consider This breed tends to be vocal, but it responds well to training.

🐾 *These irrepressibly cute dogs have a distinguished history as circus performers; they are very playful and are always eager to please.*

Maltese

The Maltese originated almost 3,000 years ago on the Mediterranean island of Malta, where this breed's isolation has led to a fabulous canine specimen. They are striking dogs with big characters and gregarious natures. They enjoy daily indoor romps and a short walk on a leash, but they are not great outdoor dogs.

Temperament Maltese are good-tempered pets, but they are inclined to be irritable with small children. They are hardy, spirited animals with a trusting, lively nature.

Appearance When trotting along, this diminutive breed looks like it is floating on air, as the Maltese is covered in long, flat, silky hair that hangs to the ground. The coat color is white, with a hint of gray or lemon. Grooming care can be time consuming, involving combing every one to two days. Also, the white hair may be difficult to keep clean.

Size & weight Height at withers 9–10 in. (23–25 cm); 4–7 lb. (2–3 kg)

Exercise needs Low

Grooming Moderate

Life expectancy 12–14 years

Points to consider These dogs may bark a lot and, despite their size, will tend to challenge bigger dogs. They should be socialized with other dogs at an early age to counteract this tendency.

Poodle (Toy)

All varieties of Poodle are closely associated with France, although they probably originated in Germany. The early Poodle varieties became valuable water-hunting companions; from there they were drawn into military service and then later used as seeing-eye and watchdogs. Some of their exotic clips arose from practicality and necessity, from the days when the breeds were working dogs. Today, Poodles have become renowned as chic accessories for fashionable ladies, particularly in France. At one time, Poodles nearly died out in America, but in the 1930s the breed was revived and has gone on to become the world's most popular dog. They are generally elegant in appearance, with a light, springy step that stems from their working retriever stock.

Did You Know?

🐾 Poodles are agile, eminently trainable, and eager to please; they often appeared in circuses in the early twentieth century. It is likely that many of the Poodle clips derive from this time, especially the pom-pom effect popular on the legs of many dogs.

Temperament Intelligent and independent dogs, Poodles need lots of mental stimulation. A short daily walk or indoor games are recommended to keep them occupied.

Appearance There are many guidelines for the clips and appearance of show Poodles. Family pets are usually left unclipped, except for regular maintenance clips, which should be done at least four times each year. The coat is curly, harsh, and can be dense; any solid color is acceptable. Poodles have straight, narrow muzzles, bright eyes, and ears covered by wavy hair.

Size & weight Height at withers 10 in. (25 cm) or under; 4–8 lb. (2–3.5 kg)

Exercise needs Moderate

Grooming Moderate

Life expectancy 12–14 years

Points to consider These dogs are prone to eye and hip problems; take care to find a reputable breeder.

Chinese Crested

The two versions of this breed, the Powderpuff and Hairless varieties, are distinctive and yet likely to be born in the same litter. This breed was thought to have originated in China in the thirteenth century (perhaps bred from African hairless dogs, which were reduced in size by the Chinese), and to have traveled to the West with traders who used them as ratters on ships. The Powderpuff variety tends to have a heavier build, but otherwise these dogs are almost identical (except for the coverage of hair). The Hairless variety is not bred for the outdoors and should wear protective clothing on cold-weather outings.

Temperament Chinese Cresteds are devoted to family and have an innate willingness to please. They are friendly and affectionate and make good watchdogs. They are good with children, though nervous of young children.

Appearance The Chinese Crested is a lean dog, with a narrow ribcage and plain or spotted skin. The Hairless variety has silky hair on the ears, head (crest), tail (plume), and lower legs (socks). Where hair is absent, the skin is soft and smooth and lightens in color in the summer. The small head has well-defined features, appealing dark eyes, and large ears that are emphasized by the long hair on the head. The Powderpuff has a slightly more robust construction, with a deep chest and better protection against cold weather in the form of a soft double coat of moderate density and length. Powderpuffs need brushing two to three times weekly, and Hairless dogs require skin protection, with the application of sun block as appropriate. In both varieties, the hair is white.

Size & weight Height at withers 11–13 in. (28–33 cm); 5–12 lb. (2–5.5 kg)

Exercise needs Moderate   **Grooming** Moderate   **Life expectancy** 13–15 years

Points to consider Hairless Chinese Cresteds are prone to sunburn and should be protected from the cold.

Did You Know?

From Africa to China and the West, the Chinese Crested has a complex history. Some sources believe that these dogs were owned and bred by the Han Dynasty in China, where they were valued as lapdogs for their affectionate, gentle nature.

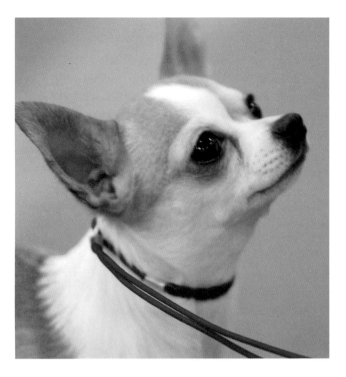

Chihuahua

Chihuahuas were "discovered" in Chihuahua, Mexico, in about 1850, after which a few were taken to North America, where they became popular lapdogs. One of the breed's progenitors was likely the Techichi, bred by the Toltecs at least as early as the ninth century A.D. The popularity of the Chihuahua has gradually increased over the years and was particularly intense after Xavier Cugat (the King of Rumbas) was seen with one in his arms. Fragile and apparently delicate, Chihuahuas are not keen on the outdoors, and most can get enough daily exercise merely by running around indoors.

Temperament Reserved with strangers and often devoted to one person, Chihuahuas can be temperamental. They are intelligent dogs, very involved in the world around them, and usually quite vocal in offering their opinion.

Appearance Known for being the smallest dog breed, the Chihuahua is only slightly longer than tall. It has an alert, terrierlike attitude, and it can move swiftly. There are two coat varieties—long-haired and short-haired. The short coat is soft and glossy, while the long coat has soft, straight to wavy hair and fringed ears. Both types require a minimal amount of grooming. Coat color varies but is most commonly fawn, red, or white. Chihuahuas have distinctive round heads, neat faces, prominent ears, and bright, intelligent eyes.

Did You Know?

🐾 It is believed that these small dogs may have come about from the crossbreeding of a Chinese Hairless dog (imported from Chinese traders) with the native Techichi in South America.

Size & weight Height at withers 6–9 in. (15–23 cm); not to exceed 6 lb. (2.5 kg)

Exercise needs Minimal

Grooming Minimal

Life expectancy 13–14 years

Points to consider This breed has no major health concerns, but there is a common breed trait of a soft spot in the skull (molera), due to incomplete frontal closure. This breed is a popular choice of pet for apartment dwellers and makes an excellent companion for an elderly person, as it does not require vigorous exercise and has a loyal temperament.

English Toy Spaniel

The English Toy Spaniel (known in the UK as the King Charles Spaniel) shares an identical early history with the Cavalier King Charles Spaniel. Popular as "comforters" or companion dogs, spaniels grew in popularity during the seventeenth century, partly because of the fashion set by King Charles II. These dogs are not overly active, but they do enjoy a walk on a leash and fun games.

🐾 *These gentle, appealing dogs are eager to please and usually shine in obedience classes. They are very affectionate with children, though they are easily overwhelmed by boisterous and young children.*

Temperament Although sometimes reserved and calm, English Toy Spaniels are also affectionate and playful. They are excellent lapdogs and are devoted to their family.

Appearance English Toy Spaniels are compact dogs with long, silky coats in an attractive combination of colors. They are shown as four varieties: the red and white Blenheim; the black, tan, and white Prince Charles; the mahogany-red Ruby; and the black and tan King Charles. With domed heads, they have undershot jaws and turned-up noses, dark, wide-set eyes, and an appealing expression.

Size & weight Height at withers 10–11 in. (25–28 cm); 8–14 lb. (3.5–6.5 kg)

Exercise needs Minimal

Grooming Moderate

Life expectancy 10–12 years

Points to consider This breed is prone to knee problems (patella luxation) and tends to have sensitivity to anesthesia; soft spot in the skull, due to incomplete closure, is also sometimes seen.

Cavalier King Charles Spaniel

Appealing and attractive small dogs, Cavalier King Charles Spaniels are among the most popular toy dogs. They were admitted to the AKC's Toy group as a separate breed in 1996. One appalling consequence of their popularity, however, is that inbreeding has increased their tendency toward fatal heart conditions. Cavaliers enjoy a long walk and run, and they are quite athletic, despite their size.

Temperament Their cheerful characters make them ideal companion dogs. They are friendly toward other dogs and pets and very affectionate toward people.

Appearance An elegant spaniel, slightly longer than it is tall, this breed combines many of the qualities of a toy and a gundog. It retains the build of the working spaniel, but everything is smaller. The silky coat, of moderate length, has a slight wave, but no curl, and is feathered around the long ears and feet. These spaniels typically have gentle expressions, with large, dark eyes, short muzzles, and long, feathered ears, low-set and close to the face. The placid nature of these animals tends to encourage the feeding of tidbits, which can lead to weight problems. The coat can appear in a variety of colors, from ruby, black and tan, and tricolor, to Blenheim (a mix of chestnut and white).

Did You Know?

🐾 Cavalier King Charles Spaniels have been popular at least since the seventeenth century, when they appeared in Van Dyck's portrait of King Charles II. Even before that date, they were known as comforter dogs and were used as lap and feet warmers!

Size & weight Height at withers 12–13 in. (30–33 cm); 13–18 lb. (6–8 kg), proportionate to height

Exercise needs Moderate

Grooming Moderate—once- or twice-weekly brushing

Life expectancy 9–11 years

Points to consider This breed has common chronic heart disease (mitrial valve insufficiency).

🐾 *These sweet-natured dogs make excellent companions for city dwellers.*

Japanese Chin

A favorite lapdog of the noble and royal ladies of China and Japan, a pair of Chins was presented to Queen Victoria by the American Commodore Matthew Perry upon his return from the East. Subsequently, traders imported more of these dogs to both Europe and North America. The cheerful and good-natured Japanese Chin has a distinctive expression and an extremely dainty character.

Temperament Japanese Chins are responsive and affectionate to those they know, but they can be reserved with strangers. A dog that enjoys a quiet existence, Chins do not make suitable pets for young children (although these dogs do like boisterous games).

Appearance Small and lively, with an aristocratic look, Japanese Chins have large wide-set eyes and a short undershot jaw. Their single abundant coat stands out from the body and is silky and straight, but the overall appearance is square. Colors are black and white or red and white. The plumed tail is arched over the back.

Size & weight Height at withers 8–11 in. (20–28 cm); 4–7 lb. (2–3 kg)

Exercise needs Low to moderate

Grooming Moderate   **Life expectancy** 12–14 years

Points to consider This breed does not tolerate heat well.

Pomeranian

The smallest of the five German Spitz breeds and retaining a lot of the character of their larger cousins, Pomeranians make good watchdogs and can produce a shrill yapping that may deter intruders. They need a daily walk or session of indoor play, and the thick double coat needs brushing once or twice a week.

Temperament The intelligent and extroverted Pomeranian is an energetic dog, although it can be reserved toward strangers.

Appearance A warm, soft undercoat is combined with a harsh outer coat that stands off the body and gives this breed a puffed-up appearance. The coat is normally one color—orange, black, tan, cream, or white. It has a small ruff, erect ears, and a tail that arches over the back and is carried flat.

Size & weight Height at withers 8–11 in. (20–28 cm); 3–7 lb. (1.4–3 kg)

Exercise needs Moderate   **Grooming** Moderate   **Life expectancy** 12–16 years

Points to consider This dog tends to bark excessively.

Pekingese

Highly prized in China during the Tang Dynasty, the Pekingese were carefully bred for centuries before making an appearance in the West A type of sacred "Foo Dog," they were known as sleeve dogs because they could be carried in the large sleeves of their masters. Many were pampered by personal servants in the imperial palaces, where they were treated like royalty. These long-haired, distinctive-looking dogs are sensitive to heat and should be kept cool in warm weather. Their exercise needs can be met with a leisurely walk.

Temperament Pekingese dogs can be playful, but they are probably not active enough to play with most children. They can be exasperatingly stubborn, but they make good-natured and devoted companions.

Appearance This is a compact, long-haired dog with a pear-shaped body, heavy forelimbs, and lighter hindquarters. It has an unhurried gait with a slight roll brought about by bowed legs. The Pekingese has a thick undercoat and a long, coarse outercoat (in any color), which is straight and stands off the body; it is profusely feathered on the ears, tail, legs, and toes, and needs a great deal of grooming. The nose appears almost squashed between the large, bright eyes.

Size & weight Height at withers 6–9 in. (15–23 cm); not to exceed 14 lb. (6.5 kg)

Exercise needs Minimal   **Grooming** Considerable   **Life expectancy** 13–15 years

Points to consider These dogs are susceptible to corneal abrasions, they are often sensitive to anesthesia, and puppies must often be delivered by cesarian. Pekingese tend to be aggressive with other dogs.

Pug

Another toy breed that can trace its history to China (it was the favored pet of the Tibetan Buddhist monasteries), the Pug is frequently seen in tiny carvings, or *netsuke*, which confirm how little the breed has changed over thousands of years. It has many of the features of the eastern mastiff breeds from which it was miniaturized, including a distinctive expression. This dog's wrinkles must be cleaned and thoroughly dried to prevent infections and dermatitis; a daily walk and occasional brush of its coat to remove dead hairs are its only other care requirements.

Temperament Pugs are highly affectionate and they make good watchdogs. They are playful and generally willing to please, but they can be stubborn and seemingly convinced of their own importance. Tough and hardy dogs, they are rarely aggressive.

Appearance Although compact, Pugs hide a big dog in a small shell. They have a large forehead with deep wrinkles, and traditionally a black mask. The coat is fine, smooth, and short, and can be apricot-fawn, black, or silver in color. Surprisingly fast for a stocky dog, their gait is strong and jaunty with a slight roll about the hindquarters. The short nose can cause breathing problems in hot weather, and in general, Pugs are not very tolerant of heat or humidity.

Size & weight Height at withers 10–11 in. (25–28 cm); 14–18 lb. (6.5–8 kg)

Exercise needs Minimal

Grooming Minimal

Life expectancy 12–15 years

Points to consider This dog wheezes and snores, and is prone to obesity and corneal abrasions.

Did You Know?

🐾 Pugs were a favorite companion of Josephine, the wife of Napoleon Bonaparte. She is said to have contrived to get her pet to carry messages to her husband during his imprisonment.

Miniature Pinscher

Developed in Germany in the 1800s, the Miniature Pinscher gained international recognition in the early twentieth century. One of the more energetic breeds, the Miniature Pinscher is an athletic, racy dog.

Temperament These dogs are self-possessed, busy, playful, and bold, and they have good watchdog abilities. They are courageous animals, who will snap at animals larger than themselves, and they retain a strong ratting ability.

Appearance With a narrow, tapering head and erect ears, this is a remarkably alert and upstanding breed. "Minpins" have a strong muzzle, small catlike feet, and a high-stepping gait. The tail is set high and frequently docked. Coat colors are clear red, stag red (with intermingling black hairs), black with rust-red, or chocolate with rust-red. The coat is smooth, hard, and short.

Size & weight Height at withers 10–12 in. (25–30 cm); 8–10 lb. (3.5–4.5 kg)

Exercise needs Moderate   **Grooming** Minimal   **Life expectancy** 12–14 years

Points to consider The Miniature Pinscher has a low tolerance to cold; it is not an outdoor dog.

Italian Greyhound

This breed is believed to have originated in areas of Turkey and Greece more than 2,000 years ago. Prized for its elegance and beauty, the Italian Greyhound's fragile proportions mean it is never raced like the larger sight hounds. A daily outdoor run or walk on a leash is enough exercise for this miniature breed.

Temperament Italian Greyhounds are equable dogs that enjoy a comfortable indoor life.

Appearance The Italian Greyhound is a sight hound in a reduced package and embodies similar characteristics to a full-sized Greyhound. However, the fine-boned structure means that fractures are a likely hazard, although these dogs are otherwise hardy. The coat is short and glossy, and grooming is minimal (requiring only the occasional brushing to remove dead hair). The head is well proportioned, with the skull and muzzle being of equal length. Large eyes and the dog's habit of holding its head on one side often give it a quizzical appearance.

Size & weight Height at withers 13–15 in. (33–38 cm); 7–14 lb. (3–6.5 kg)

Exercise needs Moderate   **Grooming** Minimal   **Life expectancy** 13–14 years

Points to consider Care should be taken in households with energetic children, as this dog can be easily injured. These are ideal dogs for city dwellers.

Toy Manchester Terrier (English Toy Terrier)

The Toy Manchester Terrier is descended from small Manchester Terriers, with a dash of Italian Greyhound, which shows itself in the breed's slightly arched back.

Temperament Although exhibiting typical terrier character traits, this breed is very gentle (though its inquisitiveness can lead it to chase small animals). Toy Manchester Terriers are lively companion dogs and especially suitable for city dwellers.

Appearance Sleek, racy, and compact, the Manchester Terrier is longer than it is tall, with a slightly arched topline and a keen, alert expression. The wedge-shaped head is topped by large, erect ears with pointed tips (when cropped). The short, dense coat is a glossy black and a rich mahogany tan.

Size & weight Height at withers 10–12 in. (25–30 cm); not to exceed 12 lb. (5.5 kg)

Exercise needs Moderate   **Grooming** Minimal   **Life expectancy** 14–16 years

Points to consider This breed sometimes displays aggression.

Toy Fox Terrier (American Toy Terrier)

The Toy Fox Terrier is the product of determined and deliberate crosses between Manchester Terriers, small Smooth Fox Terriers, and Chihuahuas. This has created a robust breed that makes an excellent companion and show dog.

Temperament Good in obedience and agility trials, this breed likes to be the center of attention. Its personality is influenced by its stock: Typically terrier, but with a milder disposition. Animated, eager to please, and loyal to its owners, these dogs are not easily intimidated. Intelligent animals, they are easy to train and have proved highly capable as hearing dogs for the deaf.

Appearance Elegant, athletic, and well balanced, this breed has a short, fine, and glossy coat with a small (but distinct) ruff; colors are white and tan, tricolor, or black and white. The large V-shaped ears are erect, pointed, and set high on the head. Large, dark eyes are set wide apart, and the head has a well-defined stop. Toy Terriers are naturally well groomed, with intelligent, eager expressions. The tail may be docked (simply for aesthetic reasons).

Size & weight Height at withers 8–11 in. (20–28 cm); 4–7 lb. (2–3 kg)

Exercise needs Moderate   **Grooming** Minimal

Life expectancy 13–14 years

Points to consider This breed has no particular health problems.

Hounds

The breeds of the hound group are among those that have worked most closely in cooperation with humans, having helped us to hunt and survive. They are particularly devoted to their masters and, in return, they have earned great respect and admiration.

The hounds are divided into two groups: sight hounds, which pursue quarry mainly by visual contact; and scent hounds, which hunt with the exceptional canine sense of smell. The French have contributed a great deal to the breeding of scent hounds, partly because successive French kings and their retainers used them to flush game from all corners of the extensive royal forests. Scent hounds are usually quite happy to coexist with other dogs and are at their happiest when using their formidable scenting abilities to follow a trail. Most scent hound breeds are squarely proportioned, standing as tall at the shoulder as their body is long (the short-legged Bassets being one notable exception). Sight hounds, in comparison, are more aerodynamic, sleek, and graceful creatures—being long-limbed and often deep-chested, supporting a large lung capacity that enables them to pursue prey at high speed. A characteristic of many of the hound breeds is their ability to produce the distinctive (and, for many people, unnerving) sound called baying.

As pets, hounds are energetic dogs that need plenty of exercise, including long daily walks and/or a long run off the leash every day. They are not especially territorial, but they do retain a strong instinct to chase prey-sized creatures—be they rabbits, squirrels, cats, or simply sticks, balls, and other toys— so they should be exercised in a secure area.

Greyhound

Greyhounds have been prized for thousands of years for their speed, agility, and keen-sighted hunting skills. They closely resemble the dogs depicted in ancient Assyrian and Egyptian carvings; and for this reason, some claim that they are the most purebred dogs on earth. They are certainly among the fastest dogs in the world, capable of reaching speeds up to 43 mph (69 km/h). Greyhound racing began to become popular in fifteenth-century England.

Temperament Greyhounds are gentle, affectionate, and intelligent dogs, sometimes timid but usually good with children. They are not always reliable with cats and smaller dogs.

Appearance With narrow waists, large chests, and long, well-boned legs, Greyhounds are streamlined dogs. They have long, narrow skulls, long muzzles, and small, neat ears. Their coats range in color from black to white, through various shades of fawn, red, and brindle (streaked or spotted with a darker color).

Size & weight Height at withers 27–30 in. (27–32 kg); 60–70 lb. (27–32 kg)

Exercise needs Considerable　　　**Grooming** Minimal　　　**Life expectancy** 10–12 years

Points to consider Without adequate attention and exercise, Greyhounds will become restless and bored, which may lead to problem behaviors. They should be exercised in fenced areas only because they chase other animals.

Pharaoh Hound

These dignified dogs have a long, venerable ancestry. Pharaoh Hounds originated in ancient Egypt, where they have existed for more than two thousand years. In Malta, where the Pharaoh Hound is the national dog, they are bred for rabbit hunting. With their keen hearing and eyesight, they make excellent watchdogs.

Temperament Pharaoh Hounds are affectionate with children and people they know, but may be wary of strangers and are not reliable with unfamiliar children. They are generally obedient and easy to train.

Appearance They are characterized by their large, pricked ears. They have intelligent, alert expressions and well-defined, tapered heads and muzzles. The neck is long and muscular, amber eyes are deep-set with good binocular vision, and the nose is flesh-colored, although it flushes when the dog is excited. The short, glossy coat is a deep red color.

Size & weight Height at withers 21–25 in. (53–63 cm); 45–55 lb. (20–25 kg)

Exercise needs Considerable

Grooming Minimal　　　**Life expectancy** 12–14 years

Points to consider These dogs are likely to chase cats.

Ibizan Hound

Tall and agile, Ibizan Hounds share the body type of the dogs that are depicted in ancient Egyptian carvings. It is said that Phoenician sailors brought these dogs to the island of Ibiza in the eighth century, and that Hannibal took some of them along on his famous campaigns across the Alps. Today, Ibizan Hounds are popular throughout Spain, where they are used as watchdogs or to hunt rabbits and hares.

Temperament Ibizan Hounds are even-tempered, affectionate family dogs, but they can be suspicious of strangers. Early, supervised exposure to children, in particular, is recommended.

Appearance Characterized by large, mobile, erect ears, Ibizan Hounds are elegant dogs with long skulls and muzzles, straight backs, and long, powerful legs. The eyes are widely set, and the nose is flesh-colored. The coat may be either smooth or wiry, with colors ranging from white to fawn, red, tan, and mixtures of these.

Size & weight Height at withers 22–29 in. (56–74 cm); 42–55 lb. (19–25 kg)

Exercise needs Considerable—daily vigorous exercise is required.

Grooming Moderate   **Life expectancy** 12 years

Points to consider Because of their great jumping ability, it is recommended that Ibizan owners have access to secure, high-fenced exercise areas.

Whippet

Whippets were originally bred to capture small game. Their speed made them famous as racing dogs—hence their nickname, the "poor man's race-horse." The breed was popularized in many mining areas of England, where, up to World War I, Whippet racing was popular. These dogs have been known to run at speeds of up to 40 mph (65 km/h). Small Greyhounds definitely form part of their genetic make-up, but the remaining parts are less certain, though terriers are likely forebears.

Temperament They are quiet, intelligent, gentle, and make alert watchdogs.

Appearance With a lithe, elegant shape, Whippets are streamlined for swiftness. They have long, lean heads, which taper to a black nose, and rose-shaped ears that flop sideways. Their coat is short, fine, and close; and, when not running, they usually carry their long tail between their hind legs.

Size & weight Height at withers 18–22 in. (46–55 cm); 27–30 lb. (12.5–13.5 kg)

Exercise needs Considerable—vigorous daily walks and runs off the leash are essential.

Grooming Minimal   **Life expectancy** 13–14 years

Points to consider Their delicate skins may be prone to lacerations. They need access to a secured area for running.

Basenji

Basenjis are small, alert hunting dogs of an ancient lineage; dogs of very similar body type can be seen depicted on the side of the pharaohs' tombs. In Africa, they are still used as pack dogs for flushing out game. Basenjis are distinguished by the strange yodel-like noise they emit, instead of a bark (and they will also wail when unhappy, though they are mostly quiet dogs). Like wolves and dingos, Basenjis come into season once, rather than twice, each year. Basenjis shed minimally, which makes them excellent pets for allergy sufferers. They are also fastidious in their cleaning habits, which are similar to those of cats.

Temperament Friendly and confident, Basenjis make good house pets, but they are stubborn in nature and have a tendency to become destructive if bored.

Appearance Basenjis have long jaws, typical of many ancient dog breeds, and wrinkled foreheads, which give them a quizzical expression. They have large, mobile, pricked ears that encourage heat loss in hot climates. The distinctive tail curls back close to the spine. The short, sleek coat evolved as camouflage and is usually tan and white, but black and red with white markings is also common. The back is short and straight, with a well-defined waist.

The tightly curled, high-set tail is a distinctive feature of the Basenji, which is an elegant, poised breed blessed with tremendous agility.

Size & weight Height at withers 16–17 in. (40–43 cm); 21–24 lb. (9.5–11 kg)

Exercise needs Moderate to considerable

Grooming Minimal

Life expectancy 15 years

Points to consider Basenjis are prone to a number of hereditary diseases and problems, so prospective owners should consider this carefully and ensure they select a reputable breeder. Some Basenjis chase cats, and most are also suspicious of strangers. They can be difficult to train.

Saluki

Because of their elegance, speed, and hunting prowess, Salukis have been prized throughout the Middle East for generations. Active dogs, capable of great stamina and speed, they need lots of space (and do not tend to do well in confined city apartments).

Temperament Salukis can be aloof, high-strung, and sensitive to noises. But despite their reserved nature, they need a lot of attention and they are usually gentle and affectionate pets. They are not reliable with young children and have a tendency to be shy with strangers.

Appearance Salukis are graceful, long-boned dogs. They have narrow skulls, bright, hazel eyes, and long, silky ears. The supple neck gives way to a muscular torso with a moderately broad back and long, strong legs. There are two types of Saluki: the feathered type (displaying a featherlike fur pattern on the low-set tail, back of the thighs, and sometimes on the shoulder), and the smooth-haired type. The coat of both types is silky. Their coloring varies from white to cream, fawn, golden red, grizzle, tan, tricolor, and black and tan.

The Saluki has typically trusting, gentle eyes and a vulnerable expression. Sensitive dogs, they require dedicated owners who can provide plenty of attention and exercise.

Size & weight Height at withers 22–28 in. (58–71 cm); 31–55 lb. (14–25 kg)

Exercise needs Great

Grooming Moderate

Life expectancy 12 years

Points to consider Salukis require a great deal of exercise and space. They are not suitable pets for households with children and they are usually too timid and sensitive for a city environment.

Did You Know?

The nomadic Bedouin Arabs used to revere Salukis and sometimes transported them on camels to protect their delicate paws from burning on hot sand.

Afghan Hound

An Afghan seen at top speed is a glorious sight, with its long, flowing coat shown off to perfection. These long-limbed, elegant dogs are, today, something of a fashion statement for some owners, though they are descendants of an ancient and robust breed of sight hound. These dogs were first brought to Europe at the end of the nineteenth century by soldiers returning from service in Afghanistan, where they were bred to hunt gazelle and desert fox in the mountainous countryside, while acting as watchdogs at night.

Temperament Sensitive creatures, Afghans thrive on attention, and they can be very high-strung. They are intelligent dogs, and often extremely independent (a trait that can make them difficult to train). They are usually gentle and can make good family pets, though they tend to be nervous with strangers.

Did You Know?

🐾 There are three varieties of Afghan hound: long- and thick-haired, the most popular type in the West; the fringe-haired variety, which is similar to the Saluki; and the short-haired, rarely seen outside Kirgiz Taigan, a former Soviet republic north of Afghanistan.

Appearance Afghans have long heads and muzzles and expressive, almond-shaped eyes that lend them a dignified appearance. The ears are covered in silky hair and are set low so that they almost appear to blend in with the body coat. A long neck gives way to a muscular body and a straight, level back. The tail is lightly feathered and curls at the end.

Size & weight Height at withers 25-30 in. (63–74 cm); 50–60 lb. (23–27 kg)

Exercise needs Considerable

Grooming Considerable—the long coat requires a great deal of grooming to prevent it becoming matted.

Life expectancy 11–12 years

Points to consider These dogs need firm handling.

Irish Wolfhound

Distinctive, rangy, and pleasantly shaggy in appearance, Irish Wolfhounds are instantly recognizable by their sheer size. For centuries, these dogs were valued for their immense strength and speed. A popular breed today, Irish Wolfhounds are not always obedient and can be a challenge to train—though they are responsive, affectionate pets.

Temperament If your home is large enough to accommodate a large dog, an Irish Wolfhound is an ideal family pet. Calm and affectionate, they are loving dogs, immensely friendly, and keen to play.

Appearance Rough-coated giants, Irish Wolfhounds have harsh, wiry topcoats. The colors may be gray, brindle, red, black, white, or wheaten. They have long heads atop muscular necks, with deep chests and long bodies. The hair on the face is wiry and reasonably long over the eyes and under the jaw. Ears are small and set well back on the head. The tail is long and slightly curved.

Size & weight Height at withers 32–34 in. (80–85 cm); 105–120 lb. (48–55 kg)

Exercise needs Moderate   **Grooming** Moderate   **Life expectancy** 9–11 years

Points to consider Their size makes them unsuitable for most city dwellers.

Scottish Deerhound

Deerhounds have outstanding hunting skills: They are capable of chasing game for miles and strong enough to fell a deer. Popular for many centuries among the Scottish nobility, the Deerhound population eventually declined in Scotland, as hunting with guns became more common.

Temperament As pets, Deerhounds are affectionate, gentle dogs with a quiet dignity. They respond quickly to obedience training, though they have a tendency to chase cats and smaller animals.

Appearance Resembling Greyhounds in shape, Deerhounds are long-haired dogs, usually dark gray in color (although the breed standard lists many alternatives). The coat is rough and slightly harsh, with a softer, insulating undercoat beneath it. The head is broad at the ears, tapering into a narrow muzzle with powerful jaws. Their dark eyes have a gentle expression, and small ears are set well back on the head. The neck is powerfully muscular and the chest is both wide and deep. The tail is long and reaches almost to the ground.

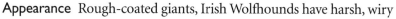

Size & weight Height at withers 28–30 in. (71–76 cm); 75–110 lb. (34–49 kg)

Exercise needs Great   **Grooming** Low to moderate

Life expectancy 12 years

Points to consider Deerhounds need plenty of space and exercise.

Borzoi

The majestic Russian Borzoi (meaning "sight hound") was bred in medieval times and beyond to hunt for Russian nobles. The long-limbed Borzois are probably descended from Greyhounds, Salukis, and Russian sheepdogs; they demonstrate exceptional strength and speed, and were thus able to track and capture wolves, hares, and foxes.

Temperament Borzois are usually reserved animals and, while they can make loyal pets for adults, they do not easily tolerate boisterous or young children. They can be snappy and irritable with strangers, though they are usually gentle and affectionate toward their owners.

Did You Know?

🐾 When Borzois were first brought to the United States, they were known as Russian Wolfhounds, but in their native Russia they were bred primarily to hunt hares and foxes.

Appearance Graceful Borzois have elegant, lean heads and long, powerful jaws. Their oblong-shaped eyes are set closely together, giving them good binocular vision, while the small ears are set well back on the head. Their sleek, wavy coats come in a wide variety of colors. The long back is slightly arched, and the tail is long and full.

Size & weight Height at withers 27–29 in. (68–74 cm); 75–105 lb. (35–48 kg)

Exercise needs Great   **Grooming** Considerable   **Life expectancy** 12 years

Points to consider Borzois can be stubborn, and the more dominant dogs can become aggressive unless trained by experienced owners. These dogs are not well-suited to an urban environment.

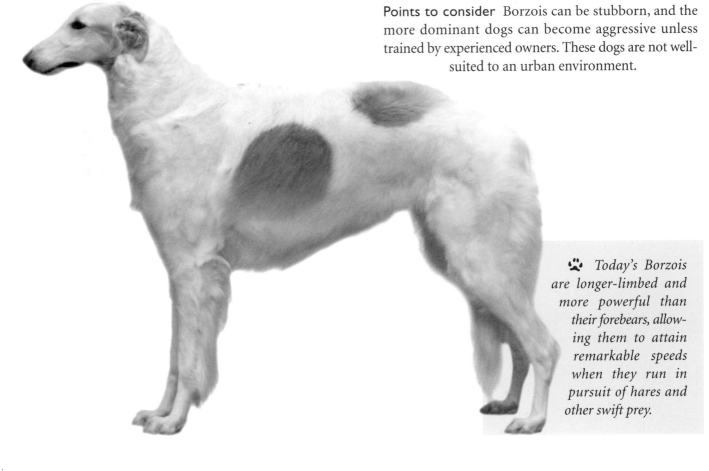

🐾 *Today's Borzois are longer-limbed and more powerful than their forebears, allowing them to attain remarkable speeds when they run in pursuit of hares and other swift prey.*

Rhodesian Ridgeback

Powerful and muscular, Rhodesian Ridgebacks are also known as African Lion dogs, as they were bred to trail big game, particularly lions. They are formidable animals and, today, they are popular as watchdogs because they are usually loyal to their owners and tend to be suspicious of strangers.

Temperament Sometimes stubborn and prone to aggression, and not always reliable with children, Ridgebacks can be rewarding, loyal pets but require a good deal of discipline and training.

Appearance Handsome dogs, Rhodesian Ridgebacks are characterized by a ridge along the back, on which the hair grows forward. Powerful in appearance, the chest is broad and deep, and the neck is muscular. The head is broad between the ears and reasonably long. Eyes are set well apart and ears hang down from high on the head. The short, sleek coat is an attractive golden-red color and, in cold climates, a thick undercoat grows for added insulation.

Size & weight Height at withers 24–27 in. (61–69 cm); 70–85 lb. (32–39 kg)

Exercise needs Rhodesian Ridgebacks are powerfully built, have tremendous stamina, and can jump surprisingly high. They require vigorous daily exercise.

Grooming Minimal

Life expectancy 12 years

Points to consider Ridgebacks are not ideal dogs for first-time owners.

🐾 *This detail at right shows the sleek back of a Ridgeback with its characteristic ridge of forward-growing hair that starts just behind the shoulders.*

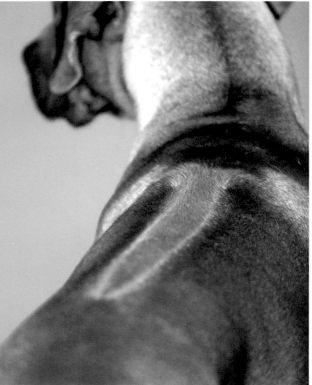

Beagle

Lively and intelligent animals, Beagles are the smallest dogs in the hound group. They are very independent and will roam, if given the opportunity (and, although rigorous training will help curb this behavior, it is not always possible to overcome). Highly vocal dogs, they howl, especially when left alone, and they love digging. Beagles were bred in Britain, as early as the fourteenth century, from small Foxhounds to create a dog suitable for hunting alongside people on foot, and were adept at chasing rabbits and hares. During the 1950s, Beagles were the most popular family pets in the United States, and this is reflected in the character Snoopy, the enigmatic Beagle in Charles M. Schulz's long-running cartoon strip, *Peanuts*.

Temperament Beagles are affectionate and friendly and make popular family pets because they are good with children. Rigorous obedience training should be started at an early age; Beagles tend to display a variety of behavioral problems—including howling, digging, and the tendency to roam.

Did You Know?

🐾 In the sixteenth century, Beagles were smaller than the breed standard today. Queen Elizabeth I had a pack of "pocket beagles" that were under 10 inches in height, and many hunters carried beagles in their saddlebags (or even in their pockets!), only releasing them later in the hunt to pursue the quarry.

Appearance The Beagle's short, weatherproof coat comes in the classic hound colors of white, tan, and black. A typical Beagle has a handsome, almost square muzzle and intelligent, dark brown eyes. The ears are large with rounded tips and hang down beside the cheeks. The body is muscular and taut, and the tail is carried up, though not over the back.

Size & weight Height at withers 13–15 in. (33–38 cm); 18–30 lb. (8–14 kg)

Exercise needs Considerable—they require daily walks and the opportunity to run off leash, but care should be taken to exercise them in fenced areas because of their tendency to roam.

Grooming Minimal

Life expectancy 13–14 years

Points to consider Some hereditary health problems; excessive barking, resistance to obedience training, and roaming can present problems.

Harrier

Harriers are descended from Beagles, Bloodhounds, and English Foxhounds. They are robust, scenting pack animals, bred to hunt foxes and hares, and now popular as family pets.

Temperament Harriers are outgoing, friendly animals that make affectionate pets. They are good with children, though sometimes too boisterous for very young children, and are friendly with strangers.

Appearance The Harrier appears similar to the English Foxhound, but smaller in size. The head is slightly narrower than that of the Beagle, and the small, oval eyes provide good binocular vision. The body is sturdy in build, with a short, dense coat, which is usually a combination of black, tan, and white.

Size & weight Height at withers 18–22 in. (46–56 cm); 48–60 lb. (22–27 kg)

Exercise needs Considerable—the Harrier needs at least two daily walks and vigorous off-leash exercise; it will howl or display destructive behavior if insufficiently exercised.

Grooming Minimal   **Life expectancy** 11–12 years

Points to consider Harriers are prone to chasing cats and other small animals.

English Foxhound

The English Foxhound is a long-established breed, dating from at least the thirteenth century. These dogs possess great energy and stamina and are capable of running ceaselessly for a full day in the field.

Temperament English Foxhounds are loyal and gentle, reliable with children, and excellent as watchdogs. Their pack and hunting instincts are, however, very strong, and they are difficult to train; barking or howling and chasing small animals are particular behavioral problems.

Appearance Rugged and robust, English Foxhounds have bodies adapted for both speed and stamina, with deep chests and powerful legs. They have square muzzles, keen brown or hazel eyes, and attentive expressions. Their large ears are carried close to the cheeks. The coat is glossy and short and usually tricolor (black, tan, and white).

Size & weight Height at withers 21–25 in. (53–64 cm); 65–70 lb. (29–32 kg)

Exercise needs Great   **Grooming** Minimal

Life expectancy 11–13 years

Points to consider English Foxhounds can be stubborn and difficult to train.

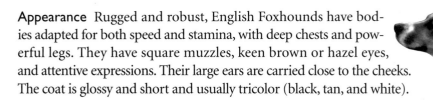

Black-and-Tan Coonhound

Bred in the United States to hunt raccoons, the Black-and-tan Coonhound excels at hunting and pursuit. The breed is probably descended from Talbot Hounds, English Foxhounds, and Irish Kerry Beagles. Tenacious tracking dogs, Black-and-tan Coonhounds will follow the scent trail of an animal, corner it, and then bay for the hunter. They are large dogs and have plenty of stamina for the pursuit of larger game, including bear.

Temperament As pets, Black-and-tan Coonhounds are friendly and affectionate and they are particularly playful and reliable with children. However, they require a great deal of exercise and have strong scent-tracking instincts—which makes them unsuitable as pets for most city dwellers—and they can be challenging to train.

Appearance Coonhounds resemble Bloodhounds in size and share the pendulous ears. They are deep-chested, muscular dogs, with strong limbs bred for endurance. The coloring of the short, dense coat is, as their name implies, mainly deep black with tan markings on the legs, the chest, over the eyes, and around the muzzle.

Size & weight Height at withers 23–27 in. (58–69 cm); 55–80 lb. (25–36 kg)

Exercise needs Great

Grooming Minimal—weekly brushing is advisable, however, and more frequent brushing is helpful when they are shedding heavily.

Life expectancy 11–12 years

Points to consider The long ears need regular checking to keep them clean and free of infection. These dogs are not well suited to a city environment.

Bloodhound

Aptly named, Bloodhounds have the finest sense of smell of any domestic animal. Affable and gentle, the Bloodhound displays exceptional tracking skills but has no further interest in its prey once it has located it. Its distinctive appearance, featuring deep facial "wrinkles" and large, drooping ears, provides the key to the Bloodhound's scent-tracking skills, because the scent is held in the facial folds and ears.

Temperament These are affectionate animals, reliable with children, and they are happy in a domestic environment (as long as they get plenty of exercise). They are not always easy to train, and some prospective owners may be put off by their tendency to drool profusely.

Did You Know?

🐾 Bloodhounds' ancestry can be traced back to the Norman Conquest of England in the eleventh century, when the invaders brought them across the English Channel. They have outstanding olfactory capabilities and can persistently follow a scent for miles. For this reason, they were often used by landowners and law enforcers to track trespassers and suspected criminals and were feared for centuries.

Appearance Bloodhounds have a permanently mournful expression because of the long dewlaps of loose skin that hang down from the face, along with pendulous, soft ears. Their large ribcages house an efficient cardiovascular system, and with powerful shoulders and strong backs, the whole frame ensures that they have great stamina. Coats are short and dense, colored red, liver, and tan, or black and tan. The white variety, dating from medieval times, was known as the Talbot Hound.

Size & Weight Height at withers 24–26 in. (61–66 cm); 80–110 lb. (36–50 kg)

Exercise needs Considerable—without several brisk daily walks and regular opportunities to follow scent trails, these dogs can become bored and possibly destructive.

Grooming Moderate—the short coat is low-maintenance, but the ears need to be checked daily and cleaned at least once each week.

Life expectancy 10–12 years

Points to consider They have a characteristic bay and can be "talkative." They also drool a great deal.

American Foxhound

The American Foxhound has a distinguished ancestry: George Washington is credited with founding the breed by crossing English Foxhounds with Kerry Beagles and French hounds to create a hardy Foxhound to suit the rugged terrain of the Americas. Each American Foxhound possesses a distinctive voice that can be recognizable to its owner. These dogs have a strong pack instinct and are highly energetic. Because of this, they cannot be left to become bored, when they are likely to howl and become destructive. Obedience training can be challenging, because they are strong-willed and easily distracted by tracking scents.

Temperament American Foxhounds are sociable and friendly, highly active, and sometimes stubborn. They can make suitable family pets and are good with children, but require a great deal of space, frequent exercise, and plenty of attention.

Appearance The coat is short and dense, in a variety of colors, most commonly a combination of black, tan, white, and gold. The head is large, with a slightly domed skull and strong jaws. Ears are set at eye level and hang loosely below the jaw line. The chest is long, but the body is otherwise compact and muscular, and the tail is long.

Size & weight Height at withers 21–25 in. (53–64 cm); 65–75 lb. (30–34 kg)

🐾 *With their domed heads and wide-set eyes, American Foxhounds typically have a refined, but gentle, expression.*

Exercise needs Great

Grooming Minimal

Life expectancy 11–13 years

Points to consider American Foxhounds are not well suited to city or suburban life: They require a good deal of outdoor exercise each day. They are not easily trained, and recall training is particularly difficult.

Basset Hound

The lugubrious Basset Hound breed originated in France, where these dogs were bred to hunt in packs. Their physique perfectly equips them to follow a scent close to the ground, and they hunt tenaciously with deliberate, but never clumsy, movements.

Temperament Bassets are gentle dogs, occasionally stubborn, but mostly happy to fit in with family life, and they are particularly friendly with children. However, their strong instincts do make them willful, so they are not easy to train.

Appearance The bodies of Basset Hounds are normal in length relative to their head size, but they have short, stubby legs and large joints. Some breeders believe they may be descended from "dwarfed" Bloodhounds. Bassets are heavy-set dogs that bear their weight evenly on large paws and walk with a rolling gait. With their large, domed heads and pendulous ears and dewlaps (which are similar to those of Bloodhounds), Basset Hounds have a very serious expression. The eyes are slightly sunken and droopy, so that the red of the lower eyelid is partially visible. The coat is short, hard, and dense, and requires only minimal grooming. Colors are black, white, and tan.

Did You Know?

🐾 The word *basset* means "dwarf" in French, which provides a clue to the breed's origins. The Basset's long ears, which flap around its face, provide vital assistance in picking up a scent, enabling the dog to follow a trail that is up to several hours old.

Size & weight Height at withers 13–15 in. (33–38 cm); 40–60 lb. (18–27 kg)

Exercise needs Moderate   **Grooming** Minimal

Life expectancy 10–11 years

Points to consider Prospective owners should be aware that Basset Hounds drool and require special attention to their ears, as well as being prone to numerous hereditary health problems and obesity. They should not be walked by children, because they are easily distracted by scents and are thus a handful on their leashes.

🐾 *Basset Hounds are sweet-natured and affectionate; their expressions are sometimes doleful, or even comical.*

Dachshund

Dachshunds were originally developed in Germany to flush out badgers from their setts. They are bred in three varieties: smooth, wirehaired, and longhaired; and in two sizes: standard and miniature. Smooth Dachshunds are thought to have origins in ancient Egypt, as sculptures from this period show short-legged dogs seated beside the pharaohs. Longhaired Dachshunds are descended from a cross between Dachshunds and short-legged spaniels, such as the Sussex. Wirehaired Dachshunds were bred by crossing Smooth Dachshunds with rough-haired Pinschers and then with Dandie Dinmont Terriers.

Temperament Intelligent, brave, and independent-minded dogs, Dachshunds need firm training from an early age, as they are not naturally eager to behave obediently and can sometimes be aggressive toward people or other dogs. Energetic and playful, they have a tendency to put on weight if allowed to indulge their love of food or if insufficiently exercised. They can be good with children if socialized with them while they are puppies.

Did You Know?

🐾 *Dachs* means "badger" in German, and Dachshunds (literally, "badger dogs") were bred to pursue badgers and flush them out of their setts. Today, German Dachshunds are a separate breed from their British and American cousins, and are slightly longer in the leg, as they are judged by their fitness to work.

Appearance Dachshunds have well-defined heads with long muzzles and expressive, intelligent eyes, framed by ears that rest against the cheek. The coats vary greatly in length and color. Shorthaired Dachshunds have smooth, glossy coats. Those of the longhaired type are soft and slightly wavy, and the ears, set just above the eyes, are covered in fine, silky hair. Wirehaired Dachshunds are characterized by rough coats and goatee beards.

Size & weight Height at withers 5–10 in. (13–25 cm); miniature 9–10 lb. (4–5 kg); standard 15–25 lb. (6.5–11 kg)

Exercise needs Low to moderate

Grooming Minimal to moderate

Life expectancy 11 years

Points to consider Dachshunds tend to be one-person dogs. They may not be reliable with children unless socialized with them while they are puppies.

Petit Basset Griffon Vendéen

This short-legged, rough-coated scent hound was bred in the Vendée region of France to hunt small game over difficult and rough terrain. It is descended from the larger Grand Griffon Vendéen and was selectively bred to retain the fearlessness and energy of its larger ancestor.

Temperament Petit Basset Griffon Vendéens are alert and lively dogs; they have an independent streak but are generally eager to please and respond well to training.

Appearance These dogs have long backs and short, straight legs. The rough, dense coat is lemon, tricolor, orange and white, or grizzled, and covers a softer undercoat. The head is twice as long as it is wide, covered with long hair that forms eyebrows and a beard around the jaws. Intelligent eyes are framed by long, pendulous ears. The body is stocky, with a deep chest and a strong, medium-length tail set high.

Size & weight Height at withers 13–15 in. (33–38 cm); 40–60 lb. (18–27 kg)

Exercise needs Moderate   **Grooming** Moderate   **Life expectancy** 15 years

Points to consider The long back means that back problems may occur.

Norwegian Elkhound

Evidence from Norway suggests that this breed is almost 5,000 years old. The most popular dogs of the Spitz family, they were bred, as their name suggests, to hunt elk.

Temperament They are courageous, intelligent dogs with plenty of stamina and, as pets, they can usually be trusted with children.

Appearance Elkhounds have wedge-shaped muzzles and small, pricked ears. The coat is thick and weather-resistant: The coarse, straight outercoat covers a soft undercoat. The color is varying shades of gray, with occasional black tips. They have a ruff around the muscular neck and a wide ribcage. The body is compact and well muscled, and a high-set tail curls over the back

Size & weight Height at withers 19.5–20.5 in. (49–52 cm); 43–50 lb. (20–23 kg)

Exercise needs Moderate   **Grooming** Moderate

Life expectancy 12–13 years

Points to consider Rigorous obedience training is recommended to eliminate youthful willfulness.

Otterhound

As their name suggests, Otterhounds were bred in Britain specifically to hunt otters. Otters are comparatively rare today, and so is the Otterhound. These dogs are exceptional swimmers (with webbed feet), and their scenting abilities are almost as good as those of Bloodhounds: They were able to dive into cold rivers to follow an otter's trail of bubbles for considerable distances.

Did You Know?

🐾 Otterhounds have long, shaggy coats that will become matted unless they are regularly brushed. Their long ears also require regular cleaning to keep them free of matting and infection.

Temperament These are energetic dogs that need plenty of space and brisk exercise. They are friendly, amiable creatures, but need firm discipline to prevent them becoming destructive—or from exercising their independent streak whenever they are near water!

Appearance Otterhounds are large dogs, with majestic heads and a dignified stance. A rough, shaggy topcoat in any hound color hides a soft undercoat that provides excellent weather protection. Long hair covers their heads, and dark, intelligent eyes peer out from under a fringe. Ears are long and covered in fine hair. The back is slightly arched and the chest is deep with a well-sprung ribcage.

Size & weight Height at withers 24–27 in. (60–67 cm); 65–120 lb. (30–55 kg)

Exercise needs Great

Grooming Moderate—sheds profusely

Life expectancy 12–14 years

Points to consider These dogs need strong discipline to curb the independent streak in their personalities. Their attractive, shaggy coats need weekly grooming to control shedding.

Working Dogs

The working dogs category includes those dogs bred for heavy work, such as pulling sleds, carrying weighty loads, and guarding flocks and settlements. All the dogs in this section are sufficiently intelligent to be trained, though they must be adequately stimulated with games and exercise to prevent them from becoming bored and destructive. It is important to note that, while working dogs were traditionally prized for their independence and initiative, these traits are not always valued in the modern domestic environment.

As may be expected, working dogs are generally quite large, and they do require plenty of exercise and space. The very strength and size (as well as the temperament) of many of the working breeds means that they are not necessarily ideal family pets. Siberian Huskies, for example, are happiest living as part of a pack, and others, like the Japanese Akita, are extremely powerful and should only be kept by experienced dog owners. By contrast, the affectionate Newfoundland, while a large dog, is even-tempered and devoted to its human family.

In 1983, the American Kennel Club pulled a number of the member breeds out of this group and reclassified them in a new group, the herding dogs (see page 125).

Boxer

Energetic, alert, and intelligent, Boxers are excellent guard dogs and tolerant family pets. They are descended from the German Bullenbeisser ("bull-biter") breed, possibly crossed with Bulldogs and Great Danes to create a tough working dog. Boxers live their life at high speed, so they need and enjoy plenty of exercise and games. They will submit to training, but tend to exhibit exuberant, puppylike behavior well into old age (and can unintentionally create mayhem, especially in close quarters). They are alert and self-confident animals (indeed, they have been successfully trained for use in the police and military), though they also make devoted family pets and are patient with small children. Boxers are very clean dogs, and some even groom themselves in a manner similar to cats.

Temperament Boxers are alert, playful, very patient, and good with children. They are loyal dogs and wary of strangers.

Did You Know?

Boxers were first exhibited in Munich in 1895, but did not become well known in the United States until after World War II, when many returned home with servicemen who had fought in Europe. The first Boxer registered with the American Kennel Club was in 1904, but the American public did not begin to take a serious interest in the breed until around 1940.

Appearance The Boxer's main identifying feature is the large head with upturned nose and slightly wrinkled face. They are well-muscled dogs, with a close-fitting, short coat, and give the impression of being aggressively built animals. Colors are fawn and brindle with white markings on the chest, face, and feet. Boxers have a blunt muzzle and large jaws with a dark mask in contrast to the head color. The triangular ears are set wide apart on top of the head and are raised when the dog is alert. Set high, the tail is usually docked and carried high.

Size & weight Height at withers 21–25 in. (53–64 cm); 55–70 lb. (25–32 kg)

Exercise needs Considerable—needs a long daily walk

Grooming Minimal

Life expectancy 11–12 years

Points to consider Hereditary deafness is an issue in a small percentage of these dogs. Heart problems and hip dysplasia can also present problems.

Mastiff

Heavyset, muscular creatures that exude power, Mastiffs are possibly the most imposing dogs in the world. They have an ancient lineage: Carvings of Mastiffs are on ancient Assyrian friezes dating from the sixth century B.C. The Romans took them to Britain, and their name probably derives from the Anglo-Saxon word *masty*, meaning "powerful." This breed is more properly called the "Old English Mastiff," since the term "mastiff" is used to describe an entire group of giant dogs (not just a single breed). Mastiffs are exceptionally powerful dogs, and they suit experienced dog owners rather than novices.

Did You Know?

Mastiffs were the original "dogs of war." In ancient Babylon, four towns were exempt from taxes in return for training Mastiffs as war dogs for the army. These dogs were trained to hunt down and capture the soldiers of an opposing army, and their descendants were used centuries later in bloodthirsty bull- and bearbaiting arenas.

Temperament Mastiffs are excellent watchdogs and demonstrate great loyalty and affection for their owners. They are generally dignified, calm, and easygoing pets, but they do need plenty of space and exercise.

Appearance The American Kennel Club stresses that a dog's height should come from the height of the body, rather than from long legs, and this sums up the Mastiff. They are heavily built, muscular dogs with sturdy, densely boned limbs, broad necks, and massive, square heads. The eyes are set wide apart on the broad head, and the heavy muzzle is black. The forehead has wrinkles, which are more pronounced when the dog is alert. Ears are small and triangular in shape, set high on the head. The short coat is easy to maintain and is usually colored apricot-fawn, silver-fawn, or a dark fawn brindle.

Size & weight Height at withers 27–30 in. (69–76 cm); 175–90 lb. (79–86 kg)

Exercise needs Moderate

Grooming Minimal

Life expectancy 9–11 years

Points to consider These dogs require a high-quality diet to fulfill their potential, as well as a large amount of space. They are fairly reliable with children, but they are large and sometimes clumsy, and therefore not ideally suited to households with young children.

The characteristically wrinkled face of this handsome Mastiff lends him a worried-looking expression, but his wrinkles deepen when he is paying attention rather than feeling nervous or insecure.

Bullmastiff

So far as is known, Bullmastiffs were bred in the later part of the nine-teenth century in England by gamekeepers who crossed the powerful Mastiff with the fast and aggressive Bulldog to create a large, power-ful dog that would overpower and hold (but not harm or maul) poachers. Alert, agile, and immensely strong, Bullmastiffs still make exceptional watchdogs. These dogs are usually reliable around children, but they are too strong for them (or even slight adults) to con-trol and are best kept by experienced dog owners.

Temperament The ferocity of their forebears has largely been bred out of today's Bullmastiffs, and they are generally calm, intelligent animals. They are very protective of their human family (some may say overly protective), but they are some-times resistant to training.

Appearance Muscular and robust, Bullmastiffs are substantial dogs with heavy bones and powerful bodies. The large, wide head has a moderate, black muzzle and characteristic wrinkle on the forehead when alert. The jaws are large with slightly pendulous flews. Small, triangular ears are positioned on top of the head and hang slightly forward. The muscular, broad neck merges with the chest, which is wide and deep. The short, hard, flat coat is fawn, red, or brindle in shades of red and fawn and requires only minimal groom-ing. The feet are large and compact with black nails.

Size & weight Height at withers 24–27 in. (61–69 cm); 100–130 lb. (45–59 kg)

Exercise needs Considerable—needs vigorous daily walk

Grooming Minimal

Life expectancy 10–11 years

Points to consider The deep chest means that this dog may be prone to gastric torsion (bloating). Their size and power can make them difficult to control, and they are sometimes resistant to training. They are not suitable for first-time owners.

Rottweiler

Rottweilers have a reputation as formidable and sometimes threatening dogs, although their ferocity has been somewhat reduced by selective breeding. It is likely that these dogs are descended from one of the drover dogs of ancient Rome, and it is thought that the Romans brought their Tibetan Mastiff ancestors to Germany more than two thousand years ago. Rottweilers need plenty of vigorous exercise, and they are not suitable pets for inexperienced dog owners because of their size and power.

Temperament Rottweilers are superb watchdogs and they respond well to obedience training, though owners must be prepared to devote considerable time to this. They are generally good-natured animals, but—if challenged by other dogs or strangers—they may show their temper and demonstrate their naturally strong urge to protect their family.

Did You Know?

🐾 In Germany, the Rottweiler is still referred to as the Rottweiler Metzgerhund, or "Rottweil Butcher's dog," because it was frequently used by butchers as a draft dog to deliver meat during the nineteenth century. It was bred in the south German town of Rottweil in the early nineteenth century.

Appearance Rottweilers are handsome dogs, mainly black, but with tan markings on the legs and face. The coat is dense and short, with an undercoat on the neck and thighs. The body is heavily set and powerfully muscular. The strong, arched neck supports a large, broad head with a short, square muzzle and robust jaws. Almond-shaped eyes are dark brown, and the ears are positioned high and wide on the head. Rottweilers have deep, broad chests, heavily boned legs, straight, slightly sloping backs, and tails that are often docked (for aesthetic reasons).

Size & weight Height at withers 22–27 in. (56–69 cm); 90–110 lb. (41–50 kg)

Exercise needs Considerable

Grooming Moderate

Life expectancy 11–12 years

Points to consider Test for eye problems. Rottweilers are extremely protective of their families and should not be considered by inexperienced dog owners.

Great Dane

Despite their name, Great Danes are really German dogs and are known as the *Deutsche Dogge* ("German Mastiff") in their homeland, where they were initially bred to hunt wild boar (one of the most powerful and dangerous of Europe's big-game animals). Some zoologists believe that the Mastiff breeds originally came from Asia. In Germany, the Great Dane has been cultivated as a distinctive breed for at least 400 years.

Temperament These elegant, powerful, dignified, and affectionate dogs thrive on family life. They tolerate children and other animals, and obedience training usually dissipates any stubbornness.

Appearance Great Danes are majestic dogs with large heads and powerful limbs. The skin is taut all over the body and the short, sleek coat may be fawn, black, blue, brindle, or harlequin (an irregular black-and-white pattern). The head is well-defined, with a large jaw and slightly pendulous lips. The ears are set high on the head. The neck is long and well arched and the chest is deep and broad. Feet are round and catlike with arched toes. The tapering tail is carried as an extension of the back.

Size & weight Height at withers minimum 28 in. (71 cm) for females; 32 in. (81 cm) for males; weight in proportion to height

Exercise needs Considerable   **Grooming** Minimal

Life expectancy 9–10 years

Points to consider Hip dysplasia and heart problems afflict the breed. These dogs have a tendency to stubbornness and need a firm hand during training. They enjoy play, but games that encourage possessive behavior should be avoided.

The large, powerful Great Dane has an almost regal bearing when standing to attention. The short coat should be glossy and smooth.

Greater Swiss Mountain Dog

The ancient Romans introduced the forebears of this rare breed to the Alpine region, where they were bred as draft animals to haul sleds or small carts through the mountainous villages. Gentle and robust, these dogs are among the earliest descendants of the Mastiff breeds; they are also related to the Saint Bernard breed.

Temperament Greater Swiss Mountain Dogs are rarely aggressive toward humans, but may display aggression toward other dogs. They make excellent, affable companions and vigilant watchdogs.

Appearance The Greater Swiss Mountain Dog is characterized by a powerful neck and shoulders and has muscular hips. It has a robust head, a lively, animated expression, powerful jaws, and medium-sized dark-brown eyes surrounded by black rims. The ears are positioned well back on the head and hang down to mid-cheek level. The hard, glossy topcoat is black with rust and white markings. The body is muscular and broad.

Size & weight Height at withers 23–28 in. (58–71 cm); 130–35 lb. (59–61 kg)

Exercise needs Moderate   **Grooming** Moderate   **Life expectancy** 11–13 years

Points to consider Greater Swiss Mountain Dogs are generally good with children, but can be difficult to handle outdoors if they are aggressive with other dogs.

German Pinscher

The origins of this alert, sometimes high-strung, breed lie with the Doberman, Miniature Pinscher, and other pinscher types, although it is also closely associated with the Standard Schnauzer.

Temperament Pinschers have natural protective instincts toward home and family. They are generally willing learners, though they need consistent discipline. The breed has all the essential qualities of a watchdog and companion, and it will not back down from a dispute with other dogs.

Appearance This medium-sized dog has erect ears, square proportions, and a powerfully muscular body built for endurance and agility. The coat is dense and smooth, usually fawn, red, or black-blue.

Size & weight Height at withers 17–20 in. (43–51 cm); 25–35 lb. (11–16 kg)

Exercise needs Moderate   **Grooming** Minimal

Life expectancy 12–14 years

Points to consider German Pinschers are energetic dogs that require a good deal of attention.

Doberman Pinscher

Elegant, agile, and intelligent dogs, Doberman Pinschers originated in Germany around 1890. Created by breeding short-haired shepherd stock with mixtures of Rottweiler, Black-and-Tan Terriers, and smooth-haired German Pinschers, Dobermans were bred with the aim of producing a terrier with the skills of a watchdog. Indeed, they are popular throughout the world as police or tracking animals. Doberman Pinschers are energetic dogs that need a great deal of stimulating exercise.

Temperament Dobermans have acquired a reputation as fearsome animals, and some may be aggressive and demonstrate fear biting, although this can usually be controlled with firm handling. Most Dobermans are affectionate, sociable, and faithful animals, but they must be well trained and are probably safest in the hands of an experienced dog owner who can provide the necessary consistent discipline.

Did You Know?

🐾 The first Dobermans were bred in the nineteenth century by Louis Dobermann, a German tax collector who used them for protection while he went about his unpopular business.

Appearance Dobermans are characterized by their wedge-shaped muzzle, lean head, and strong, almost square body silhouette. The ears naturally hang at the back of the head, but are often cropped in the U.S. so that they stand erect. With dark, almond-shaped eyes and a long jaw, the Doberman has a keen, alert expression. The neck is reasonably long and gives way to a deep chest and robust body, capable of great stamina. The short, thick coat is black, brown, blue, or fawn, and the tail is short.

Size & weight Height at withers 24–28 in. (61–71 cm); 66–88 lb. (30–40 kg)

Exercise needs Considerable   **Grooming** Moderate

Life expectancy 10–12 years

Points to consider Hereditary heart disease may be a problem. Although these dogs can be fine with the children of their own family, they may be aggressive with children they are unfamiliar with.

Akita

These large, versatile hunting dogs are an extremely popular breed in Japan, where they have been bred for more than 300 years. The first record of these dogs is from the early seventeenth century, when a famous nobleman who was exiled to Japan's rugged northern mountains is said to have developed the precursors to the Akita. These dogs were traditionally used to hunt bear, deer, and wild boar. They are dignified, aloof animals, powerfully built and very confident. Today, they are most widely used in police work or as watchdogs. Males are especially prone to exerting dominance and have a tendency to fight with other dogs, but rigorous early training can lessen this tendency. They are devoted to their human family, but they are probably not ideal dogs for inexperienced owners. They require a great deal of exercise and stimulating play, and a well-fenced yard is a necessity to keep this independent, alert breed happy.

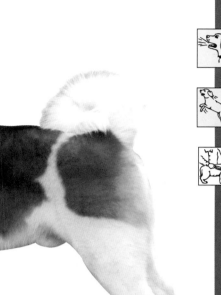

Temperament These dogs are generally brave, alert, mild-tempered, and good-natured (though they tend to be aggressive toward other dogs).

Appearance Akitas are typical Spitz dogs, with slightly vulpine facial features. The head is massive; it is broad with a deep muzzle, deep-set triangular eyes, and small, pricked ears. The muscular, thick neck gives way to a wide, deep chest and heavily boned body. The feet are round and catlike. Akitas have double coats that can be any color. The harsh outercoat is about two inches long on the body and covers a dense, soft undercoat. The tail is carried high and is either curled over the back or against the flank.

Size & weight Height at withers 24–28 in. (61–71 cm); 75–110 lb. (34–50 kg)

Exercise needs Great—long daily walk and off-leash run

Grooming Considerable   **Life expectancy** 10–12 years

Points to consider This breed has occasional hereditary eye problems. Akitas tend to be aggressive toward other dogs; they are sometimes stubborn and difficult to train.

Did You Know?

🐾 In Japan, dogs are classified by size, and *akita inu* (as this breed is called in Japan) means "large dog." There are many dogs in the medium (*shika*) and small (*shiba*) categories, but only one large breed, the Akita. This dog is a national treasure of Japan, where it is a symbol of good health, happiness, and longevity—upon the birth of a child, the family will usually receive a small statue of an Akita.

Alaskan Malamute

Malamutes have been bred in the Arctic regions of Alaska for generations for use as sled-pullers and draft animals. They are true pack animals, with the instinct either to lead or be led, so it is important that they receive rigorous obedience training as puppies. Malamutes are immensely strong animals that thrive on an outdoor life and have the stamina for plenty of exercise. They remain superb competitors in the popular sport of sled-dog racing.

Temperament Alaskan Malamutes are friendly, devoted companions that make affectionate pets.

Appearance Malamutes have beautiful, thick guard coats over a two-inch, oily undercoat that protects them from the rigors of the Arctic winter. The color is usually solid white or has shadings of gray, black, sable, or red. Their bodies are substantial and muscular, with powerful shoulders, deep chests, and strong-boned legs. The neck is broad and the head is wide with a pronounced stop and tapered muzzle. Almond-shaped eyes are small, while the ears are pricked and well-furred, designed to retain body heat. Tails are bushy, carried over the back.

Size & weight Height at withers 23–28 in. (58–71 cm); 75–123 lb. (34–56 kg)

Exercise needs Very considerable   **Grooming** Considerable   **Life expectancy** 12 years

Points to consider These dogs have strong pack instincts and need rigorous training. They require a great deal of exercise and are not well-suited to an urban environment.

Anatolian Shepherd Dog

Anatolian shepherds used their dogs to protect their flocks from wolves and other predators, not to herd them. The powerful Anatolian Shepherd Dog (also known as the Turkish Shepherd Dog) is descended from ancient mastiff-type dogs and is an excellent, territorial guard dog, but must be rigorously trained from an early age.

Temperament They are intelligent and can be strong-willed, so they are not always reliable as companion dogs.

Appearance Rugged and large, Anatolian Shepherd Dogs are impressive animals, built for endurance and speed. They are heavily built, with large heads, muscular, thick necks, and long backs. The coat can be any color and is rough with a thick, protective undercoat. Thick fur forms a ruff around the neck. The head is wide with a square muzzle, black lips, and neat, triangular ears that hang down. The tail is carried low and has a natural curl.

Size & weight Height at withers 28–32 in. (71–81 cm); 90–150 lb. (41–68 kg)

Exercise needs Great   **Grooming** Moderate   **Life expectancy** 10–11 years

Points to consider Not ideal companions. They are not a good choice for a family with small children.

Siberian Husky

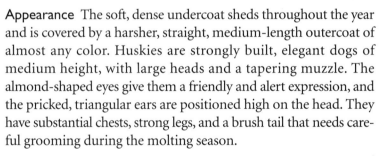

Supreme pack animals with seemingly limitless stamina, Siberian Huskies have been used to herd reindeer and pull sleds in Siberia for more than three thousand years. They were developed and bred by the seminomadic Chukchi people. World famous as exceptional working dogs, Huskies are energetic animals that need a great deal of exercise. They enjoy adventure in the form of digging and jumping fences—so a secure enclosed yard is a necessity. These dogs rarely bark, but instead vocalize with a wolflike howl.

Temperament Siberian Huskies are dignified dogs with equable temperaments. Husky puppies were raised by the women of the Chukchi people, and it has traditionally been said that this is the reason for the Husky's relaxed temperament and ease in a family environment. Friendly and gentle, Siberian Huskies display none of the overprotective qualities of watchdogs, but in the presence of other dogs, they will tend to exercise the domineering behavior typical of pack animals.

Did You Know?

🐾 Siberian Huskies were imported to Alaska by fur traders at the turn of the twentieth century, and in 1910 a team of Siberian Huskies won a grueling 400-mile race driven by John "Iron Man" Johnson. From that date, Huskies continued to capture most international sled-racing titles.

Appearance The soft, dense undercoat sheds throughout the year and is covered by a harsher, straight, medium-length outercoat of almost any color. Huskies are strongly built, elegant dogs of medium height, with large heads and a tapering muzzle. The almond-shaped eyes give them a friendly and alert expression, and the pricked, triangular ears are positioned high on the head. They have substantial chests, strong legs, and a brush tail that needs careful grooming during the molting season.

Size & weight Height at withers 20–23 in. (51–58 cm); 35–60 lb. (16–27 kg)

Exercise needs Very considerable—long daily walk and run

Grooming Moderate   **Life expectancy** 11–13 years

Points to consider No hereditary health problems. They shed constantly and require a great deal of exercise.

Samoyed

Samoyeds are descended from hardworking and hardy Siberian Spitz dogs used by their nomadic owners to herd and guard flocks of reindeer. They lived closely with their human masters, sharing their tents, and remain very affectionate dogs today. Samoyeds need plenty of exercise, and their spectacular coats shed throughout the year.

Temperament These affectionate dogs are alert and intelligent, and love to play. Obedience training is advisable from an early age to curb their naturally strong will. They are usually good with children.

Appearance The Samoyed's thick, soft undercoat is covered by a rougher, weather-resistant outercoat. A ruff frames the small, finely chiseled head, with its well-defined features, dark eyes, and black nose. The ears are set wide

apart and are small and erect. With strong shoulders and muscular bodies, Samoyeds have long, bushy tails that curl over their backs.

Size & weight Height at withers 19–23 in. (48–58 cm); 50–66 lb. (23–30 kg)

Exercise needs Moderate

Grooming Considerable   **Life expectancy** 12–14 years

Points to consider The coat sheds constantly and is hard to keep clean; excessive barking can be a problem.

Kuvasz

The Hungarian Kuvasz is descended from the herding and guarding dogs used by nomadic shepherds in the Tibetan region during the Middle Ages. Many medieval European rulers kept these dogs as their companions.

Temperament A natural watchdog, the Kuvasz is suspicious of strangers and very protective of its human family. These dogs are independent and require firm handling by an experienced owner.

Appearance The Kuvasz is a large, muscular, and powerful dog. The broad neck supports a large head with a wedge-shaped muzzle. The black nose and dark eyes contrast with snowy hair on the face. Ears frame the face, hanging forward from high on the head. The profuse white coat is composed of a medium-coarse topcoat over a fine undercoat. The body is slightly longer than it is high, with well-muscled limbs and a long, bushy tail.

Size & weight Height at withers 26–30 in. (66–76 cm); 70–115 lb. (32–52 kg)

Exercise needs Considerable   **Grooming** Considerable   **Life expectancy** 11–13 years

Points to consider Profuse sheddings, high-maintenance grooming, and difficulty in obedience training are characteristic of this breed.

Great Pyrenees

Also known as the Pyrenéan Mountain Dog, this magnificent white breed is probably related to several other European guarding mastiffs, such as the Hungarian Kuvasz and the Italian Maremma, as well as the St. Bernard and the Newfoundland. They have been used for many centuries to guard flocks in the rocky, inhospitable Pyrenees, as well as to haul sleds. When first adopted as household pets, Great Pyrenees were often rather aggressive, though selective breeding over recent years has significantly reduced this trait.

Did You Know?

🐾 Intelligent and hardy, the Great Pyrenees was used as a messenger dog by both the Americans and the French during World War II.

Temperament Great Pyrenees are gentle, faithful, and affectionate family pets, and they make very good watchdogs. However, they are often slow to mature—both physically and mentally—and it is important that they are well socialized and trained from an early age.

Appearance Keen-eyed and alert, Great Pyrenees have a friendly, dignified demeanor. They are substantial dogs—immensely strong, with great stamina. The beautiful white topcoat is profuse, long, and flat, and provides vital protection against the elements. It almost forms a mane around the regal, wedge-shaped head. Small, triangular ears hang down from eye level against the head. The body is muscular, and the thick tail reaches the floor or may curve over the back.

Size & weight Height at withers 25–32 in. (64–81 cm); 85–132 lb. (39–60 kg)

Exercise needs Moderate to considerable

Grooming Considerable

Life expectancy 9–11 years

Points to consider This breed has no major hereditary health problems. Potential owners should be prepared for constant shedding and daily grooming to prevent matting.

Newfoundland

"Newfies" are large, gentle, dolorous-looking, charming dogs that demonstrate great devotion to their owners. They are water dogs that were traditionally used by fishermen to pull their nets ashore. Today, Newfoundlands retain a love of water and they are exceptional swimmers despite their large size. They are used by the coastal emergency services in France, and there are many stories about these dogs rescuing drowning people. However, they are equally happy on land, where they also work as draft animals, hauling fishing nets and carts.

Temperament These friendly dogs relish family life. They are docile, gentle, obedient, and very good with children.

Appearance Newfoundlands are large dogs with great, shaggy, bearlike coats. The double coat is dense, flat, oily, and water-resistant, and must be groomed regularly to maintain its condition. The Newfies' torso is massive, designed to house a large pair of lungs. The large, wide head sits on top of a strong neck and is covered with fine hair. The benign eyes are deep set, and the muzzle is square. The legs are powerfully muscular and the feet are webbed, which enables the dog to swim strongly. The thick tail acts as a rudder when the dog is in the water.

Did You Know?

🐾 Newfoundlands have long captured the imagination of artists and writers. The noted Victorian landscape painter Sir Edwin Landseer included Newfoundlands in many of his paintings, and J. M. Barrie, the author of *Peter Pan*, cast a Newfoundland as nanny to the Darling children, Wendy, John, and Michael.

Size & weight Height at withers 26–28 in. (66–71 cm); 100–150 lb. (45–68 kg)

Exercise needs Considerable

Grooming Considerable

Life expectancy 9–11 years

Points to consider These dogs will always rescue a swimmer—whether or not they need it! Their large size makes them unsuitable for small homes; considerable shedding and a tendency to obesity may put off some potential owners. Newfoundlands are very affectionate and dislike being left alone, when they can develop a number of problem behaviors.

Portuguese Water Dog

Portuguese Water Dogs were used to herd fish into nets, pull fishing nets from the water, retrieve lost tackle, and carry messages between boats. Their coats are profuse, providing insulation against cold water.

Temperament These dogs are cheerful, energetic creatures, but they can be stubborn.

Appearance Elegant dogs that are black or dark brown, Portuguese Water Dogs are sometimes mistaken for Poodles. Their single coats are thick and wavy, and although the tail is often trimmed, a plume remains at the end, which enables it to float when in the water. They have well-muscled shoulders and long, deep chests. The domed head is reasonably small and the face finely chiseled. The dog pictured here sports the "lion" clip, popular for this breed.

Size & weight Height at withers 17–23 in. (43–58 cm); 35–60 lb. (16–27 kg)

Exercise needs Considerable **Grooming** Considerable **Life expectancy** 12–14 years

Points to consider This breed can be challenging to train; excessive barking can be a problem.

Bernese Mountain Dog

Gentle giants, Bernese Mountain Dogs were bred in Switzerland to pull carts and herd livestock.

Temperament These dogs are friendly, confident, and alert, but they tend to be aloof with strangers. They are faithful and intelligent animals and fit in well with family life—as long as there is enough space.

Appearance Bernese have glossy, long coats that are mainly black, with rust-colored and white markings. A white marking on the chest typically forms a Swiss cross. They are large, substantial dogs with robust limbs, strong, muscular necks, and large heads with a long, powerful muzzle. Dark brown eyes have a friendly, inquiring expression, and the medium-length ears hang close to the head. The tail is thick and bushy.

Size & weight Height at withers 23–27 in. (58–69 cm); 87–90 lb. (39–41 kg)

Exercise needs Moderate to great

Grooming Considerable—coats need regular brushing **Life expectancy** 8–10 years

Points to consider These large dogs are not ideally suited to city life.

Saint Bernard

As mountain rescue dogs, the powers of Saint Bernards are almost legendary, and these massive dogs—equipped with the famous brandy barrel—are credited with saving hundreds of lives. The breed was probably developed by breeding the Asian "Molasser" dogs that the Roman armies brought to Helvetia (Switzerland) during the first two centuries A.D. with the native dogs that existed in the region during that time. They are large, powerful dogs with plenty of stamina and they need a good, high-quality diet—especially while they are still growing.

Temperament Saint Bernards are gentle and trustworthy dogs that are easily trained and make fine family pets. They need ample space and exercise, and though they are good with children, their very bulk means that constant supervision is necessary in order to avoid accidents.

Appearance Saint Bernards have a reassuring bulk and an intelligent expression that is emphasized by the white blaze on the face. The large, wide head is characterized by wrinkles on the forehead and a short muzzle; the flews of the lower jaw hang slightly. Saint Bernards are copious salivators. The wide neck gives way to a broad chest and back, with a strong tail that curves slightly at the tip. Saint Bernards can have either rough or smooth coats, and coloring is orange, red-brindle, or brown-brindle.

Size & weight Height at withers 25.5 in. (65 cm) for females; 27 in. (69cm); 110–200 lb. (50–91 kg)

Exercise needs Considerable—require regular daily walks (they prefer more frequent, short walks to long ones)

Grooming Considerable   **Life expectancy** 8–10 years

Points to consider Hereditary hip and heart problems. This breed drools a lot, and their size should be considered.

Did You Know?

🐾 Saint Bernards were first used as rescue dogs in the Swiss Alps by monks at the hospice at Saint Bernard Pass. The monks first brought the dogs to the hospice sometime between 1660 and 1670, probably to serve as watchdogs and as companions during the lonely winter months. The monks also used the dogs as draft animals and as pathfinders in the heavy mountain snowdrifts, which led to the discovery of their keen rescue instincts.

Standard Schnauzer

Known as the "Mittelschnauzer" in its native Germany, the Standard Schnauzer is the granddaddy of the giant and miniature breeds. Used for a variety of farm jobs, the Standard Schnauzer is rather too large to qualify as a terrier, and although it is a good ratter, it is more often used to herd livestock. The harsh coat requires a great deal of attention and must be stripped regularly.

Temperament These alert, friendly dogs respond very well to obedience training, but are not reliable with children.

Appearance Schnauzers are distinguished by their rough, wiry, black-and-white or pure black coats. The hair is longest on the face, where it forms a beard and eyebrows, giving the dog a slightly mischievous expression. They have a square, rugged build, with a relatively long chest and a short, stubby tail that is usually docked.

Size & weight Height at withers 17–19 in. (43–48 cm); 32–34 lb. (14–15 kg)

Exercise needs Great   **Grooming** Considerable   **Life expectancy** 12–14 years

Points to consider Grooming can be time-consuming; not suitable for households with young children.

Giant Schnauzer

With their bearded faces, Giant Schnauzers have an almost avuncular air, and their very size gives them an authority lacking in small dogs. Like all schnauzers, this breed had its beginnings in the neighboring Germanic kingdoms of Württemberg and Bavaria. Giant Schnauzers were traditionally used as cattle-herding and driving dogs and—by the first decade of the twentieth century—as watchdogs at German breweries.

Temperament Strong and quick to learn, these dogs benefit from early obedience training. They make loyal family pets, although they may be suspicious of strangers or unfamiliar animals.

Appearance Giant Schnauzers have a square, rugged silhouette and bodies capable of great stamina. They have harsh, wiry topcoats in shades of gray over a softer undercoat. The long head is covered in coarse hair (forming the impression of a beard and bushy eyebrows) narrowing gradually from the ears to the black nose. Triangular ears fold neatly forward. The body is stocky and powerful and the high-set tail is usually docked.

Size & weight Height at withers 23–27 in. (58–69 cm); 55–80 lb. (25–36 kg)

Exercise needs Considerable   **Grooming** Considerable

Life expectancy 12–14 years

Points to consider Schnauzers are often wary of children.

Komondor

With their unusual corded coats, Komondors are distinctive dogs that have been used for centuries as herders and—even more so—as guardians of sheep and cattle flocks in their native Hungary. They are independent, strong animals. It is common for a working Komondor puppy to be raised with a flock of sheep, being sheared at the same time as its charges. Komondors are most suited to experienced dog owners with plenty of space.

🐾 *The unique tassled coat of a fully mature Komondor takes up to two days to dry and requires a lot of maintenance.*

Temperament As companions, these dogs are courageous, territorial, and devoted, but they require training to socialize them from an early age.

Appearance The Komondor's coat takes two years to grow to maturity and, once the heavy, white cords have grown to their full length, they need plenty of care. The dense coat covers the whole body from head to tail, providing exceptional protection against bad weather and rough conditions; the skin underneath is an interesting shade of gray. Komondors are substantial dogs, well-muscled, with great agility and power. They have deep chests, muscular necks, and strong jaws.

Size & weight Height at withers 25–27 in. (64–69 cm); 40–60 lb. (18–27 kg)

Exercise needs Considerable—a long daily walk is required

Grooming Considerable

Life expectancy 10–12 years

Points to consider The grooming required for this breed is time-consuming. Komondors are not reliable with young children.

Non-Sporting Dogs

The category of non-sporting dogs encompasses dogs of a wide variety of shapes, sizes, and temperaments. These dogs do not quite fit into any of the other breed categories. Most are companion dogs that have been selectively bred, mainly for their looks, though a few breeds were once bred for a working purpose. (For instance, the Dalmatian was used as a carriage dog in the eighteenth century.) Many became companion dogs when the work they were trained for became outdated. Poodles, for example, are often pampered companions today, but were once used as water retrievers, and Bulldogs have been out of work in Britain since 1835, when bull-baiting was banned.

The most notable feature of the non-sporting category is the great diversity of breeds—a testament to the tastes and perseverance that have driven dog breeding down the centuries.

American Eskimo Dog

Despite its name, this dog is not descended from working sled dogs, but has been selectively bred as a companion dog from the medium-sized Nordic (Spitz) breeds. Around the turn of the twentieth century its intelligence, agility, and quickness to learn made this breed a common sight in circuses in the United States, where it was much favored by circus performers.

Temperament American Eskimo Dogs are alert and intelligent animals that make excellent guard dogs and are usually tolerant with children. Although these dogs are protective of their home and family, they generally will neither bite nor display aggressive behavior.

Appearance American Eskimo Dogs are handsome, luxuriant, white animals. They have elegant, finely featured heads, topped by small, erect, well-furred ears. The dense, soft undercoat is topped by a thicker, profuse, straight topcoat, which forms a distinct ruff around the neck. The body is compact and elegant, and the tail is carried curled over the back. The head has a tapered muzzle, black, oval eyes with black rims, and a black nose.

Size & weight Height at withers: Toy: 9–12 in. (23–30 cm), Miniature: 12–15 in. (30–38 cm), Standard: 15–19 in. (38–48 cm); weight in proportion to height

Did You Know?

🐾 This breed acquired its present name in 1917; previously it was known as the German Spitz, the name by which is still known in Germany. The breed originated in Pomerania, an area that covers parts of Germany and Poland.

Exercise needs Moderate

Grooming Considerable

Life expectancy 12–13 years

Points to consider This breed has no hereditary health problems. Shedding can be a nuisance.

Keeshond

Also known as the "Dutch Barge Dog," Keeshonds originated in the Netherlands, where they were the symbol of patriotic dissidents in the years before the French Revolution. They are handsome dogs, with abundant, rough coats that form a striking ruff around the shoulders and neck. Owners must ensure that these dogs do not overheat in hot weather. They have excellent hearing and are good watchdogs.

Temperament Keeshonds are intelligent dogs that learn quickly from obedience training. They are affectionate and tolerant and make excellent family pets.

Appearance Keeshonds are probably descended from Spitz-type dogs, as they share the characteristics of foxlike heads, pointed ears, and profuse coats. They are medium-sized dogs, sturdy, with a square silhouette. The harsh outercoat is a mixture of gray, black, and cream, and the breed standard specifies desirable markings on the face, legs, and body. The head is wedge-shaped, with a dark muzzle and dark "spectacle" markings around the almond-shaped eyes. The small, triangular ears are carried erect, and the thick, bushy tail is carried curled over the back.

Size & weight Height at withers 16–19 in. (41–48 cm); 55–66 lb. (25–30 kg)

Exercise needs Low to moderate

Grooming Considerable

Life expectancy 12–13 years

Points to consider There are some breed-related health concerns. Grooming is time-consuming—the coat will become matted if not brushed daily.

Schipperke

Small and energetic, this Belgian dog once worked on the canal boats of Flanders chasing vermin, and its name means "little captain." The Schipperke is physically similar to Spitz dogs, with a foxlike face and erect ears, though it is probably descended from the Belgian black sheepdog.

Temperament The Schipperke is a lively, intelligent breed that makes an affectionate family pet, although it can be suspicious (and noisy) with strangers and very stubborn.

Appearance The Schipperke's shiny coat is thick and harsh, and stands up around the neck to create a ruff, with "culottes" on the back and thighs. Longer than they are tall, Schipperkes have deep chests and powerful legs, with small, round feet. The head is reasonably wide with a pronounced stop and long, tapered muzzle; the small ears are erect. Dark brown eyes give the dog an alert expression. The outer coat is black, though the undercoat may be slightly lighter.

Size & weight Height at withers 10–13 in. (25–33 cm); 7–18 lb. (3–8 kg)

Exercise needs Moderate   **Grooming** Moderate   **Life expectancy** 13–14 years

Points to consider These dogs have no common hereditary health problems.

Löwchen

The Löwchen is also known as the "Little Lion Dog" because of the distinctive way its wavy coat is sometimes trimmed around the legs and loins. Löwchens are truly European dogs, being descended from French Bichons, and were used during the Middle Ages as affectionate companion dogs.

Temperament Löwchens are gregarious, intelligent dogs who love playing with children and are confident in their dealings with other dogs.

Appearance The Löwchen's coat only needs to be trimmed for show purposes and is naturally soft, long and wavy in any color. They are small compact dogs, slightly longer than they are high, with round heads and short muzzles. The eyes are deep set and inquisitive, while the nose color depends on the shade of the coat. The ears hang down the side of the head and are well-fringed. The high-set tail is clipped to leave a tuft at the end and is often carried over the back when the dog is moving.

Size & weight Height at withers 11–14 in. (28–36 cm); 9–18 lb. (4–8 kg)

Exercise needs Moderate   **Grooming** Considerable

Life expectancy 13–14 years

Points to consider These dogs have no common hereditary health problems.

Shiba Inu

The smallest and oldest of the Japanese dog breeds, the Shiba Inu was bred for many centuries as a highly skilled hunting dog. Although the breed came close to extinction during World War II, this is now the most popular native breed in Japan (where these dogs are still used to hunt small animals).

Temperament Agile, lively, and intelligent, Shiba Inus are affectionate pets for experienced and patient owners. They sometimes demonstrate aggression toward other dogs and tend to be aloof with strangers, but they are very devoted to those they know.

Appearance Shibas are striking dogs with thick double coats in shades of red, fawn, brindle, black, black-and-tan, and white. They are sturdy animals with muscular bodies, deep chests, and powerful legs. The head is a triangular shape, with the characteristic pointed Spitz muzzle, dark triangular eyes, and small, pointed, erect ears that are set high. The thick tail is carried curled over the back.

Size & weight Height at withers 13–15 in. (33–38 cm); 17–23 lb. (7–10 kg)

Exercise needs Moderate

Grooming Moderate

Life expectancy 12–13 years

Points to consider Newly developed teeth occasionally cause problems. Intensive training is required to correct dominant, and sometimes aggressive, behavior, and these dogs are better in the hands of experienced owners than novices.

Finnish Spitz

With their rich, golden coats, pointed muzzles, and erect ears, these handsome animals bear more than a passing resemblance to foxes. They are vigorous dogs, used by Finns for generations as hunters and retrievers. In fact, this breed is the national dog of Finland, where it is still used as a worker: These dogs employ their exceptional hearing to listen out for wing beats, which tell them that a bird has landed, and then bark loudly (a notable Spitz characteristic) to alert the hunter.

Temperament Friendly, intelligent, and alert, they make excellent watchdogs and outgoing family pets. They are easily trained and usually very obedient, although excessive barking is not easily corrected.

Appearance The Finnish Spitz has a glorious red double coat: The undercoat is a slightly lighter hue than the abundant topcoat and makes the whole coat glow. The body is compact and square, with a bushy tail that is carried curled over the back. The muzzle is pointed, the lively eyes almond-shaped and dark, and the ears are erect.

Size & weight Height at withers 15–20 in. (38–51 cm); 31–35 lb. (14–16 kg)

Exercise needs Considerable   **Grooming** Moderate   **Life expectancy** 12–14 years

Points to consider Excessive barking is a common complaint.

Chow Chow

The Chow Chow is considered one of the oldest recognizable breeds of dog—dating back at least two thousand years (and quite possibly longer) to the Han Dynasty in China. In ancient times, Chow Chows were used as hunting, herding, and pulling dogs, as well as for protection. Today, they are popular pets and guard dogs. They are probably descended from Spitz dogs, and they are distinguished as one of only two dog breeds to possess a blue-black tongue (the other being the Chinese Shar-Pei).

Temperament Chows are loyal dogs and are often aloof with strangers, but they respond well to firm, gentle handling. They are intelligent and independent.

Appearance Chow Chows have either thick, harsh coats, which give them a cuddly look (although they are anything but!) and form a ruff around the shoulders and neck, or, less commonly, smooth coats. They have well-proportioned heads and small, apparently scowling faces—this is caused by the slightly wrinkled forehead and pads of skin at the inner corner of each eye. A broad, short muzzle ends in a black nose. Small, rounded ears sit high on the head, and the compact body gives way to a thick tail, which is carried over the back.

Size & weight Height at withers 17–20 in. (43–51 cm); 45–75 lb. (20–34 kg)

Exercise needs Moderate—daily walk of 1–2 miles

Grooming Considerable

Life expectancy 11–12 years

Points to consider The small, tight eyes are prone to problems.

Lhasa Apso

Lhasa Apsos were bred exclusively in Tibet for many centuries and were used by monks and nobility as indoor guard dogs. Introduced to the West in 1921, this is now an exceptionally popular breed. Their distinctive long coats were once trimmed to resemble the flowing mane of a lion, and they require a great deal of grooming. The fur picks up dirt and dust from the floor. It does not molt, but mats naturally and therefore requires daily attention.

Temperament The Lhasa Apso was bred as a companion for monks, and it is a breed well-suited to domestic life, though these dogs do not tolerate young children and they are wary of strangers. Although these dogs enjoy human company, they are extremely self-reliant and are equally happy to occupy themselves.

Appearance The long, hard, slightly wavy coat of the Lhaso Apso is its most distinguishing feature. The outer coat reaches to the floor if left untrimmed and may be in almost any color, including grizzle, honey, sandy, slate, black, white, brown, or parti-color. The head is held proudly upright and is also covered in long hair. Long ears hang down the side of the head, and the eyes are dark and friendly. The muzzle is rounded and reasonably short. The tail is carried to one side over the back.

Size & weight Height at withers 9–11 in. (23–28 cm); 13–15 lb. (6–7 kg)

Exercise needs Moderate—daily walk of 1–2 miles

Grooming Considerable

Life expectancy 12–14 years

Points to consider These dogs are sometimes prone to back problems; test for eye disorders. They are not recommended for families with young or boisterous children.

Did You Know?

🐾 Lhasa Apso means "hairy barking dog," an apt summary of the dog's appearance and voice. (It still barks aggressively at unfamiliar sights and sounds.) The Tibetans compared these dogs to the mythological Snow Lion, and they were considered sacred, often being given to honored guests as a gift.

Standard Poodle

Poodles are an ancient breed. They were bred throughout Europe as retrieving water dogs—the name coming from the German *pudel* or *pudeln*, meaning "to splash." The breed is thought to have originated in Germany, where it was used as a water retriever. German Poodles were also used as working dogs to pull carts, and thus became larger and stronger than their French cousins (which were mainly companion dogs, and so became the smaller Toy and Miniature Poodles).

Temperament Poodles are delightful companion dogs, having great intelligence and being highly trainable— a characteristic that has led to their popularity as circus performers. Standard poodles make good family pets.

Appearance The thick, curly coat of the Poodle is often clipped in the "lion clip," which traditionally kept the joints and organs covered and warm, while freeing the legs for swimming. The coat, which can be any solid color, does not molt and must be regularly trimmed and washed. Standard Poodles are long-limbed and elegant, being squarely built, with a proud carriage. The head is small with a long, straight muzzle, dark, lively eyes, and long ears which hang from eye level or just beneath. The feet are small and well padded, while the tail is carried high.

Size & weight Height at withers 15 in. (38 cm); 45–70 lb. (20.5–32 kg)

Exercise needs Moderate to great

Grooming Moderate to considerable

Life expectancy 11–13 years

Points to consider This breed is sometimes prone to hip dysplasia and eye problems.

Tibetan Spaniel

These small dogs resemble Pekingese (and may well feature in their ancestry), but they are certainly not true spaniels. Introduced to the West in the mid-nineteenth century, their name may be derived from their pendant ears, which are similar to those of spaniels. In their native Tibet, they are reputed to have been used as "prayer dogs" and were trained to turn the monks' prayer wheels.

Temperament Tibetan Spaniels are confident and friendly dogs—faithful to their owners, but sometimes aloof with strangers.

Appearance Tibetan Spaniels are leggier, perhaps more handsome versions of Pekingese. With slightly longer muzzles, these attractive dogs do not suffer the same respiratory problems as the Pekingese does. Their heads are proportionately small, with wide-set, dark eyes and long, well-feathered ears that hang from high on the head. The silky double coat forms a shawl or ruff around the head and neck and is balanced by the fluffy tail, which is carried curled over the back. The coat can be any color. Longer than they are high, Tibetan Spaniels have slightly bowed front legs.

Size & weight Height at withers 10 in. (25 cm); 9–15 lb. (4–7 kg)

Exercise needs Moderate—short daily walk

Grooming Moderate

Life expectancy 13–14 years

Points to consider This breed has no hereditary illnesses and makes an adaptable pet.

Sweet-natured "Tibbies" are sensitive and responsive companions and are intelligent, alert, and quick learners in obedience classes. They are a deservedly popular breed as family pets.

Tibetan Terrier

Medium-sized, feisty animals, Tibetan Terriers were used as herding dogs in the remote, rocky landscapes of Tibet, and they have large, flat feet that helped them cope with the inhospitable landscape. They are hardy, robust animals with engaging temperaments and were traditionally given as good-luck gifts to travelers in Tibet's inaccessible Lost Valley.

Temperament These dogs are intelligent, loyal, and affectionate, though sometimes reserved with strangers. They are reliable family pets but not tolerant of young children.

Appearance Long hair disguises most of the Tibetan Terrier's features, leaving only a small black nose to face the world. The profuse, thick coat, which does not quite reach to the ground, provides excellent protection against harsh Tibetan climates.

Size & weight Height at withers 13–16 in. (33–41 cm); 17–23 lb. (7–10 kg)

Exercise needs Moderate—daily walk of 1–2 miles

Grooming Considerable   **Life expectancy** 13–14 years

Points to consider This breed has no hereditary disorders. They do not respond well to young children.

Bichon Frise

Classified in Britain as a toy breed, this tiny dog is probably descended from the French water-spaniel, the Barbet. Throughout history, Bichons have been popular among sailors, who traded them from continent to continent. Bichon Frises are robust dogs, and despite their small size, they used to round up sheep in Norway. This is exceptional, however, and Bichon Frises are happiest in families where they enjoy lots of playful exercise.

Temperament The Bichon Frise is renowned for its cheerful and confident temperament. Bichons are charming and intelligent companion dogs, and are easily trained. Evenly tempered, they are sensitive and good with children.

Appearance A black nose and dark eyes peer out from under a cloud of fluffy, white hair, giving this dog a humorous and inquisitive expression. The coat is long and loosely curling, and it requires careful grooming to prevent the curls from matting. They are compact dogs with gracefully arched necks and a finely chiseled face just visible beneath the profuse hair. The tail curls gracefully over the body.

Did You Know?

🐾 Although it originated in the Canary Islands and was once known as the Tenerife Dog, the Bichon Frise is French, its name meaning "fluffy little dog" (and a properly groomed Bichon certainly lives up to its name). From the fourteenth century, the Bichon breeds became popular with royalty and are seen in a great many paintings, especially those of Goya.

Size & weight Height at withers 9–11 in. (23–28 cm); 7–12 lb. (3–5.5 kg)

Exercise needs Minimal

Grooming Considerable

Life expectancy 13–14 years

Points to consider Pay extra attention to the teeth and gums, as these dogs are prone to gum disease.

🐾 *Grooming may be time-consuming and must not be neglected, as the Bichon's coat mats readily.*

Boston Terrier

Despite the fact that they are descended from fighting dogs (resulting from a cross between an English Bulldog and a white English Terrier), Boston Terriers are lively, intelligent animals that make good family pets. Bred in Boston, Massachusetts, the breed was registered with the American Kennel Club in 1893 and was originally used for ratting, as well as being a popular companion dog.

Temperament Boston Terriers are energetic dogs that relish human company, although males in particular are territorial around other dogs. Their overall gentle nature has earned them the nickname of "the American gentleman" among dogs.

Appearance Boston Terriers are compact dogs with smooth, glossy coats. The length of the legs must balance the length of the body to give the dog its characteristic square silhouette. They have square heads with short muzzles and a face free from wrinkles. The round eyes are wide-set, and erect ears are positioned on the outside edge of the skull. The short, fine coat requires only minimal grooming, and it should be red-brindle or black-brindle in color—ideally with white markings on the blaze,

around the eyes, and on the forechest. The tail is low-set, either tapering or screw, and should never be carried above the horizontal.

Size & weight Height at withers 15–17 in.; (38–43 cm); 15–25 lb. (7–11 kg)

Exercise needs Moderate—daily walk of 1–2 miles

Grooming Minimal

Life expectancy 12–13 years

Points to consider The comparatively large head size of this breed means that cesareans are sometimes required at whelping.

Did You Know?

🐾 Boston Terriers are one of very few breeds to have originated in the United States. They were selectively bred by crossing two fighting dogs, the English Bulldog and the white English Terrier, at the end of the nineteenth century.

Chinese Shar-Pei

The Chinese Shar-Pei is a unique breed that looks quite unlike any other. It is possibly related to the Chow Chow, as this is the only other breed having a blue-black tongue. The Shar-Pei has been bred in China for over two thousand years (although the ban on dog ownership in mainland China in the 1960s nearly led to its extinction). These dogs have become popular in the United States, with some 6,000 AKC registrations per year at the end of the 1990s.

Did You Know?

🐾 Shar-Pei literally means "sand skin," a good description of the characteristic prickly coat, which is rough and short and stands on end. Shar-Peis were also known as the "Chinese fighting dog," and their loose skin was a distinct advantage, as opponents found it hard to get a firm hold.

Temperament Used in dog fighting, herding, and guarding in their native China, Shar-Peis are now primarily companion dogs, valued for their calm temperaments and independent natures. Although they are occasionally aggressive and do not tolerate young children, they can be affectionate and devoted pets.

Appearance Shar-Peis are characterized by their large, wrinkled head (sometimes described as melon-shaped) and frowning expression. The hippopotamus-shaped muzzle is well padded, and the small eyes are deep-set and widely spaced. Small, shell-like ears hang close to the side of the head. The neck is set well into the shoulders, which are covered with folds of loose skin, with a dewlap around the neck and chin. The short, harsh, straight coat should never be trimmed and is one of four solid colors: cream, fawn, red, or black. The thick tail is high set, and may be carried over the back.

Size & weight Height at withers 18–20 in. (46–51 cm); 45–60 lb. (20–27 kg)

Exercise needs Moderate

Grooming Minimal

Life expectancy 11–12 years

Points to consider These dogs are prone to eye problems and skin conditions. They need firm discipline to bring out the best in their temperaments.

🐾 *The irresistible cuddly, wrinkled Shar-Pei puppy quickly grows into a powerful, well-built dog that can be stubborn and deceptively strong—and occasionally aggressive—so make sure you start obedience training early on and avoid games that might encourage dominant behavior.*

French Bulldog

The origins of French Bulldogs are the center of one of many Anglo-French disputes: The British believe they are descended from British Bulldogs, while the French allege that they are an ancient native French breed. Whatever the truth, both English and French bulldogs share the same short muzzle and squat, yet powerful, body shape. French Bulldogs are energetic and intelligent dogs, smaller than their British cousins and originally bred for ratting.

Temperament These dogs are lively and alert animals. They make affectionate household companions and good watch-dogs; they are usually best as loyal companions to a single owner, with whom they will enjoy a close bond.

Appearance French Bulldogs are distinguished by their erect, batlike ears and short, undocked tail. They have solid, compact bodies, large, broad heads, and short muzzles. The eyes are widely spaced, the jaws broad and undershot, and the nose is black. They have short, fine coats that are easy to groom and come in shades including brindle, pied, and fawn.

Size & weight Height at withers 12 in. (30 cm); 24–28 lb. (11–12.5 kg)

Exercise needs Moderate—short daily walk

Grooming Minimal

Life expectancy 11–12 years

Points to consider This is a charming breed, with no particular health problems. The ears and facial skin require regular attention, but they are otherwise relatively low-maintenance dogs.

Bulldog

Bulldogs are among the most instantly recognizable breeds, and their typical personality belies their somewhat fearsome appearance. They were bred for centuries to bait bulls for sport, and when the sport was banned in Britain in 1835, Bulldogs nearly became extinct. They have been selectively bred to enhance their appearance, almost to the point of discomfort: This breed is notorious for enduring difficult births and for suffering from respiratory problems, especially in hot weather.

Temperament Bulldogs are affectionate, dignified, and loyal. They are generally good-natured dogs that lack the capacity for vigorous exercise, but they enjoy playing with children and are appealing companion dogs.

Appearance Thick-set, substantial dogs, Bulldogs are characterized by their short-faced head, almost stumpy limbs, and wide shoulders. The head is massive, both broad and square in shape, with widely spaced eyes and a very short muzzle. The large jaws are undershot and the black lips, or flews, hang over the lower jaw; the lower jaw turns up to give the Bulldog its distinctive, apparently resolute expression. The neck is short and very broad, extending to muscular, wide-spaced shoulders. The forelegs are slightly shorter than the hind legs, and the tail is either straight or screwed. The fine, short coat is close-fitting and may be in any color; it requires only minimal grooming.

Size & weight The AKC does not prescribe a specific height range for this dog, though it says: "the circumference of the skull in front of the ears should measure at least the height of the dog at the shoulders," and height averages 12–16 in. (30–41 cm); 40–50 lb. (18–23 kg)

Exercise needs Minimal

Grooming Minimal

Life expectancy 7–9 years

Points to consider Bulldogs are sometimes prone to breathing difficulties.

Did You Know?

🐾 Bullbaiting probably began in England in 1204 after one Lord Stamford was entertained by the sight of a butcher's dog tormenting a bull. Stamford decided to provide a field for bullbaiting tournaments, as long as the butcher pledged to provide one bull each year. This undeniably cruel sport was popular for more than 600 years, but Bulldogs are now known for their gentleness.

Dalmatian

Few dogs have captured the public imagination in quite the same way as the Dalmatian—it's obviously something about the spots! This breed is probably descended from dogs imported by merchants to Dalmatia (a region of Croatia) and ancient Greece from India. Throughout the ages, Dalmatians have demonstrated their excellent working abilities as war dogs, sentinels, hunters, retrievers, draft dogs, and shepherds. They were used as coach and carriage dogs in Britain during the eighteenth and nineteenth centuries (trained to run alongside carriages to protect the occupants against thieves and highwaymen), but they were equally popular as a kind of fashion accessory among the wealthy. In the United States, Dalmatians are best known as firehouse dogs, as they were employed to control the horses that pulled fire wagons during the nineteenth century.

Did You Know?

🐾 In 1959, when the animated movie of Dodie Smith's book, *101 Dalmatians*, was released, the number of Dalmatians registered with the American Kennel Club doubled. In 1997, when the movie was remade with real dogs, registrations were three times their usual number!

Temperament Dalmatians are lithe, outgoing dogs, capable of great stamina and speed. They need plenty of exercise and enjoy the rough and tumble of family life, although males may demonstrate aggressiveness toward other dogs. They tend to be stubborn and unresponsive to obedience training.

Appearance Dalmatians are predominantly white dogs with black or liver-colored spots (although they are born completely white). They are of robust build, with deep chests, well-sprung ribcages, and reasonably long, muscular limbs. They have long, elegantly arched necks, well-defined heads, and square muzzles. The nose matches the color of the dog's spots: Thus, a black-spotted Dalmatian has a black nose, and a liver-spotted dog, a brown nose. Ears are positioned on the back of the head and hang down, while the eyes are wide-set, bright, and inquiring.

Size & weight Height at withers 19–24 in. (48–61 cm); 50–55 lb. (23–25 kg)

Exercise needs Considerable

Grooming Minimal

Life expectancy 12 years

Points to consider Hereditary deafness can be a problem.

Sporting Dogs

The sporting group includes breeds that have been classified as working dogs or gun dogs in other contexts and earlier times; among them, pointers, setters, and retrievers. They have all been bred to accompany huntsmen, either to help them in the task of flushing out game prior to the shoot, to point the way to downed game, or to retrieve it quickly and gently, without damaging it.

Many are kept purely as companion dogs today, or are trained to do very different work. (Labrador Retrievers, for example, were traditionally bred as water dogs, but they are now among the most popular household pets, and their intelligence also makes them excellent working companions for blind people.) As a group, the sporting dogs are lively, alert animals that require plenty of exercise and stimulation.

American Cocker Spaniel

With more finely chiseled features than their English cousins, from whom they are descended, American Cocker Spaniels are among the most popular purebred dogs in the United States today. They are characterized by long, glossy coats, which must be brushed every day to avoid matting and to retain shape.

Temperament Affectionate and lively, American Cocker Spaniels make excellent family pets and are very adaptable, coping as well with city life as with more rural surroundings. These are the smallest members of the sporting dog category, and they exhibit an accommodating, playful, and obedient personality. They are usually gentle and reliable with children.

Appearance Their dense, fine, slightly wavy coats are feathered on the chest, abdomen, legs, and ears, and short on the face. Colors range from solid black or brown of varying shades to these colors mixed with white. The head is well defined, and the top of the head is rounded with a definite stop. The eyes are large and appealing, and the ears are long and set low. The tail, which may be docked, is carried level with the long back.

Size & weight Height at withers 13–15 in. (33–38 cm); 24–28 lb. (11–13 kg)

Exercise needs Moderate

Grooming Considerable—regular professional help is desirable

Life expectancy 13–14 years.

Points to consider The popularity of this breed has led to overbreeding, and care must be taken to select a reputable breeder. Many carelessly bred Cocker Spaniels exhibit serious behavioral problems.

Did You Know?

🐾 The first spaniels probably arrived in America with the Pilgrims in 1620. Although they have been exhibited since the 1880s, American Cocker Spaniels were not recognized by the American Kennel Club as a separate breed until 1946.

English Cocker Spaniel

Energetic and instantly recognizable dogs, English Cocker Spaniels retain their basic gundog instincts and love to play games of seek and retrieve. The breed was developed in Britain around the end of the eighteenth century for small-game retrieving, but was not actually recognized until dog shows began in the late nineteenth century.

Temperament These are generally affectionate dogs, whose size makes them ideal companion dogs for city dwellers (although they also relish life in the country). They thrive on exercise—and particularly on games that provide mental stimulation—and it is vital that they are not allowed to become bored, when they may develop behavioral problems. They are usually gentle and reliable with children. Because of overbreeding, some animals may be high-strung and stubborn and will not tolerate teasing by young children, so check the family history before acquiring a puppy.

Appearance English Cocker Spaniels have silky, moderately long, wavy coats that require daily attention in colors varying from dark brown, black, and liver (all with white markings) to light brown. They have elegant, well-defined heads with large, soulful eyes and pendulous ears that hang from eye level. The ears, legs, and body are well feathered, and their paws are round and firm.

Size & weight Height at withers 15–17 in. (38–43 cm); 26–34 lb. (12–15 kg)

Exercise needs Moderate to considerable

Grooming Considerable

Life expectancy 13–14 years

Points to consider Hereditary eye and kidney problems are common. A small percentage of solid-colored dogs may be prone to "rage syndrome," a rare behavioral disorder characterized by sudden attacking for no apparent reason. Like their American cousins, these dogs have been overbred, and care should be taken to choose a puppy from a reputable breeder to avoid the risk of aggression and other behavioral problems.

Did You Know?

🐾 English Cocker Spaniels were originally known as "cocking spaniels," because they were used to flush woodcocks from hedges, thickets, and undergrowth.

English Springer Spaniel

Lively English Springer Spaniels are agile, medium-sized dogs that have been bred for at least 400 years to flush out and retrieve game over rough terrain. They are energetic dogs that thrive on work and love physical activity—whether it is chasing a ball in a park or retrieving birds from lakes and marshes. Kindly, alert eyes and a trusting expression, along with an extrovert and affectionate nature, ensure that they are popular family pets. Their great energy means that they require long walks every day, with a chance to play off the leash as often as possible—and if there is water around, they are likely to venture in for a swim, whatever the weather! Fortunately, these dogs are endowed with a dense undercoat under the wavy topcoat, which provides excellent all-weather protection.

Did You Know?

🐾 It is likely that all spaniel breeds are descended from English Springer Spaniels, who get their name from their ability to "spring," or startle, game birds. Spaniels were separated into two distinct types, cockers and springers, at the end of the nineteenth century. In the early years of the twentieth century, English Springers were briefly known as Norfolk Spaniels, named after a Duke of Norfolk who bred them.

Temperament Typically, English Springers are intelligent and respond well to obedience training; they thrive on mental and physical stimulation, without which they become bored and possibly destructive.

Appearance English Springers have wavy, smooth topcoats that should never appear coarse. Colors are either black and white or liver and white. Their bodies are compact and muscular, full of power and stamina, and tails (usually lively and wagging) are carried low. Heads are well-shaped with eyes set wide and long, floppy spaniel ears hanging from eye height. Their cheeks are flat and the upper lip naturally hangs lower than the jawline.

Size & weight Height at withers 19–20 in. (48–51 cm); 40–50 lb. (18–23 kg)

Exercise needs Considerable

Grooming Moderate to considerable

Life expectancy 12–14 years

Points to consider This breed has some hereditary eye and ear problems; occasional behavioral problems may be seen in carelessly bred families.

Sussex Spaniel

These melancholy looking, yet cheerful and devoted companion dogs are not common in either North America or Britain. Bred as hunting dogs, Sussex Spaniels are heavyset and have considerable stamina. They enjoy long walks and are happy in urban environments as long as they are given plenty of exercise every day. Their rich, liver-colored coats are very dense, so these dogs are not happy in hot, humid environments.

Temperament Sussex Spaniels are friendly dogs. They may appear suspicious of strangers, but they will reward their family with years of affection and are especially gentle with children. They should be socialized early with other dogs to prevent them from showing aggression.

Appearance Sussexes are heavily built spaniels with short, strong legs and long, muscular bodies. Their rich, golden-liver coat is slightly wavy, and the ears and front legs are well feathered. Strong, square heads top short, thick necks, and large lobe-shaped ears hang from eye height.

Size & weight Height at withers 13–15 in. (33–38 cm); 35–45 lb. (16–20 kg)

Exercise needs Considerable   **Grooming** Considerable   **Life expectancy** 12–13 years

Points to consider The eyelids and flews are prone to infections.

Spinone Italiano

These are very appealing dogs, with kindly and alert light brown eyes peering out from under a fringe of hair, with a long mustache and beard adding character to the dog's expression. Spinones have been bred since the twelfth century in northern Italy and their primary use was in retrieving game. They are powerful dogs with an immensely thick coat that is both impervious to extremes of weather and almost thorn-proof.

Temperament They are dignified dogs that are naturally patient, docile, and hardworking and enjoy playful, vigorous exercise.

Appearance The Spinone's overall shape is square; they have well-muscled bodies, deep chests, and broad, powerful thighs. The coat, which is usually all white or a combination of white and chestnut or white and orange, is dense and wiry, ideally about 1.5 in.(4 cm) long, although the soft hairs on the face are longer. Ears are triangular in shape and hang low on the head. The short, stumpy tail extends straight out from the back.

Size & weight Height at withers 22–27 in. (56–69 cm); 71–82 lb. (32–37 kg)

Exercise needs Moderate to considerable   **Grooming** Considerable   **Life expectancy** 12–13 years

Points to consider These dogs drool a great deal.

American Water Spaniel

Originally bred around the turn of the nineteenth century in the Midwest as a duck hunter, the American Water Spaniel excels at retrieving game from lakes and rivers and can be trained to do this from a boat. A sturdy, well-muscled dog, its color, coat, and build probably indicate the breed's descent from the Irish Water Spaniel and the Curly-Coated Retriever.

Temperament American Water Spaniels can be intelligent, affectionate dogs when they are provided with plenty of training and structured play. They require a great deal of stimulation and do not do well left alone for long periods. Given an active enough environment, they can make good family pets and play well with children if they are socialized with them early.

Did You Know?

🐾 The American Water Spaniel is the state dog of Wisconsin and was the first breed to be developed in the United States as an all-around hunter. It boasts the remarkable ability to retrieve from boats, launching itself into swiftly moving waters to swim out to collect game.

Appearance Coats are dark brown and closely waved or marceled (consisting of uniform waves), and eyes usually match the color of the coat. Typically, floppy spaniel ears are set above the eye line, but not too high, on the well-proportioned head.

Size & weight Height at withers 15–18 in. (38–46 cm); 25–45 lb. (11–20 kg)

Exercise needs Considerable—must have plenty of regular exercise

Grooming Considerable

Life expectancy 12 years

Points to consider This breed has no major hereditary health problems. Behavioral problems, including whining, barking, and destructive scratching, chewing, and digging, are likely if these dogs are underexercised or left alone for long periods.

Irish Water Spaniel

Distinguished by an intensely curly coat that appears to repel water—ideal for their original work of retrieving water fowl—these dogs possess great stamina and are outstanding swimmers. Because of their high energy, they are not suitable as indoor pets, but are ideal for anyone who can provide long daily walks in the country. The curly topknot of hair gives these dogs an almost comical appearance.

Temperament Playful, lively, and exuberant, Irish Water Spaniels seem to have a tremendous zest for life and are always keen to play—but these inquisitive dogs need rigorous obedience training.

Appearance The curly coat is a dark liver color and has an oily quality. These are the tallest of the spaniels and have a square-shaped body with a deep chest. The head is high-domed, with a strong muzzle and alert brown eyes peering from under a fringe of curls. The tail tapers to a smooth point.

Size & weight Height at withers 21–24 in. (53–61 cm); 45–65 lb. (20–30 kg)

Exercise needs Great   **Grooming** Considerable   **Life expectancy** 12–14 years

Points to consider Unsuitable for city dwellers.

Welsh Springer Spaniel

These lively, alert spaniels were first identified in Wales during medieval times, when they were known as "starters," as their job was to startle, or spring, game.

Temperament Welsh Springer Spaniels are loyal dogs that can be boisterous, but are usually responsive to obedience training. They love company and are full of energy, especially as puppies, when they may overwhelm small children with their strength and playfulness—though they are otherwise good with children.

Appearance Welsh Springers are characterized by attractive glossy coats of liver and white, which are flat and wavy, with feathering over the front legs. Hair on the face and tail is smooth. Ears are smaller and smoother than those of the English Springer Spaniel and are set low. A well-defined straight muzzle ends in a neat tip.

Size & weight Height at withers 17–19 in. (43–48 cm); 35–45 lb. (16–20 kg)

Exercise needs Considerable

Grooming Moderate   **Life expectancy** 13–14 years

Points to consider Hip and eye testing is advisable; these dogs require plenty of exercise and suit a rural environment.

German Shorthaired Pointer

Athletic, muscular, and alert, German Pointers appear poised for action. Descended from a nineteenth-century cross between heavy German Pointers and the lighter, leaner English Pointers, these are energetic dogs that require plenty of exercise.

Temperament German Shorthaired Pointers are lithe, intelligent dogs that love field work and stimulating games.

Appearance They have well-defined heads with large noses and well-opened nostrils, ideal for scenting. Their coats are short and dense and require little maintenance. Colors include black, liver, and either of these colors mixed with white. Short, stumpy tails extend directly from the muscular torso, and the chest is deep and broad.

Size & weight Height at withers 21–25 in. (53–64 cm); 45–70 lb. (20–32 kg)

Exercise needs Considerable   **Grooming** Minimal   **Life expectancy** 12–14 years

Points to consider These dogs require a great deal of exercise.

German Wirehaired Pointer

The German Wirehaired Pointer was developed as an all-around gundog, equally at home on land or water and adept at retrieving, flushing, and pointing. They are intelligent and energetic hunters that appreciate a good deal of exercise, and they make very good watchdogs.

Temperament Loyal and affectionate toward those they know, these dogs are also stubborn and protective.

Appearance The coat is dense, harsh, wiry, flat, and impervious to weather and water. Although the hair on the face is finer, German Wirehaired Pointers are distinguished by a small, coarse "beard." The coat is black and white, liver, or liver and white (although the American Kennel Club prefers liver-colored coats). They are sturdily built, medium-sized dogs, with an almost square muzzle.

Size & weight Height at withers 22–26 in. (56–66 cm); 55–70 lb. (25–32 kg)

Exercise needs Great   **Grooming** Moderate

Life expectancy 12–14 years

Points to consider These dogs are stubborn and difficult to train.

Pointer

Pointers are dignified dogs that embody powerful grace, speed, agility, and devotion. It is clear from artistic evidence that they were bred as early as the mid-seventeenth century in England for their clean profiles and calm intelligence, which enable them to point toward scented game. They have been bred to overcome a dog's natural instinct to descend upon and seize game; instead, they are trained to stand and point, allowing accompanying hounds to chase and seize the game.

Temperament Gentle and loyal dogs, Pointers are excellent around children. They thrive on plenty of exercise, so are usually happiest living in the country. These dogs are reasonably obedient and largely good-natured, although they can appear suspicious of strangers.

Appearance Pointers have short, smooth coats that are easy to maintain. Colors are liver, lemon, black, or orange, either in combination with white or solid-colored. They have neat heads, with distinctive, slightly concave muzzles, which give them a well-defined silhouette, and an elevated nose for scenting. Their hearing is exceptional and their high-set ears hang loosely, close to the head.

Did You Know?

🐾 The hunting instinct is evident in Pointers as young as two months of age. Their body language gives huntsmen a good idea of where quarry is located: Pointers hold their heads high when sniffing for a scent and low when pointing to game.

Size & weight Height at withers 23–28 in. (58–71 cm); 45–75 lb. (20–34 kg)

Exercise needs Great—enjoys long walks and a good run

Grooming Minimal   **Life expectancy** 12–13 years

Points to consider This breed can be overly sensitive and timid.

Brittany

Elegant and rugged spaniels with expressive faces, Brittanys are the most popular breed of dog in their native France. In the 1930s, the breed was introduced into the United States, where they have been bred as shooting dogs—their intelligence and keenness to work making them both successful and popular, especially among bird hunters. Despite their spaniel-type looks, they are natural pointers, with dense, wavy coats.

🐾 *The Brittany is alert and ready for action—whether work or play. The breed is named for the province in northwestern France where they were first bred.*

Temperament They are generally happy dogs with attractive temperaments, keen to interact with other animals as well as humans.

Appearance Wavy coats are either orange and white or liver and white in either clear or roan patterns. Tails are short and sometimes docked. Brittanys are compact dogs and they have a slightly squarer face than other spaniels, with floppy ears set high on the head.

Size & weight Height at withers 17–20 in. (43–51 cm); 30–40 lb. (13–18 kg)

Exercise needs Considerable

Grooming Moderate   **Life expectancy** 12–14 years

Points to consider Test for hip dysplasia. These dogs will become destructive and bark excessively if they are underexercised.

Vizsla

Noble hunting dogs, Vizslas (also known as Hungarian Pointers) are an ancient breed—with illustrations of very similar dogs dating from as far back as the tenth century. They were bred as hunters and were particularly valuable in falconry. After the introduction of firearms, Vizslas became skilled gundogs.

Temperament Vizslas are intelligent, gentle dogs that show good protective instincts and are rarely aggressive. They are sociable with both other dogs and humans, and they usually respond well to training, though they can be stubborn. Their character is best summed up by their name: *Vizsla* means "alert and responsive" in Hungarian.

Appearance Vizslas have short, dense coats that are an unusual light rusty-copper color.

Their bodies are muscular and strong, with a well-arched chest. Paws are rounded, compact, and almost catlike. The head is lean and muscular, with the broad muzzle tapering to a square, brown nose and a furrow down the center of the forehead. Tails are usually docked. Ears are wide and silky and hang from above eye level, close to the cheeks.

Size & weight Height at withers 21–24 in. (53–61 cm); 48–66 lb. (22–30 kg)

Exercise needs Considerable

Grooming Minimal   **Life expectancy** 13–14 years

Points to consider With thin coats, these dogs do not fare well in extreme cold. They need a great deal of exercise.

Did You Know?

🐾 The national dog of Hungary, the Hungarian Vizsla was nearly extinct before 1945. The sleek, attractive breed survived and flourished because many émigrés took their pets with them when they emigrated to North America and other parts of Europe. The wire-haired variety was developed in the 1930s and is particularly popular in Canada, but it is not recognized by the American Kennel Club.

Weimaraner

Classic pointers, Weimaraners were developed in the German city of Weimar during the nineteenth century, at the court of Grand Duke Karl August of Weimar. They were bred specifically as hunting dogs for the nobility, and even in the early years of the twentieth century, their use was strictly limited to members of Germany's exclusive Weimaraner Club. Naturally, these dogs were considered highly prestigious.

Temperament They are handsome, dominant dogs, and should undergo rigorous obedience training at an early age to keep them under control. They are highly protective, especially of children, and they make good family pets, given the right home. They are large animals and need plenty of exercise and stimulating games, so are probably happier in a rural environment. As a breed, they are alert, courageous, and friendly dogs, but they are too stubborn and boisterous for first-time owners.

Did You Know?

Weimaraner puppies are striped at birth and have blue eyes. The stripes fade after a few days, and their eyes change to the breed's characteristic amber color by the time they are two or three months old.

Appearance Weimaraners have an unusual and beautiful coat that varies between mouse-gray and silver-gray, with an almost metallic sheen. The coat is short, dense, and barely sheds, making Weimaraners an excellent choice of dog for allergy sufferers. They are powerfully built animals, well-muscled, with deep chests and a dignified bearing. Their heads have long muzzles and wide-set, pale-colored eyes (amber, light blue, or gray). The ears are large, high-set, and slightly folded. Tails on working dogs are usually docked.

Size & weight Height at withers 23–27 in. (58–69 cm); 70–86 lb. (32–39 kg)

Exercise needs Great

Grooming Minimal

Life expectancy 11–14 years

Points to consider While Weimaraners can make excellent family pets, they are too exuberant for very small children, and obedience training is a challenge. Prospective owners should be prepared to devote plenty of time to training and exercise.

Field Spaniel

Field Spaniels are solid, medium-sized dogs, bred in England from Cockers and Sussex Spaniels. Selective breeding to emphasize the length of the back and short, heavy legs meant that Field Spaniels became useless as working dogs, and by 1945 the breed was almost extinct. The breed was revived twenty years later, and today these dogs make excellent family pets who love human companionship— but they should be socialized with children at an early age.

Temperament Field Spaniels are energetic and very enthusiastic when it comes to outdoor activity. They are receptive to training.

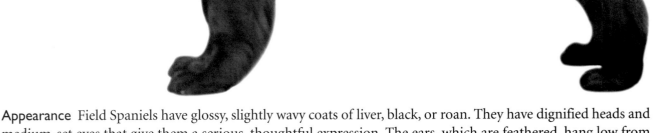

Appearance Field Spaniels have glossy, slightly wavy coats of liver, black, or roan. They have dignified heads and medium-set eyes that give them a serious, thoughtful expression. The ears, which are feathered, hang low from the head and the short, straight tail is carried low.

Size & height Height at withers 16–19 in. (41–48 cm); 35–55 lb. (16–25 kg)

Exercise needs Considerable

> *Field spaniels have serious, yet gentle eyes and can give the appearance of thinking carefully. Their soft, pendulous ears are long and require regular checking and occasional trimming. These gentle dogs love their human companions and dislike long periods left alone.*

Grooming Considerable

Life expectancy 13 years

Points to consider These dogs are very energetic and may not do well in an urban environment, though they are calm indoor pets if exercised sufficiently.

Irish Setter

Little is known about the early history of the Irish Setter, a breed that gained in popularity in the early eighteenth century, but these dogs are probably descended from some combination of Irish Water Spaniel, Irish Terrier, English Setter, Spaniel-Pointer, and Gordon Setters.

Temperament Lively and playful, Irish Setters are beautiful dogs who love to interact with people and other animals. They are slow to mature mentally and sometimes appear excitable, but they are extroverts full of irrepressible energy and affection. These animals are eager to please, but it is sometimes hard for them to overcome their natural instincts, and as a result, training can be long and drawn out, and recall training is usually challenging.

Appearance The finely chiseled head ends in a long, elegant muzzle, with a neat black or chocolate-colored nose. They have a long, silky topcoat of deep chestnut, which is straight and fine on the head, on the front of the legs, and at the ear tips, but well-feathered over the rest of the body, and will require regular attention to avoid matting. They have an athletic build, with a deep, narrow chest and well-sprung ribs.

Size & weight Height at withers 25–27 in. (64–69 cm); 60–70 lb. (27–32 kg)

Exercise needs Considerable

Grooming Moderate to considerable   **Life expectancy** 12 years

Points to consider Irish Setters are prone to hip dysplasia and eye problems. Overbreeding has led to a number of problems including behavioral disorders, so care must be taken to select a reputable breeder. This breed demands patience during training.

Did You Know?

🐾 The Earl of Enniskillen, a nineteenth-century fancier of this breed, was one of many who considered Irish Setters the most beautiful of all dogs. Famous American owners include the movie star Mary Pickford, and the breed's popularity increased dramatically with the 1962 release of the movie *Big Red*.

English Setter

Beautiful dogs with soulful eyes, English Setters have been bred since at least the fourteenth century, initially as hunting dogs. Today, they are lively, energetic dogs that thrive on companionship and appreciate very long walks.

Temperament These dogs are gentle and sweet-natured and are especially calm around children.

Appearance English Setters are graceful, strong dogs, with long, slightly wavy topcoats that come in a range of colors: orange belton, blue belton (white with black markings), tricolor (blue belton with tan on muzzle, over the eyes, and on the legs), lemon belton, and liver belton. They have a deep, well-ribbed chest that allows for great stamina and rounded, compact feet with arched toes.

Size & weight Height at withers 24–25 in. (61–64 cm); 55–66 lb. (25–30 kg)

Exercise needs Considerable   **Grooming** Moderate to considerable   **Life expectancy** 12–13 years

Points to consider Skin allergies are common.

Gordon Setter

Robust, dignified dogs, Gordon Setters are the strongest and heaviest of the setters, built for stamina rather than speed. They were developed in Scotland from at least 1620 where they were popular as hunting dogs.

Temperament Bred to scent out game and wait for the hunter, Gordons are patient creatures, never aggressive unless someone they love is under threat. They are energetic dogs that love to be outside and they are devoted to their owners, but they can be strong-willed.

Appearance The head is reasonably heavy and well defined, with long ears set low and close to the head. Gordons are black and tan in color, and their long coats are flat (apart from on the ears and legs, where the coat curls attractively). They have short, well-sprung backs, and short, feathered tails. Their dark brown eyes lend a keen, yet imperturbable, air to their expression.

Size & weight Height at withers 23–27 in. (58–69 cm); 45–80 lb. (20–36 kg)

Exercise needs Considerable

Grooming Moderate to considerable

Life expectancy 12–13 years

Points to consider Gordons are not suited to city life.

Chesapeake Bay Retriever

As its name suggests, the Chesapeake Bay Retriever was bred to retrieve game along the shores of Chesapeake Bay. A strong, powerful animal, its jaws are perfectly adapted to carry birds gently yet firmly, and its dense double coat provides protection against the cold—often icy—conditions in which it works.

Temperament Bright, courageous dogs with a love of water, Chesapeake Bay Retrievers are generally respectful to strangers and calm with children—although they can be tricky to train, as they are also independent creatures. With sufficient training and exercise and early exposure to children, they can make good family pets.

Did You Know?

🐾 Chesapeakes are descended from two Newfoundland puppies who were rescued from an English ship that was wrecked off the coast of Maryland in 1807. The British sailors gave the puppies as a gift to the American men who showed them hospitality. The puppies and/or their offspring were probably bred with local dogs around the Chesapeake Bay to produce this hardy breed.

Appearance The dark-brown or yellow-brown coat is thick, short (but not curly), and contains a good quantity of natural oils; it is especially wavy on the shoulders, loins, and back, but the tail should not be feathered. The broad skull is covered in short hair. Eyes are wide-set and very clear, usually yellowish or amber in color, and give the dog an inquisitive demeanor; ears hang loosely from high on the head. Feet are strong and slightly webbed, which aids their swimming ability. These dogs are powerfully built, of medium height, and have great stamina.

Size & weight Height at withers 21–26 in. (53–66 cm); 55–80 lb. (25–36 kg)

Exercise needs Considerable—a daily walk of 2–3 miles

Grooming Moderate—coat sheds in the spring and needs daily brushing

Life expectancy 10–12 years

Points to consider These dogs tend to suffer from eye problems in old age. They are energetic and not suited to city life. To prevent aggressive, dominant behavior from developing, owners should be prepared for firm, intensive training of young puppies, and tug-of-war games should be avoided.

Wirehaired Pointing Griffon

Originated by the Dutch breeder Eduard Korthals during the nineteenth century, the Wirehaired Pointing Griffon is nevertheless considered a French breed—as the major portion of its development took place in France. It is a classic hunting dog and is also happy to retrieve game and chase rodents.

Temperament This dog is obedient, faithful, and hardworking, and makes an excellent family pet. Training and firm control are essential, as some can be headstrong.

Appearance Griffons owe their rugged appearance to their topcoats, which are wiry, thick, and impervious to harsh weather; the AKC considers it preferable for these dogs to be colored steel gray with brown markings, but there are several variations. They have square, bearded muzzles, and friendly ears peer out from under moderately long facial hair.

Size & weight Height at withers 20–24 in. (51–61 cm); 50–60 lb. (23–27 kg)

Exercise needs Great   **Grooming** Moderate   **Life expectancy** 12–13 years

Points to consider These dogs can be destructive if insufficiently exercised.

Clumber Spaniel

Originally used to track and retrieve game, Clumber Spaniels were named after the Duke of Newcastle's home, Clumber Park, where a number of these dogs were sent by a French duke during the French Revolution. With their long, low backs and massive heads, Clumber Spaniels probably number Basset Hounds and Alpine Spaniels among their forebears. They have impressive scenting talents and stamina, and need vigorous exercise and training to prevent them from becoming bored.

Temperament Dignified dogs, Clumber Spaniels are affectionate and gentle with those they know, and they rarely show aggression to strangers.

Appearance With an abundant silky coat, Clumbers are predominantly white and have feathered tails. They have large heads and a pensive expression, with floppy ears set low. They have powerful hind legs and large feet that are well covered with hair.

Size & weight Height at withers 17–20 in. (43–51 cm); 55–85 lb. (25–39 kg)

Exercise needs Moderate

Grooming Considerable   **Life expectancy** 12–13 years

Points to consider These dogs are good family pets but require patience during training.

Golden Retriever

Golden Retrievers combine good looks with affectionate, sensible, and equable temperaments, and they are one of the best-loved breeds in the world. This dog was developed in the late nineteenth century by crossing a Tweed Water Spaniel (now extinct) with other breeds (including a Newfoundland, Irish Setters, and other water spaniels).

Temperament Goldens demand attention from their owners, but they repay it with utter devotion and obedience. They are easy to train and their instinct to retrieve remains strong—and they will often bring their owners unexpected gifts! Golden Retrievers are such amenable, intelligent dogs that they are often selected to work as seeing-eye dogs for the blind or in other areas of pet therapy. They are reliable with children of all ages and enjoy plenty of play.

Appearance The distinctive golden coat may vary in hue from cream to pale gold or almost auburn, and may become lighter with age. It is usually flat or wavy, with feathering around the forelegs, and requires daily brushing to rake out dead hair; it is advisable to trim the hair around the feet, neck, and tail. The head is covered in short, straight hair, and the powerful muzzle is distinguished by a large black nose, with dark flews that droop naturally on the lower jaw. The eyes appear kindly and alert. Neat ears hang low and well back on the head.

Size & weight Height at withers 21–24 in. (53–61 cm); 55–75 lb. (25–34 kg)

Exercise needs Moderate to considerable

Grooming Considerable—these dogs shed profusely

Life expectancy 12–13 years

Points to consider Hereditary problems may include allergic skin conditions, eye problems, hip dysplasia, and epilepsy. This breed has become extremely popular, and overbreeding has caused problems ranging from health concerns to aggression. Goldens are not especially energetic, but they must be exercised well every day, because they tend to gain weight easily.

Did You Know?

🐾 Golden Retrievers are excellent swimmers, and during the nineteenth century they were bred to retrieve waterfowl. Their powerful muzzles hide a gentle mouth, ideal for game retrieval, and the thick tail is used as a rudder when swimming.

Curly-Coated Retriever

Curly-Coated Retrievers are possibly the oldest retrieving breed in the world, and although they are not now so common in their native Britain, they were a longtime favorite among gamekeepers. Robust, intelligent dogs, they are popular family pets in the United States. The Curly-Coated Retriever was bred to retrieve waterfowl.

Temperament Hardworking, loyal, and even-tempered, Curlies make keen watchdogs. They benefit from stimulating training and should be kept active and exercised.

Appearance These dogs are either black or liver-colored, and their tight curls cover the whole body apart from the face, where the hair appears straighter. Eyes are almond-shaped and help give the dog an alert expression.

Size & weight Height at withers 23–27 in. (58–69 cm); 65–80 lb. (29–36 kg)

Exercise needs Considerable   **Grooming** Moderate   **Life expectancy** 11 years

Points to consider They are not suited to city life.

Flat-Coated Retriever

Versatile gundogs, Flat-Coated Retrievers excel at field trials and make excellent companions. The breed declined in popularity during the twentieth century, eclipsed by Labradors and Goldens, but numbers are now increasing.

Temperament This cheerful, lively breed is a faithful family pet that responds well to training and is eager to please.

Appearance Liver or black in color, the fine, straight coat lies flat over a dense, waterproof undercoat. The head has a gently sloping stop, and eyes seem constantly alert and quizzical. The tail is well feathered, as are the strong legs that end in round feet with arched toes.

Size & weight Height at withers 22–24 in. (56–61 cm); 55–80 lb. (25–36 kg)

Exercise needs Considerable

Grooming Moderate to considerable   **Life expectancy** 11–13 years

Points to consider This breed is susceptible to bone cancer.

Labrador Retriever

These dogs originated in Newfoundland, Canada, where they were used to retrieve fishing nets and were known as the "small water dog" (to distinguish them from their larger Newfoundland cousins). Early-nineteenth-century salt-cod traders brought them to England, where landowners began breeding them and training them for use as gundogs. They have a natural instinct for hard work and make excellent retrievers. Their innate intelligence has made them the breed of choice as seeing-eye dogs. Inactive dogs are prone to boredom and weight gain so their diet must be carefully supervised.

Temperament One of the most popular breeds, Labrador Retrievers make excellent family pets, as they are equable, gentle, and intelligent dogs that are reliable with children of all ages. Lively puppies respond well to obedience training.

Appearance Black, yellow, or chocolate, Labradors' coats are short, straight, and dense, with a soft undercoat to protect them from the elements. They require minimal grooming, although the dense undercoat sheds profusely in the spring. Strongly built, with a well-developed, broad head, powerful neck, and kindly brown eyes, Labrador Retrievers are characterized by their tapering "otter" tail and well-developed foot pads.

Size & weight Height at withers 21–24 in. (53–61 cm); 55–80 lb. (25–36 kg)

Exercise needs Considerable

Grooming Minimal

Life expectancy 12–13 years

Points to consider These dogs are prone to eye and hip problems in old age, and they tend to gain weight easily.

Did You Know?

🐾 Labrador Retriever bitches selected to work as seeing-eye dogs are specially chosen for their intelligence and equable temperament, and they begin their training as six-week-old puppies. The average working life of a guide dog is eight or nine years, and training is rigorous—beginning with a sighted "puppy walker," who accustoms the dog to traffic, noises, urban scenes, and crowds (and all the everyday situations encountered by a blind person). When the dog is a year old, it learns how to deal with crossing roads, to judge height and width so that the owner does not bump into obstacles, and how to cope with traffic.

Terriers

The word "terrier" comes from the French, meaning "to go to ground." Terriers were traditionally small, aggressive dogs that were bred for pursuing vermin such as rats, badgers, and foxes. In the nineteenth century, small dogs like Yorkshire Terriers were bred almost exclusively for the sport of ratting, when owners competed to see how many rats their terriers could kill in a given time. Many members of the modern terrier group, such as the Airedale, Fox, or Kerry Blue, are considerably larger, as they are also descended from hunting breeds.

In the days when transport and local communications were poor, terriers were bred regionally, and selective breeding emphasized whatever features would best equip the animals to cope with local conditions. The Lakeland Terrier, for example, from the Lake District of northern England, is especially nimble, enabling it to cope with the rocky outcrops of the local hills and dales. Similarly, the appealing small Scottish breeds (among them, the Skye, West Highland White, and the eponymous Scottish Terrier) have exceptionally thick double coats to protect them against the more severe conditions of a Highland winter. The terriers that originated in Ireland are larger than those from Britain, partly because they were crossbred with hunting dogs to circumvent a law forbidding peasants to own hunting dogs. Today's Irish terriers, such as the Kerry Blue and the Soft-coated Wheaten, are all-round working dogs, skilled at retrieving, guarding, and herding.

Self-confident, captivating dogs, terriers make terrific family pets and provide constant entertainment. As a group, terriers are feisty dogs with tremendous energy. Though most are affectionate, they can be noisy, sometimes intolerant of children, and some may nip when irritated—so owners should remember this when training and socializing a terrier puppy.

Airedale Terrier

With their grave, yet friendly, expressions and their good-natured playfulness, Airedales are popular family pets. The breed originated in the mid-nineteenth century in Yorkshire, England, when the Old English Broken Haired Terrier was crossed with the Otterhound to produce a large, alert dog used by miners and mill owners to hunt otters. They are the largest dogs in the terrier group, a fact that has earned them the nickname "King of Terriers."

Temperament Airedales are hard workers, but they can also be stubborn dogs and they need firm discipline from an early age. Confident and outgoing, they are very protective of their family (and often very vocal about it!), and thus they make excellent watchdogs. Owners should be aware that these dogs are often suspicious of other dogs, and they may be keen on fighting.

Appearance Airedales have a black-and-tan outercoat that is wiry, stiff, and dense. It provides excellent all-weather protection over a softer and shorter undercoat, but must be groomed regularly to prevent knotting. The head and legs should always be tan-colored, while the back is usually black. The head is long and framed by a soft beard on the strong jaws. V-shaped ears fold forward above the level of the skull, and wide-set dark eyes are balanced by a neat black nose. The body and thighs are muscular and the feet are round and compact.

Size & weight Height at withers 22–24 in. (56–61 cm); 44–50 lb. (20–23 kg)

Exercise needs Considerable

Grooming Moderate to considerable

Life expectancy 13 years

Points to consider Always supervise these dogs during play, as they tend to become overexcited.

Did You Know?

🐾 Alert, responsive Airedale Terriers were among the earliest breeds to be used as police dogs. During World War I, they were steady and reliable enough to work as messengers along the front line, and they were also used to help locate injured soldiers.

Irish Terrier

Bred since the seventeenth century as hunting dogs, Irish Terriers excel as water retrievers and are successful competitors in field trials.

Temperament Playful and charming, Irish Terriers can be both headstrong and affectionate. They are excellent family companions, but will not shirk from a confrontation with other dogs, so it is very important that they receive obedience training.

Appearance Once known as the "Irish Red Terrier," these dogs have dense, wiry, water-resistant outercoats that are a beautiful dark gold color (formally referred to as red or red-wheaten) and need plucking twice a year. They have long heads with a flat skull, topped by triangular ears that fold forward, level with the dark eyes. Irish Terriers are characterized by muscular chests, reasonably long bodies, and a tail that is carried high.

Size & weight Height at withers 18 in. (46 cm); 25–27 lb. (11–12 kg)

Exercise needs Considerable

Grooming Moderate

Life expectancy 13–14 years

Points to consider This breed has a tendency to dominant behavior and requires thorough training at a young age.

🐾 *This Irish Terrier has characteristically bushy eyebrows and beard and neat, forward-folded, high-set ears.*

Kerry Blue Terrier

With their long facial whiskers and narrow heads, these distinctive blue-black terriers are the national dog of Ireland. Initially bred as ratters, they make impressive watchdogs and loyal companions.

Temperament Kerry Blue Terriers can be strong-willed, even aggressive, but once obedience-trained they make affectionate, lively pets and excellent watchdogs.

Appearance The Kerry's coat is soft, silky, and very thick and requires regular trimming; there is no undercoat, and the facial whiskers need daily grooming. Comparatively small heads top long, powerful necks. They have small dark eyes and understated ears that fold forward onto the forehead.

Size & weight Height at withers 17–19 in. (43–48 cm); 33–40 lb. (15–18 kg)

Exercise needs Moderate

Grooming Moderate to considerable

Life expectancy 13 years

Points to consider This breed is known for its assertiveness and stubborn nature. It requires firm training and is not suitable for households with young children.

Did You Know?

🐾 Kerry Blue Terriers generally have black fur at birth, and the color changes gradually until the dog is mature, at about two years old. The head, ears, tail, and feet of the mature dog are usually darker than the body color.

Lakeland Terrier

These affable, courageous, and hardworking dogs originated as fox-hunting dogs in the Lake District of England (where foxes are infamous for raiding sheepfolds). Tough and competitive, they appreciate challenging games. And, as they were bred to cope with rocky terrain, their agility is impressive.

Temperament As a family dog, the Lakeland Terrier may try to demonstrate a single-minded and stubborn attitude, so early training is recommended.

Appearance Lakelands have long, strong necks, and short, well-muscled backs. They need regular grooming to maintain the dense, wavy topcoat; twice-yearly stripping will ensure that the coat retains its shape. Colors range from wheaten; red; blue and tan; black and tan; or simply black. Triangular ears fold forward above the dark or hazel eyes, and a long mustache covers the strong jaws.

Size & weight Height at withers 14–15 in. (36–38 cm), 15–17 lb. (7–7.5 kg)

Exercise needs Moderate

Grooming Considerable

Life expectancy 13–14 years

Points to consider These are independent dogs that need patient owners and good training. They will become destructive if left alone for long periods.

🐾 *This cheerful Lakeland Terrier sports a friendly grin, but appearances can be deceptive: Lakelands are often hostile toward strangers, though they are friendly and sociable as pets, thriving on plenty of attention.*

Miniature Schnauzer

With their bushy eyebrows and abundant, long beards, Miniature Schnauzers have an air of gravity and paternal concern that is unusual in small dogs. They are originally from southern Germany and are descended from the same stock as Standard Schnauzers, with the addition of Affenpinscher and Miniature Pinscher bloodstock in their ancestry (which reduced their size). Miniature Schnauzers were used for a variety of farm jobs, such as herding, guarding, and rat catching.

Temperament Calm and reliable—and less noisy than many terriers—they are affable dogs that enjoy human company and the routine of family life, though they must be socialized at an early age with children.

Appearance Miniature Schnauzers have an almost square profile; they are roughly as tall as they are long, and they hold their rear legs (in particular) very straight. They have wide, powerful necks, comparatively long chests, and compact, round, catlike feet. The harsh, rough topcoat extends to bushy eyebrows and a beard that covers the dog's powerful muzzle. The coat needs regular grooming and trimming to keep it in shape (especially as this breed tends to get messy while eating). The undercoat is far softer and provides excellent warmth; Miniature Schnauzers do not cope well in hot climates. Ears are an elongated triangular shape and flop forward alongside the eyes, which appear high-set and bright.

Size & weight Height at withers 12–14 in. (30–36 cm); 10–18 lb. (4.5–8 kg)

Exercise needs Moderate   **Grooming** Moderate

Life expectancy 13–14 years

Points to consider Miniature Schnauzers are highly vocal, and excessive barking should be discouraged in early training.

Did You Know?

🐾 Schnauzers get their name from their most distinctive feature: *Schnauzer* is German for "nose" or "snout." Miniature Schnauzers' long muzzles are emphasized by their splendid beards.

Scottish Terrier

Feisty and independent, Scottish Terriers are small dogs with big characters. Like many other terriers, "Scotties" were bred to pursue and kill vermin. They are courageous animals (sometimes nicknamed "Diehard") that are very agile—despite their short legs and thickset bodies. Scotties were first bred in the early 1800s, and the Scottish Terrier Club was formed in 1892, when the breed standard was established.

Temperament Scotties are very loyal to their immediate human family and are often suspicious of strangers (although they are rarely aggressive). Some dogs have short tempers and will not tolerate teasing by children.

Appearance The color of the long coat can be black, wheaten, or brindle of any shade. The outer coat is rough and dense and extends to eyebrows and a beard, which give the dog its dignified appearance. The beard needs daily care and the whole coat should be trimmed twice a year. The head is long, and this is sometimes accentuated by the Scottie's beard. Ears are held erect, as is the tapering tail. Almond-shaped eyes have a keen, piercing expression. The body is robust and strong, and the hindquarters are especially powerful for a dog of this size.

🐾 *The Scottie's wiry, long coat does not shed a great deal, but it needs weekly brushing and quarterly trimming.*

Size & weight Height at withers 10 in. (25 cm); 18–22 lb. (8–10 kg)

Exercise needs Moderate to considerable

Grooming Moderate

Life expectancy 13–14 years

Points to consider Scotties must be supervised carefully as they like to chase small animals; they are sometimes irritable and snappy with small children.

Sealyham Terrier

One of the most ancient terrier breeds, Sealyhams are originally from Sealyham in Pembrokeshire, in west Wales. They are descended from various terrier breeds, as well as the Corgi. These dogs were outstanding hunters of badger and otters, being able to work in underground burrows, aboveground, and in water.

Temperament Sealyham Terriers are fearless and bossy dogs, and they may be prone to aggression (unless properly trained). In general, they are loyal family pets and are good with older children.

Appearance Sealyhams are white terriers, although black or brown markings on the head and ears are permissible. With short legs and long bodies, they present a rectangular silhouette. They have slightly domed heads, dark, deep-set eyes, and ears that are set well back on the head and hang down beside the cheeks. The coat is long, hard, and wiry over a dense protective undercoat, and long hair on the face gives the head an almost square shape; eyebrows and beard are bushy.

Size & weight Height at withers 10 in. (25 cm); 22–24 lb. (10–11 kg)

Exercise needs Low to moderate

Grooming Considerable

Life expectancy 13–14 years

Points to consider These dogs need training to discourage their tendency toward aggressive behavior.

🐾 *These white, bearded dogs enjoy digging and exploring. After a romp in the park they will probably return home needing a thorough brushing to restore their appearance!*

Wire Fox Terrier

For almost 100 years, Smooth and Wire Fox Terriers were considered to be of the same breed. In 1984, however, the AKC divided these dogs into two breeds, as it is now believed that they are descended from different sources. Like its smooth counterpart, the Wire Fox Terrier is an enthusiastic digger and was bred to flush foxes and vermin from their holes.

Temperament Wire Fox Terriers are alert dogs with keen expressions and hardy constitutions. They are not particularly affectionate toward people, although socialization and training from an early age are helpful.

Appearance With their long, square muzzles and dense facial whiskers (which form a small beard), Wire Fox Terriers have a rather serious demeanor. They are strongly built dogs with a dense, wiry coat that may be crinkly. The color may be white, white and tan, or black and white. These dogs present an almost square silhouette, with their straight backs and forelegs, and they should carry their tails erect, but never curled over.

Size & weight Height at withers 14–15 in. (36–38 cm); 15–20 lb. (7–9 kg)

Exercise needs Considerable   **Grooming** Moderate   **Life expectancy** 13–14 years

Points to consider These dogs may be prone to deafness.

Soft-Coated Wheaten Terrier

With their round head, black nose, and appealing eyes, Soft-coated Wheaten Terriers look like cuddly bundles of fun—which, by and large, they are. Hardy Irish farm dogs, they are used for guarding, herding, and hunting.

Temperament They are affable, intelligent, playful dogs and are gentle with children. Their steady temperament and responsiveness to obedience training makes these dogs popular as family pets.

Appearance Their soft, silky coats are thick, wavy, and the color of ripening wheat—hence the breed's name. The coat is thicker on the head and legs and does not shed or undergo any seasonal changes in texture or length. Grooming, however, is a year-round necessity, involving daily brushing and quarterly trimming. The head is reasonably long, covered with profuse soft hair and ending in a distinct black nose. Ears are small and V-shaped, and the tail is sometimes docked.

Size & weight Height at withers 17–19 in. (43–49 cm); 30–40 lb. (13–18 kg)

Exercise needs Moderate to considerable

Grooming Considerable   **Life expectancy** 13–14 years

Points to consider This breed may have hereditary health problems, and it is essential to seek a reliable breeder.

Welsh Terrier

Similar in appearance to both the Lakeland and Airedale terriers, the Welsh Terrier is a long-established breed that was once commonly known as the Old English Terrier or the Black-&-Tan Wire-Haired Terrier. It was bred as a sporting dog in Wales for hunting otter, fox, and badger.

Temperament Welsh Terriers are energetic and affectionate; they enjoy vigorous walks and play and are easily trained. They are rarely aggressive, although they will not easily back down from a fight with another animal.

Appearance The thick, wiry black-and-tan coat covers a fine undercoat that provides excellent protection against the elements. With sturdy, muscular legs, the Welsh Terrier presents a compact, square silhouette. The head is moderately long, with a large black nose and a shaggy beard. The ears fold forward above the dark, deep-set eyes.

Size & weight Height at withers 15–20 in. (38–51 cm); 20–22 lb. (9–10 kg)

Exercise needs Considerable   **Grooming** Moderate   **Life expectancy** 12–14 years

Points to consider Early training is essential to curb possessive behavior.

Border Terrier

Border Terriers were bred as working dogs. They were developed as early as the seventeenth century on the border between England and Scotland as a dog tough enough to follow foxes and fast enough to keep up with horses. They have tremendous stamina and energy.

Temperament Border Terriers benefit from firm, early training to curb any aggressive tendencies toward other dogs. Friendly, reliable, and alert, these dogs react well to children and are affectionate family pets.

Appearance Border Terriers have a rough, dense topcoat that protects them against weather and rough terrain. The coat may be red, grizzle and tan, wheaten, or blue and tan. They have broad heads and short muzzles, with keen, friendly expressions. Small, V-shaped ears fold over from the top of the head. Their legs are sturdy and well muscled.

Size & weight Height at withers 11–13 in. (29–33 cm); 11–15 lb. (5–7 kg)

Exercise needs Moderate   **Grooming** Moderate

Life expectancy 13–14 years

Points to consider These dogs love to chase small animals, so they should not be walked by children.

Norfolk Terrier

These small, appealing terriers have short legs and long bodies. They were bred in Norfolk, in the east of England, primarily for rat catching and rabbiting, but also to pursue foxes and badgers.

Temperament Although they are one of the smallest terrier breeds, Norfolk Terriers are utterly fearless and seem constantly alert. They are intelligent dogs that make good family companions.

Appearance Norfolk Terriers are protected by straight, wiry, thick coats that are wheaten, red, black and tan, or grizzle-gray in color. The coat is longer and rougher on the neck and shoulders and should be stripped regularly. With a round face and a short muzzle, Norfolk Terriers are characterized by their triangular ears, which flop forward.

Size & weight Height at withers 9–10 in. (23–25 cm); 11–12 lb. (5–5.5 kg)

Exercise needs Considerable for their size

Grooming Moderate

Life expectancy 13–14 years

Points to consider These dogs chase small animals, so caution should be exercised outdoors.

🐾 *Who could resist the appealing expression of this sociable, alert Norfolk Terrier? These dogs love to play and are apparently tireless.*

Norwich Terrier

Norwich Terriers are identical in almost every respect to their Norfolk cousins—apart from their ears, which are held erect (as opposed to flopping forward).

Temperament Like the Norfolks, Norwich Terriers are cheerful, brave dogs, and they relish games and stimulating training. They enjoy regular exercise and are usually good with children.

Appearance The coat is the same as that of Norfolk Terriers and needs only a short brush every day to keep it clean. Although they are descended from the same mix of Cairn, Border, and Irish Terriers as the Norfolks, Norwich Terriers are distinguished by their ears, which are held erect.

Size & weight Height at withers 10 in. (25 cm); 12 lb. (5.5 kg)

Exercise needs Moderate   **Grooming** Moderate   **Life expectancy** 13–14 years

Points to consider Norwich Terriers chase small animals.

Australian Terrier

The tenacity of these small, spirited dogs belies their size. Australian Terriers were bred as farm dogs, and they are apparently scared of nothing. One of the smallest of the working terriers, the Australian Terrier was bred as a worker and companion, and it is able to navigate rough terrain.

Temperament Willing to take on small vermin and snakes, Australian Terriers are also unafraid of confrontations with larger dogs, and they seem to especially enjoy teasing cats. However, these dogs are generally friendly and affectionate companions and they respond well to training. They also make good watchdogs.

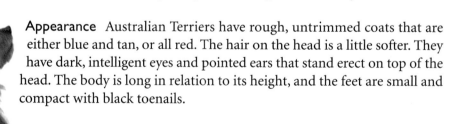

Appearance Australian Terriers have rough, untrimmed coats that are either blue and tan, or all red. The hair on the head is a little softer. They have dark, intelligent eyes and pointed ears that stand erect on top of the head. The body is long in relation to its height, and the feet are small and compact with black toenails.

Size & weight Height at withers 10–11 in. (25–28 cm); 12–14 lb. (5.5–6.5 kg)

Exercise needs Moderate

Grooming Moderate

Life expectancy 13–14 years

Points to consider Australian Terriers should not be walked by children.

Cairn Terrier

Rugged and hard-working, little Cairn Terriers originated on the Isle of Skye in the Scottish Highlands, where they were bred to hunt vermin. They worked alongside larger packs of hounds and were bred small so that they could flush game and vermin from small holes. Cairn Terriers are hardy dogs with few health problems, and they are comparatively long-lived.

Did You Know?

🐾 Cairn Terriers are among the longest-established pure terrier breed, dating back to at least the sixteenth century. In the Highlands and Islands of Scotland, landowners used to mark boundaries or graves with small piles of stones, or cairns, in which small wild animals made their homes. Cairn Terriers were employed to chase vermin from the cairns.

Temperament Irresistibly cute, their sweet appearance belies a bossy terrier temperament (although they are eager to please and respond well to obedience training). As puppies they are especially lively and may take up to two years to settle down to family life. They adapt well to city living and make terrific pets for adult households. They are not always reliable with children and they have a tendency to excessive yapping and barking, especially if left alone for too long.

Appearance Cairns are well protected against both poor weather and inhospitable environments by their profuse, rough outercoats, which cover a softer, dense undercoat. The coat requires regular brushing and occasional stripping to maintain its shape. Cairns may be of any color—from cream or gray to tan, red, and black—although white is not acceptable. They have broad heads, with muzzles in proportion, and are well covered with shaggy hair. Ears are carried erect on top of the head, and tails are also erect, but should not curl over.

Size & weight Height at withers 9–11 in. (23–28 cm); 13–14 lb. (6–6.5 kg)

Exercise needs Moderate

Grooming Moderate

Life expectancy 14 years

Points to consider Cairn Terriers often display dominant behavior and should not be walked by children, as they sometimes fight other dogs.

🐾 *The wide-set, slightly sunken eyes, shaggy eyebrows, and small, pointed ears of this Cairn Terrier are typical features of this breed, which is among the smallest, yet most fearless and tenacious, of terriers.*

Dandie Dinmont Terrier

This breed's imaginative name comes from a character in Sir Walter Scott's 1814 novel *Guy Mannering*, which features one of these appealing terriers. They were originally bred in the north of England to pursue and kill badgers.

Temperament Dandie Dinmonts are feisty and independent dogs. They thrive on companionship and make good watchdogs, but are wary of children and strangers.

Appearance With a long back and short legs, Dandie Dinmonts are long, low terriers. Their outercoats are wiry and cover a soft, dense undercoat; they require daily grooming to comb out tangles and knots. The color of the coat is either mustard (varying from a reddish brown to fawn) or pepper (from a dark bluish black to a light silvery gray). Dark, intelligent eyes peer out from the soft, silky hair, which covers the head, muzzle, and the large, domed forehead. The tail is 8–10 inches long (20–25 cm) and slightly curved.

Size & weight Height at withers 8–11 in. (20–28 cm); 18–24 lb. (8–11 kg)

Exercise needs Moderate　　　**Grooming** Considerable　　　**Life expectancy** 13–14 years

Points to consider Dandie Dinmonts can be snappy and unfriendly and should be socialized early.

Skye Terrier

These long-coated dogs are named after the Scottish island from which they originated. As working dogs, they were used to track otter, badgers, and weasels, but their size now makes them popular urban dogs.

Temperament Skye Terriers are intelligent and loyal, though they may be cautious with strangers. The most famous was probably Greyfriars Bobby, the devoted Skye Terrier that lay on his master's grave in Edinburgh, Scotland, for fourteen years after his master's death in the 1850s—despite the offers of a home.

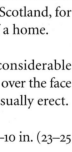

Appearance Skyes have profuse, long, straight coats that require considerable grooming. They are black, gray, fawn, or cream in color. The guard hair over the face is shorter than that on the body, but it covers the eyes. The ears are usually erect.

Size & weight Height at withers is ideally 9–10 in. (23–25 cm); 19–23 lb. (8.5–10.5 kg)

Exercise needs Moderate

Grooming Considerable

Life expectancy 13 years

Points to consider These dogs are inclined to be snappy, especially with strangers.

Parson "Jack" Russell Terrier

Named after the nineteenth-century country parson who developed the breed (the Reverend John Russell), the Jack Russell is a very popular dog. Descended from Wire Fox Terriers, it was intended to be small enough to pursue foxes underground, with legs long enough to accompany horses on the hunt. Today, there are both smooth- and wire-haired varieties. Since April 2003, the American Kennel Club has officially referred to these dogs as Parson Russell Terriers.

Temperament Tenacious in the pursuit of prey, these dogs are feisty and motivated with strong hunting instincts. They have lively, intelligent personalities and are devoted to their owners.

Appearance Small and alert, they are fit working dogs that are mainly white in color, with patches of black and brown. The thick, harsh outer coat requires minimal grooming, although the wire-haired variety needs more attention. Jack Russells are longer than they are tall, with muscular bodies, strong necks, and slightly pointed muzzles. Ears are pointed and may be erect or folded forward. Tails should be long enough to "provide a good handhold"—owners once dragged Jack Russells out of foxholes by their tails.

Size & weight Height at withers 12–14 in. (30–36 cm); 13–17 lb. (6–7.5 kg)

Exercise needs Moderate to considerable

Grooming Minimal

Life expectancy 13–14 years

Points to consider Despite their small size, these dogs are energetic and love to run, and they are not ideally suited to city life. They chase small animals and thus should not be walked by children.

Smooth Fox Terrier

The Smooth Fox Terrier is a robust breed, descended from various terriers, the Greyhound, and the Beagle. A classic working dog, bred to "go to ground" to flush out foxes and smaller vermin, Smooth Fox Terriers will often exhibit a strong urge to dig—so, if you plan to own one of these dogs, you will need to ensure that your yard fencing is secure!

Temperament Smooth Fox Terriers are energetic dogs that love to run and are probably happiest living among wide open spaces. They are feisty and need firm handling.

Appearance Smooth Fox Terriers have short, thick, straight coats that require only occasional brushing. Coloring is mostly white (sometimes white and tan, black and tan, or black and white). According to the AKC, brindle, red, or liver markings are "objectionable." The head is essentially long and narrow. Triangular ears flop forward onto the brow, framing appealing dark eyes. The body is taut and muscular, and the tail, which may be docked, is carried perpendicular to the body.

Size & weight Height at withers 15 in. (38 cm); 15–20 lb. (7–9 kg)

Exercise needs Considerable   **Grooming** Minimal

Life expectancy 13–14 years

Points to consider These dogs are independent and can be challenging to train; they tend to chase small animals and should not be walked by children.

West Highland White Terrier

These appealing white dogs are very popular companions throughout the world, and they thrive on attention and regular exercise. West Highland Whites are descended from light-colored Cairn Terriers, which were selectively bred in the 1880s to produce the "Westie." Westies achieved worldwide fame when one was used with a black Scottish Terrier to advertise Scotch whisky.

Did You Know?

West Highland Terriers were selectively bred so that their light color would be clearly visible on the Scottish moors, making them easily distinguishable from the game they were chasing. With strong instincts, Westies will take off in pursuit of a cat or rabbit whenever they get the chance.

Temperament Confident and playful, Westies are alert and fearless, but they can be excitable and so benefit from firm training (which also helps to ensure that they do not try to dominate their family). Generally good with children, they have been known to nip when irritated. All in all, they are exuberant, intelligent little dogs that fit in well with family life.

Appearance Westies have small, round faces that are covered profusely with fine hair. With their black, button eyes (set wide) and black nose, they have an irresistibly cute appearance. The ears are small and pricked, and the tail is 5–6 inches long. The long, coarse outercoat covers a soft, almost furlike insulating undercoat, and needs regular brushing to keep it clean. Stripping and clipping are especially necessary if the dog is to be exhibited or shown. The body is compact with a deep chest, broad back, and well-muscled loins.

Size & weight Height at withers 10–11 in. (25–28 cm); 15–22 lb. (7–10 kg)

Exercise needs Moderate

Grooming Moderate to considerable

Life expectancy 14 years

Points to consider Westies can be high-strung and should be socialized with children at an early age.

🐾 *This adorable Westie knows just how handsome he is. Keeping him white and fluffy, though, is a daily challenge! Westies are inquisitive and love to get as dirty as possible—but they often dislike water and refuse to cooperate at bathtime. Be careful not to use perfumed shampoos or dry products on your Westie, as there is a breed tendency to skin allergies. Brushing is best!*

Bedlington Terrier

The silhouette of the Bedlington Terrier reveals a dog built for speed, and these dogs were used by Gypsies in northern England as a racing dog during the nineteenth century. This breed also has excellent hunting skills: It was originally developed as a game dog in the county of Northumberland, in England.

Temperament These are intelligent dogs that require mental stimulation and vigorous exercise if they are not to become destructive. They are generally loyal and courageous dogs, good with children they know and protective of their home and family.

Appearance Bedlingtons are elegant dogs with almost sheeplike curly coats and a distinctive topknot that covers the dog's muzzle. Colors are liver, sandy, tan, and blue (or combinations thereof). They have long, narrow heads and deep-set, gentle eyes. The ears are medium sized and triangular in shape, hanging low down the side of the cheeks. The back is naturally arched, and the well-muscled hind legs resemble those of a Whippet.

Size & weight Height at withers 15–17 in. (38–43 cm); 17–23 lb. (7.5–10.5 kg)

Exercise needs Considerable

Grooming Considerable

Life expectancy 14–15 years

Points to consider These dogs sometimes have hereditary health problems and can be snappy and hostile if they are not well trained and socialized.

🐾 *It is not difficult to see why these dogs are so often compared to sheep with their soft, curly coats and distinctive head profile. Bedlingtons often appear sensitive in disposition—and they usually are.*

Bull Terrier

Originally known as "Bull and Terriers," these dogs were bred to fight, and they were probably developed from crossing a Bulldog with the now-extinct White English Terrier. Though they are relatively small dogs, Bull Terriers are famed for their tenacity and bravery: Once their jaws are locked around something or someone, they are reluctant to let go.

Temperament Contrary to their fierce reputation, these dogs are extremely affectionate and friendly, and an experienced dog owner will find them rewarding companions. They make excellent watchdogs and enjoy stimulating training and exercise, although they are not always easy to train. Without proper training and sufficient exercise and attention, they can become aggressive and destructive.

Appearance Bull Terriers have long, distinctive heads that curve downward from the tip of the skull to the nose. They are strongly built, muscular dogs with strong necks and compact, rounded feet. Glossy, short, flat, and rough, their coats require little grooming. All-white terriers are popular, but colored varieties range from fawn to red, a tricolor mix of brindle and white, and black and brindle.

Size & weight Height at withers 21–22 in. (53–56 cm); 45–60 lb. (20–27 kg)

Exercise needs Considerable

Grooming Minimal

Life expectancy 11–13 years

Points to consider White Bull Terriers are especially prone to hereditary deafness and heart disease, while colored ones may be prone to inherited juvenile kidney failure. Because Bull Terriers are likely to fight other dogs, this is not a suitable breed for the prospective first-time owner. This breed can be highly challenging even for the most experienced owners, and thorough training is essential from an early age.

A strong, well-muscled build is one of this breed's desired characteristics. The head is long and curved, while the tapering neck is muscular and arched. These Bull Terriers are fine examples of this feisty, athletic breed.

Miniature Bull Terrier

Miniature Bull Terriers are simply a smaller version of the standard Bull Terriers, and they follow the same breed standards. They are descended from small Bull Terrier pups bred in the 1930s, and their small size makes them ideal for city dwellers.

Temperament Miniature Bull Terriers are courageous dogs that can be acquiescent to discipline, although they may be irritable and do not generally tolerate young children well.

Appearance These dogs have the characteristic long muzzle of the Bull Terrier, with narrow, deep-set eyes and erect ears. With broad chests and powerful thighs, these small dogs are substantially muscled. Colors range from white to fawn, red, tricolored, and brindle/black.

Size & weight Height at withers 10–14 in. (25–36 cm); 24–33 lb. (11–15 kg)

Exercise needs Moderate   **Grooming** Minimal   **Life expectancy** About 15 years

Points to consider These dogs may be short-tempered and do not do well left alone.

American Staffordshire Terrier

American Staffies are descended from the British Staffordshire Bull Terrier, but were selectively bred to enhance their bulk and strength. They were introduced into the United States as early as 1870, where they became known as "Pit Dog," "Pit Bull Terrier," and, later, as "American Bull Terrier" and then "Yankee Terrier." The breed was accepted for registration in the AKC Stud Book in 1936.

Temperament Although this terrier was originally bred as a fighting dog, careful breeding over recent years has curbed the breed's more aggressive instincts. These dogs must be socialized from an early age to accustom them to other dogs and humans, but they are usually loyal and obedient. They are protective of their families and are especially gentle with children, though they are often on their guard around other dogs.

Appearance A slightly furrowed brow gives American Staffordshire Terriers a quizzical expression. They have round faces with well-muscled cheeks and immensely powerful jaws. Ears stand erect on top of the head and are often cropped (which, at one time, would help prevent damage during dog fights). The coat is smooth and short and appears in combinations of liver, black, white, and tan. The body is muscular and heavily boned.

Size & weight Height at withers 17–19 in. (43–48 cm); 40–50 lb. (18–23 kg)

Exercise needs Considerable   **Grooming** Minimal

Life expectancy 11–12 years

Points to consider These dogs need experienced owners.

Staffordshire Bull Terrier

Bred for dog fighting in nineteenth-century England from a cross between a bulldog and a terrier, Staffordshire Bull Terriers are muscular and agile dogs that benefit from vigorous daily exercise.

Temperament Staffies have acquired a poor reputation for aggression. They are intelligent dogs, and their pugnacious instincts can be controlled by careful training—but they are not dogs for inexperienced dog owners. They can be very affectionate, especially around children, but they will often try to dominate other dogs.

Appearance Heavily built dogs, Staffordshire Bull Terriers are muscular, and they give off the impression of robust power. They have short, broad heads, with almost square muzzles and immensely strong cheek muscles. Their short, smooth, and dense coats are fawn, red, white, black, blue, or brindle, sometimes with white.

Size & weight Height at withers 14–16 in. (36–41 cm); 24–38 lb. (11–17 kg)

Exercise needs Considerable **Grooming** Moderate **Life expectancy** 11–12 years

Points to consider They are often aggressive and require experienced owners.

Manchester Terrier (Standard)

Bred as ratters in nineteenth-century Manchester, England, these glossy-coated terriers are happy in either town or country—as long as they receive plenty of exercise.

Temperament Alert and dominant dogs, Manchester Terriers can be short-tempered animals. Though they are not ideal with small children, they are generally very devoted dogs, but reserved with strangers.

Appearance Their smooth, glossy coats are thick and dense, rather than soft. Manchesters have sharp faces, high-set ears that fold forward, and tan markings on the face and legs. Their tails taper to a point and are carried low. They have short bodies with slightly curved backs that lend them an elegant stance.

Size & weight Height at withers 15–16 in. (38–41 cm); 12–22 lb. (5.5–10 kg)

Exercise needs Considerable **Grooming** Minimal

Life expectancy 13–14 years

Points to consider These dogs have a tendency toward dominant and aggressive behavior and must be trained at an early age.

Herding Dogs

The herding group (sometimes called the pastoral group) is composed of dogs bred to guard livestock from predators and intruders. From the cradle of human civilization in the Euphrates basin to the hills of the Himalayas and the great plains of Africa, early humans bred small, agile dogs to drive their herds and protect them from wolves and other predatory beasts. Today, the great majority of herding dogs never see a farm animal, but many of their instincts remain and they enjoy games of chase and fetch, often "herding" their human family and relishing training exercises.

The herding group is the most recent addition to the American Kennel Club listings. Added in 1983, this group encompasses several dogs that were previously categorized in the working group. Their sizes vary, from the redoubtable Corgi to the burly Old English Sheepdog.

Herding dogs are intelligent, loyal pets that were bred to work, so they appreciate plenty of exercise and mental stimulation to prevent boredom. They are devoted to their human families and are generally reliable with children.

Bouvier des Flandres

Bouvier means "cow herd" in French, and these dogs are the descendants of cattle dogs used for centuries by farmers in northern France and Belgium. They are good all-around farm dogs and excellent watchdogs, capable of performing a variety of working tasks. They were also used in the French Army Medical Corps during World War I.

Temperament They are loyal and devoted companions and will be calm indoors—as long as they receive vigorous and stimulating daily exercise and games. They are powerful dogs, and can appear aggressive in the face of unknown situations or people.

Appearance This dog comes in all colors and sizes (its ancestors may have included the mastiff, sheepdog, and spaniel). It is a compact, powerful dog, short-coupled and of square proportion. The coat is weatherproof, double, and tousled, requiring combing once or twice weekly and trimming and shaping every three months. The large head has a distinctive beard and mustache.

Size & weight Height at withers 23–27 in. (58–69 cm); 69-90 lb. (31–41 kg)

Exercise needs Moderate   **Grooming** Moderate   **Life expectancy** 11–12 years

Points to consider This breed is not well suited to an urban environment.

Puli

The Hungarian Puli is lively and obedient, an excellent housedog, and full of energy with an inquisitive nature. A hardy dog bred for herding flocks on the plains of Hungary, most now come from breeding programs in Britain and the United States. This dog requires plenty of exercise and firm discipline.

Temperament Smart, headstrong, and tough, the Puli can be aggressive toward other dogs and reserved with strangers. Pulis are excellent watchdogs and great barkers.

Appearance Pulis are compact and square proportioned, with a distinctive corded coat that is virtually waterproof. The weatherproof, dense undercoat is soft and covered by the abundant outercoat, which becomes corded at maturity but may be brushed out. Colors range from black to shades of gray and apricot. The dog's round head is virtually hidden by shaggy hair; indeed, only a shiny black nose peers out from under the dog's "dreadlocks."

Size & weight Height at withers 16–17 in. (41–43 cm); 25–35 lb. (11–16 kg)

Exercise needs Moderate   **Grooming** Considerable

Life expectancy 12–16 years

Points to consider This dog barks a great deal and is easily bored; grooming is very time-consuming.

Border Collie

The most popular working dogs in Britain and recognized around the world as the top sheepherding dogs, Collies are the result of careful selective breeding from herding and fetching stock. The standards established for this breed in 1906 were, unusually, not based on physical attributes, but on working ability. The Border Collie was first recognized in 1955 by the AKC for inclusion in the Miscellaneous Class.

Temperament These dogs must have daily stimulation or else they will revert to destructive and occasionally aggressive behavior. They have strong predatory instincts, which is what gives them their herding talents (once trained). Intelligent and responsive dogs, they are generally not happy as urban house pets and will become snappy if bored.

Appearance Border Collies are of a medium size and are strongly boned with an athletic appearance. They combine grace and stamina with agility and ability. The coat can be rough (long and flat), or smooth and short all over the body. Colors vary, including black, brown, red, black and white, tricolor, or merle; eyes are deep-set and brown (except in merle dogs, which may have blue eyes). The head is well defined, with a tapering and slightly blunt muzzle.

Size & weight Height at withers 18–22 in. (46–56 cm); 30–45 lb. (14–20 kg)

Exercise needs Considerable

Grooming Moderate

Life expectancy 10–14 years

Points to consider Preferably, these dogs should have access to a large yard, and they are not well-suited to an urban environment.

Collie

Evidence from 1800 suggests that this breed has been around for some time; its name is thought to derive from the Gaelic word for "useful." The rough and smooth varieties derive from two different crosses, and both varieties were formerly smaller. However, breeding has ensured that Collies are now taller and have a more refined look. Rough Collies were usually black or black and white until influenced (in 1867) by the progeny of a dog named Old Cockie, who is thought to be responsible for the sable coat color. The rough-coated version became popular during the reign of Queen Victoria and has a history as a working sheepdog, although it has gained fame more recently as a movie star. The smooth Collie lacks the glamour of the rough and has not achieved the same popularity, but makes an excellent household pet.

Temperament Collies have friendly temperaments and are affectionate with children. The Collie requires vigorous exercise every day, daily physical and mental stimulation being necessary to avoid frustration.

Appearance This dog is an active, strong, and lithe herder with ambitious speed changes. The two coat varieties both have a plentiful, soft undercoat. The smooth variety has a short, hard, and flat outercoat. The rough Collie has straight and long hair, abundant at the ruff, and requires more demanding grooming care (needing to be brushed and combed at least every other day, especially when shedding). Their faces show intelligence and are expressive, so much so that their expression is listed in official breed standards as a critical factor.

Did You Know?

🐾 The 1943 Hollywood movie *Lassie Come Home*, starring the young Roddy McDowell and Elizabeth Taylor, was the precursor to more movies and a TV series that set the rough Collie on the road to stardom.

Size & weight Height at withers 22–26 in. (56–66 cm); 50–75 lb. (23–34 kg)

Exercise needs Considerable

Grooming Considerable—smooth variety needs minimal care

Life expectancy 8–12 years

Points to consider These dogs are prone to Collie Eye Anomaly (CEA). Merles should not be bred to merles, as the resulting homozygous merle is bad for the health of the resulting offspring.

Shetland Sheepdog

This breed probably comes from the same stock as the Collie and Bearded Collie, but isolation in the remote Shetland Islands kept the breed pure. The "Sheltie" resembles a rough Collie in miniature, but it is a separate breed. A small, alert, rough-coated, and long-haired working dog, the Sheltie is rarely used for herding today, but retains the instincts of a watchdog.

Temperament Shelties are loyal, affectionate, and responsive, but they may appear reserved toward strangers.

Appearance Shetland Sheepdogs are elegant and fine-featured. Their small bodies are well proportioned and covered with a long, harsh coat, and they have an attractive mane and frill around the shoulders. The head is tapered, with a long, well-defined muzzle and dark, almond-shaped eyes (giving the dog a gentle expression). Ears are semierect, and these dogs often tilt their heads in a quizzical manner.

Size & weight Height at withers 13–16 in. (33–41 cm); 20 lb. (9 kg)

Exercise needs Moderate   **Grooming** Considerable   **Life expectancy** 12–14 years

Points to consider Shelties sometimes bark excessively, especially if bored.

Belgian Tervuren

The first Terv was registered in the United States in 1918, but the breed died out during the 1930s and had to be recreated from the long-haired offspring of Malinois parents. Today, these dogs are often used by security services and in assistance work with the blind or disabled. With outstanding scenting abilities, they are also useful as drug-sniffing dogs. They thrive on stimulating work, play, and exercise.

Temperament Tervs are alert and watchful dogs. Active, affectionate, and dependable companions, they are intelligent and obedient and they respond well to training. They make good watchdogs.

Appearance Tervurens have square proportions and appear heavily set. They have long muzzles, pricked ears, and almond-shaped eyes. The tail is raised slightly when moving, and held low when at rest. Coloring is gray, fawn, or red, with darker hair on the face. The dense undercoat and abundant outercoat are straight and of medium hardness.

Size & weight Height at withers 22–26 in. (56–66 cm); 60–65 lb. (27–30 kg)

Exercise needs Considerable   **Grooming** Moderate

Life expectancy 10–12 years

Points to consider The Terv makes a devoted companion to a single person, but tends to be possessive.

Belgian Sheepdog

The Belgian Sheepdog began as a working farm dog and was officially named the "Groenendael" after the kennel that had selectively bred these dogs since 1893. It gained a reputation as a useful police dog in the United States, and Groenendaels were used as sentry dogs, messengers, and draft dogs during World War I.

Temperament Typically playful and alert, as well as tough and independent, this breed has a tendency to be domineering with other animals and possessive of its owners.

Appearance An elegant, alert, and agile dog with an intent expression, the Groenendael has almond-shaped eyes and a flat skull with a moderate stop. The long muzzle and narrow jaw, together with rigid, erect ears, gives the dog a slightly vulpine appearance. A dense undercoat is covered by an abundant black topcoat, which is long and well feathered around the shoulders, legs, and tail. The medium-length tail is raised in a slight curve when the dog is moving. The dog has a smooth, effortless gait and a tendency to run in circles rather than in a straight line.

Size & weight Height at withers 22–26 in. (56–66 cm); 60–65 lb. (27–30 kg)

Exercise needs Considerable   **Grooming** Moderate   **Life expectancy** 10–12 years

Points to consider This dog is not a good choice for inexperienced dog owners.

Canaan Dog

The Canaan Dog is an ancient breed that was used by Bedouins as a herder and watchdog. In recent times Canaan Dogs have been used for mine detection, sentry duty, as messengers, and as Red Cross helpers. During World War II, they were used to locate wounded soldiers.

Temperament The Canaan Dog has good guarding and hunting instincts, but needs plenty of exercise (involving strenuous game sessions and challenging training). It may be distrustful of strangers and other dogs.

Appearance The short, soft, undercoat varies in density according to climate and requires brushing once a week to remove dead hairs. With a slight ruff, Canaans have a bushy tail that curls up over the back when excited. This dog is highly adaptable to different climates. The body is spare with a clear, sharp outline.

Size & weight Height at withers 19–24 in. (48–61 cm); 35–55 lb. (16–25 kg)

Exercise needs Considerable

Grooming Minimal   **Life expectancy** 12–13 years

Points to consider This dog is very territorial and tends to bark a lot.

Australian Shepherd

Despite its name, the modern-day version of this breed was actually developed in the United States. It is thought that the forebears to these dogs may have traveled to America along with Basque shepherds (from the region of the Pyrenees Mountains, between France and Spain), who came to the United States via Australia.

Temperament Australian Shepherds are even-tempered working dogs with considerable charisma and strong herding and guarding instincts. They need regular exercise to keep fit (but they will not pester you to go outside). Affable animals, they greet friends and strangers openly. This breed performs well in obedience and agility competitions. Intelligent dogs, they need a good deal of mental stimulation, and human contact is vital for their emotional well-being.

Appearance This is a medium-sized dog with a medium-length, coarse double coat that is easy to groom and fairly weather resistant. Coat colors can be blue merle, red merle, black, or red, with tan in the head and lower leg area.

Tails are docked or naturally bobbed. Eyes are set wide, and the ears fold forward. Muscular and powerful, this breed combines stamina with speed and intelligence.

Size & weight Height at withers 18–23 in. (46–58 cm); 35–44 lb. (16–20 kg)

Exercise needs Considerable

Grooming Moderate

Life expectancy 12–15 years

Points to consider This breed may be susceptible to cataracts, as well as to Collie Eye Anomaly (CEA).

Belgian Malinois

One of the varieties of the *Chien de Berger Belge* (Belgian Shepherd Dog), this breed gained popularity in the United States from 1959, when this dog began to be registered as a separate breed. It is sometimes used as a police dog. These dogs need a lot of exercise and mental stimulation.

Temperament They are alert, confident dogs that can be very friendly with members of their family, but are generally not good with strangers and can be aggressive toward other dogs.

Appearance A sturdy dog, fairly square in proportion, it has almond-shaped eyes and a flat skull. The ears are stiff and erect. The tail is raised, with a slight curve when the animal is moving. A smooth gait gives the impression of effortlessness. Coat color is rich fawn to dark mahogany, with black tipped hairs and a black mask and ears. The short, straight, hard coat, with its dense undercoat, needs weekly brushing (more often when the animal is shedding).

Size & weight Height at withers 22–26 in. (56–66 cm); 60–65 lb. (27–30 kg)

Exercise needs Considerable   **Grooming** Moderate   **Life expectancy** 10–12 years

Points to consider This is a high-energy breed with the need for regular mental and physical stimulation.

Australian Cattle Dog

Also known as the Queensland Blue Heeler, this dog is a relatively recent import to Europe and North America. True working dogs, with stamina and agility to match, they persuade cattle to move by nipping at their heels.

Temperament Alert and trustworthy, Australian Cattle Dogs enjoy a large amount of exercise, but are also obedient. Naturally wary of strangers and dominant, these dogs require early socialization.

Appearance With a compact and sturdy build, Australian Cattle Dogs have wedge-shaped heads, strong necks, powerful jaws, and large teeth. A broad chest and powerful loins give them the stamina and power needed for a day's work herding cattle. The double coat is weather resistant, with a short, dense undercoat and short outercoat of blue mottling or red speckles.

Size & weight Height at withers 17–20 in. (43–51 cm); 35–45 lb. (16–20 kg)

Exercise needs Considerable

Grooming Moderate

Life expectancy 10–13 years

Points to consider This breed requires firm handling.

German Shepherd Dog

German Shepherds are among the best-known herding dogs, but they are instantly recognizable today as police dogs, having been trained and used by security forces around the world. They are one of the most numerous breeds in the world, thanks to a dedicated breeding program instituted by Max von Stephanitz at the end of the nineteenth century. A popular dog in Britain, it was formerly known as the "Alsatian Wolfdog" (in a deliberate attempt to distance the breed from anything German during World War I)—but the "Wolfdog" tag was later dropped (as too many people seemed to fear them for their name).

Temperament German Shepherds are characterized by athleticism, courage, and intelligence, qualities that have made them excellent police dogs. They have been bred in a conscious effort to produce a good sheepherding dog, but they are also used as seeing-eye dogs, watchdogs, and companions. Devoted and faithful pets, they are known to concentrate intently on a task. Shepherds need early obedience training and daily challenges through play and training to keep them mentally and physically stimulated and to prevent problem behaviors.

Did You Know?

🐾 The Roman historian Tacitus mentioned a "wolflike dog of the country around the Rhine," which may well be the ancestor of today's German Shepherds. However, without doubt, the most famous of these dogs was Rin Tin Tin, the star of twenty-two movies in the early days of Hollywood. Rescued by an American pilot in 1918, Rin Tin Tin was born in a trench in France during World War I and was clearly an exceptional dog. His owner, Lee Duncan, believed that they shared a strong bond that enabled Rin Tin Tin to perform amazing stunts and to cope with the demands of a working movie set.

Appearance German Shepherds are substantial, powerful, and versatile dogs with a strong, rhythmic gait. Secondary sex characteristics are obvious, with distinct masculine or feminine looks. The thick double coat is of medium length, and colors include black, black and tan, sable, and occasionally white and cream (although the latter colors are not acceptable in show dogs). With erect, mobile ears, a long muzzle, and deep-set eyes, these dogs emanate intelligence and 0watchfulness.

Size & weight Height at withers 22–26 in. (56–66 cm); 75–95 lb. (34–43 kg)

Exercise needs Considerable

Grooming Moderate

Life expectancy 10–12 years

Points to consider German Shepherds can make excellent pets, but must be rigorously trained and well exercised to avoid behavioral problems.

Bearded Collie

A hardy and active working dog that was finally recognized as a separate breed in its native Britain in 1944, the Bearded Collie has built up an impressive record as a show dog ever since. Its origins are similar to that of the Rough Collie, although (like most long-haired herders) it is thought to be descended from the Magyar Komondor of Central Europe.

Temperament Bred as a companion and servant, the Bearded Collie is a devoted family member and has an unspoiled temperament. Beardies are lively and cheerful, and they retain the basic instincts of a worker.

Appearance This is a medium-sized dog with a long, flowing coat that follows the shape of the body and hides a lean and athletic physique. All shades of gray, brown, and sandy (including slate gray or reddish fawn, black, or blue), with or without collie markings, can be seen. The undercoat is soft, furry, and close, while the outer coat is strong and flat, with no tendency to curl, and parts naturally down the spine. Hair is sparse on the nose ridge but longer at the sides: A long beard is a typical characteristic.

Size & weight Height at withers 20–22 in. (51–56 cm); 40–60 lb. (18–27 kg)

Exercise needs Considerable

Grooming Moderate

Life expectancy 12–13 years

Points to consider Easily bored, these dogs need stimulating exercise. They respond well to obedience training but require great patience while they are puppies.

Did You Know?

🐾 Also known as the Mountain Collie, the Hairy Mou'ed Collie, or the Highland Collie, the Bearded Collie was bred to herd cattle in the Highlands of Scotland. Most, if not all, modern award-winning Beardies are descended from a single champion named Jennie of Bothkennar.

Old English Sheepdog

Old English Sheepdogs were bred early in the nineteenth century in the west of England as drovers' dogs for driving animals to market. These drovers' dogs were tax exempt, and their tails were docked to prove their occupation (a practice that some believe is the origin of the nicknames "bob" and "bobtail"). Old English Sheepdogs make good watchdogs.

Temperament With an easy, extroverted temperament, this breed is faithful, intelligent, and can be good with children (although it has a tendency to herd them like flock). They are affectionate dogs, and early training should curb their habits of overexuberance. Firm handling is necessary in training.

Appearance This distinctive dog has an abundant coat that can be any shade of gray, grizzle blue, or blue merle, with or without white markings. They are thickset animals with square proportions and a compact body that is surprisingly agile and powerful. The loins are higher than the shoulders. The undercoat is waterproof and the shaggy outercoat is harsh textured. Coat care involves brushing and combing every day to avoid matting.

Size & weight Height at withers 21–25 in. (53–64 cm); 60–67 lb. (27–30 kg)

Exercise needs Considerable   **Grooming** Considerable   **Life expectancy** 12–13 years

Points to consider With their exercise and grooming requirements, these dogs are a major commitment.

Polish Lowland Sheepdog

An active herder that looks like a smaller version of a Bearded Collie, the Polish Lowland Sheepdog is equally trainable and intelligent. These dogs are possibly descended from Asian herding dogs, and they nearly became extinct during World War II (although a careful breeding program has ensured their survival).

Temperament Alert and self-confident, this breed needs a dominant master and consistent training. They can be boisterous, but they are generally self-controlled dogs and make wonderful companions.

Appearance Medium- to small-sized dogs, they are usually born without a tail. They have broad loins and a deep brisket. They are well muscled, with a long, harsh coat and dense undercoat, which can be any color. Long hair hangs over the eyes.

Size & weight Height at withers 17–20 in. (43–51 cm); 43 lb. (20 kg)

Exercise needs Considerable   **Grooming** Considerable

Life expectancy 13–14 years

Points to consider This breed requires experienced owners.

Briard

This is a very old breed of French working dog, having originated from French sheepdogs. (The word *Briard* means "from the French province of Brie.") Originally deployed as herd protectors, Briards were also expected to tackle wolves, should they appear. Introduced to the United States by soldiers returning home after World War I, they didn't gain real popularity in America until the 1960s. Like all herding dogs, they require vigorous and stimulating daily exercise, such as a long walk or jog, as well as a play session that includes an element of training.

Temperament They are loyal and protective toward their human family, although they may be reserved with strangers or aggressive toward other dogs.

Appearance Square and powerful dogs, Briards have broad, deep chests, housing an excellent cardiovascular system that gives them their strong stamina and endurance. They have large heads and wide muzzles, and a distinctive mustache and beard. Large eyes appear alert and composed. High-set ears are covered with abundant hair. Briards are longer than they are tall, and they sport a long outercoat that has a very dry texture. The coat comes in black, slate gray, and various forms of fawn. They have two dew claws on each hind leg.

Size & weight Height at withers 22–27 in. (56–69 cm); 75–100 lb. (34–45 kg)

Exercise needs Considerable

Grooming Considerable

Life expectancy 10–12 years

Points to consider This breed must be given adequate exercise to avoid behavioral problems.

🐾 *The Briard's long hair typically lies flat over the face, naturally parted at the center, veiling the eyes, and hanging from the muzzle.*

Pembroke Welsh Corgi

Probably developed in the twelfth century as a cattle dog, the ancestors of Pembroke Corgis may have been brought to western Wales from Holland by Flemish weavers. They are practical dogs with plenty of stamina for a day's work nipping at the heels of cattle.

Temperament Pembroke Corgis are now well established as a house and show dog, demonstrating an eagerness to please, boldness, and friendliness. They are not ideal companions for small children, as they do not tolerate teasing.

Appearance Low set, the Pembroke is intelligent with a foxy expression. The coat is of medium length, with a coarser outercoat. Colors are red, sable, fawn, and black and tan, with or without a white flash. The Pembroke sheds heavily and should be brushed at least twice a week.

Size & weight Height at withers 10–12 in. (25–30 cm); 25–30 lb. (11–14 kg)

Exercise needs Moderate   **Grooming** Moderate   **Life expectancy** 11–13 years

Points to consider Pembroke Corgis are reserved with strangers and inclined to bark a lot.

Cardigan Welsh Corgi

Welsh Corgis are among Britain's most ancient breeds, and the Cardigan Corgi has been used by Welsh farmers for centuries to herd cattle. Although quite small, this breed still needs a fair amount of exercise. This dog has speed, endurance, and intelligence, and it makes a good watchdog.

Temperament This low-set, handsome dog is an easygoing and well-mannered pet at home, but it can be scrappy with other dogs and has a tendency to bark excessively.

Appearance Cardigan Corgis have a double coat—a soft, thick undercoat, and a harsh outercoat. Colors are all shades of red, sable, and brindle, with white flashings common. The tail is fairly long and set in line with the body. Wide-set eyes and large, erect ears give these dogs a foxlike appearance.

Size & weight Height at withers 10–12 in. (25–30 cm); 25–38 lb. (11–17 kg)

Exercise needs Moderate   **Grooming** Minimal   **Life expectancy** 10–12 years

Points to consider These dogs are inclined to be snappy.

2

Are You Ready For Your New Best Friend?

Before embarking on the great adventure of dog ownership, you should take a little time to examine your lifestyle and think about the kind of dog that would suit you best. With more than 400 breeds to choose from, as well as the option of a mongrel, or mutt, there is bound to be a dog to suit you. All too often, however, owners discover that the dog they have acquired does not meet their expectations. A common problem occurs when an unprepared owner never thought about the fact that the cute, small puppy she brought home would grow into an enormous hairy creature that drools and sheds hair. Other new owners may realize that they simply cannot keep up with the exercise demands of their dog. Sometimes, owner and dog are temperamentally unsuited for each other. (In cases such as these, irresponsible owners sometimes abandon their pets to their fates on the streets, or, equally sadly, present their dogs to the vet to be put down.) These situations can easily be avoided by considering what you want from pet ownership and what you can realistically give a dog. Dogs' basic needs are reasonably straightforward—they require food, shelter, exercise, and affection. But a large dog usually costs more to keep than a small one, and an energetic Collie requires more exercise than a Pekingese. Prospective owners must carefully consider the relative importance of these and many other factors before making the decision to adopt a dog—and then setting about finding their new best friend.

The idea of coming home to an enthusiastic welcome from a lovable dog is very appealing. But remember:

🐾 *Can you take on the commitment of exercising energetic dogs like Boxers (left), Dalmations, or Labradors (above)? Do you have time to spend grooming an Afghan Hound (below) every day ?*

This same creature will be longing for exercise and playtime with you, and will not understand that you are tired after a long day at work. If you are out all day, are you able (and willing) to pay for a dog walker? Will you want to go for a long walk every day, whatever the weather? Even small lapdogs need a short walk every day and to relieve themselves several times each day; if you are not physically fit, this may be overwhelming. If you have children, this should also be a consideration. Many children love animals, but they must be taught to respect them rather than seeing them as "toys." Some small children find animals, especially large dogs,

🐾 *All dogs require daily exercise. Energetic dogs may need several miles of walking or hours of off-leash play. If you can't provide this, can you afford a dog walker to help? Do you have access to an exercise environment that meets Fido's needs?*

overpowering, and if your child is sensitive in this way, it may be better to wait a few years before acquiring a pet. If you do decide to take the plunge, it is essential that you select a dog whose temperament is suitable for children of the relevant age group—now and in the future.

That said, the benefits of dog ownership are undeniable. Many studies have shown that dog owners are happier, live longer, and are less prone to stress and heart attacks than people without pets. Dog owners succumb to fewer minor infections (possibly because they are less run down by stress) and enjoy a more optimistic outlook on life. Such simple actions as stroking an animal lower blood pressure and slow the heartbeat, and owning a dog allows many people who live alone to impose a structure to their day that it might otherwise lack. Older single people often find that a dog offers them companionship, a sense of security, and utter devotion—blessings that most of us desire to enrich our lives.

Finally, do you enjoy going for long walks and relish spending an hour or so in the fresh air, whatever the weather? Dog owning is an enormous pleasure, but it carries with it responsibilities. And if these responsibilities are not for you, then, realistically, neither is dog ownership.

Lifestyle and Space

These are very general factors to consider before you even begin to make a decision about the type of dog you would like to own. Choosing a dog that will suit your home and lifestyle is important, because becoming a dog owner should be a happy and gratifying experience for both you and the dog!

Dogs are sociable creatures and they thrive on human company, so you need to think about how a potential pet will cope if you are at work all day. Dogs left alone for more than four hours a day get bored, and this may manifest itself in antisocial behavior such as howling or scratching. More importantly, it is simply not fair on the dog to be cooped up all day without stimulation or exercise. If you are out all day and are unable even to visit your dog, it would be kinder in the long run to consider a less demanding pet. Also, if you travel a great deal, think about what you will do with your dog—do you have a friend or neighbor who can dog-sit for you?

If you live in a city apartment, far away from green spaces, parks, or a designated dog run, it is probably best not to consider a large or energetic breed. A Labrador requires a good two hours of exercise and playtime every day, whereas a smaller, less energetic breed, such as a Pekingese, may be happy with a brisk walk around the block (and is probably, therefore, better suited to urban living). In purely spatial terms, a Great Dane would dwarf a compact apartment, whereas a small Toy breed would fit those surroundings

All dog owners, but especially those who are house-proud, must accept that, despite years of human intervention, some doggy characteristics are unchangeable and, periodically, every dog rolls in something smelly, chews up something we humans may regard as inappropriate, or simply sheds hair liberally over the soft furnishings. Be aware that long-haired breeds will not only shed, but will require more grooming than short-haired dogs, and this can be time consuming.

Do you have space for a Great Dane (above, left), or would a Toy breed (above) be more comfortable?

Could you tolerate a dog that barks or howls for attention (above)? Can you spare two hours each day to exercise a fun-loving Labrador (right)?

a little better. If you have outdoor space, is it secure enough to contain a dog? And, if you are a keen gardener, try to accept that sometimes your beloved pooch may express his opinion of your flowers or plants by digging them up—or worse!

Paws for Thought: Before You Look for a Dog

🐾 Do you have children in your household, or as regular visitors? Make sure you choose a suitable dog that will be comfortable with boisterous play and tolerant of teasing. Be prepared to spend time with your children teaching them how to respect and care for an animal.

🐾 How much exercise can you provide for your dog? Don't underestimate the commitment you are undertaking. Choose an appropriate dog for your lifestyle, and be prepared to hire a dog walker if you are out for long periods during the day.

🐾 Are you willing to undertake time-consuming (and, perhaps, expensive) grooming?

🐾 Is shedding an important consideration, either because of additional cleaning work in your home or because of a potential allergy sufferer?

🐾 Do you have the space and facilities for a large dog?

🐾 Can you afford the expense of a dog, including essential equipment, food, veterinary treatment, pet insurance, and kennel fees? Add up the initial expenses and make a weekly or monthly budget for the routine costs, and consider the financial commitment carefully before you go ahead.

🐾 Do you travel a lot? If so, who will look after your pet while you're away?

🐾 *Puppies can be trained not to jump on your furniture; older dogs, too, can be trained out of bad habits. Nevertheless, dogs will shed their hair on your rugs and soft furnishings whenever they brush past. If shedding concerns you because you suffer from allergies, don't rely on a low-shedding breed to solve your problem. If the prospect of extra housework troubles you, consider how much shedding you can tolerate, and whether you'll mind cleaning up after muddy paws. Remember, your dog can't help it!*

Children

If you have children, consider how they will react to a dog. Children must be trained to respect animals, and similarly, you must choose a breed of dog that will be able to cope with playful children without becoming irritated. Labradors are among the most popular family pets because they are an equable, friendly breed that is able to

Having a pet dog teaches children about responsibility and the need to care for other creatures, and—as dogs have comparatively short lives—they will learn about death, too. Playing with dogs teaches children to interact nonverbally, and, by observing and learning about a dog's body language for clues as to his intentions, children can also become more sensitive in their dealings with people. Dog ownership can bring tremendous joy to children's lives, but don't be tempted to acquire a dog just because your child wants one. You, the adult, must be prepared to take responsibility for the dog's welfare when the novelty wears off.

accept—and thrive on—the rough and tumble of family life. If you acquire an older dog, check its background to see that it has been around children all its life; older dogs that lack experience with small children may be frightened by them and could lash out by nipping or biting.

Some dogs (and their owners) may be distressed when they are apart, but it is easier for a young dog to learn that boarding at kennels is only a temporary measure. Older dogs may be puzzled or traumatized by the change of scene and "owners," but a decent kennel will be able to cope with this. Consider taking your pet for a one-night trial to acclimate him before your vacation, so that a longer stay won't make him feel abandoned.

> 🐾 *Your veterinarian is usually the most reliable source of information about local kennels.*

Vacations

We all love vacations, but dogs—as creatures of habit—generally do not. For the family dog, vacation time means that either they must endure a long car journey to visit a strange place, or they must stay at home; alternatively, they must be put into a kennel. Consider your vacation habits and think how they would affect your pet. Do you have a reliable friend or neighbor who could look after your dog while you are away? If not, ask your vet or other dog-owning friends for recommendations of local kennels (and visit them well in advance of your vacation to check that they are suitable). All good kennels should allow potential customers to inspect them. When visiting a kennel, take note of whether or not the staff are happy in their work, as this is a critical sign of a well-run establishment. The dogs should appear well groomed and exercised, and the kennels should offer secure, weatherproof accommodations, adequate food, and a daily exercise and play program. Your dog may be happier sharing a kennel and playing with other dogs, so check the kennel's policy on this. Prices vary according to facilities.

Time and Money

Like all successful relationships, your rapport with your dog will benefit from time spent getting to know each other, and this is best achieved by playing

with your dog, taking him for daily walks, and—not least—by training him. These activities can eat into one's leisure hours and, if you feel that you already short of "personal down time," then you will want to think long and hard before committing yourself to looking after a dog.

Many would-be owners have preconceived ideas about the type of dog they would love: An elegant Afghan Hound, for example, may seem like an attractive option, but are you prepared to invest the time necessary to keep its coat beautiful? Similarly, an intelligent

🐾 *Even if you don't intend to show your pet, a long-haired dog needs a lot of grooming. Mud and parasites pose extra challenges in rural areas.*

Collie sheepdog will guard your home and provide loyal companionship, but will also need stimulating games and copious exercise and cannot be left in the house all day while you're out at work.

Dogs quickly become part of the family, but, like all dependent family members, they cost money. Although they may not pester you for the latest shoes or DVDs, dogs need food, equipment, and the regular attention of a veterinarian. Furthermore, the very animal on whom you lavish attention may herself be quite a valuable individual simply in monetary terms: Pedigree animals do not come cheap, and their very price may affect your choice of breed. Don't be tempted to look for a bargain, though.

Choosing a Dog:
the Importance of Good Breeding

Having decided that you can offer a dog a good home, you will need to choose what sort of dog would suit you best. Different breeds have very different characteristics, ranging from very obvious physical differences to wide variations in character and behavior. Naturally, these differences will vary according to the age, sex, and background of the dog. If you are not sure what sort of dog you want, visit a rescue center where the staff will be happy to offer advice and let you mingle with adult dogs. Dog shows are also useful, as prospective owners can meet breeders, compare different breeds, and talk to owners. Most owners and breeders are happy to share their experience and knowledge with rookie owners—though, of course, they'll be biased in favor of their own breed! Your local vet is another source of advice and will be able to put prospective owners in touch with local breeders or pet-rescue centers.

The most significant advantage of acquiring a pedigree dog is that its looks, size, and (to an extent) its behavior will be predictable. If you take time to study the characteristics of individual breeds, you will be able to narrow down your choice to find a breed that suits your lifestyle. Some breeds are susceptible to

hereditary defects, but breeders and owners are usually alert to potential problems, and a reputable breeder will take steps to avoid perpetuating genetic defects in new litters. Some breeds, such as Collies, are relatively independent and

🐾 If you have white rugs and you strongly dislike the distinctive odor of wet dogs, a water-loving Scottish Deerhound (above) isn't the dog for you. When choosing a puppy (below), the relative size of the paws provides an indication of how large the dog may become as an adult.

resourceful, while others will quickly become bored or anxious without human company and may become destructive or howl loudly if left alone for long periods. Other dogs, like Deerhounds, will always dive into a pond or river if they see one, making walks (and their aftermath) a messy business. Some will need extensive grooming to maintain a healthy coat. All of these factors should be considered carefully.

Crossbreeds can make excellent pets if they combine the best qualities of each parent. But be prepared to put in some time researching particular crosses to make sure you don't end up with a dog with the *worst* characteristics of each parental breed.

Dogs of completely mixed parentage are known as mutts or mongrels and are often healthier animals than pedigree dogs. They are less prone to hereditary health problems and may live longer. However, it is more difficult to predict the temperament, and a small mongrel puppy may quickly (and unexpectedly) shoot up to become a large dog. A useful tip on this is to check the size of a puppy's paws: Relatively large paws are a sign that the puppy will become a large adult.

🐾 Your young child may find this Komondor adorable, but he is large and powerful and won't tolerate boisterous games or teasing, so he's not an ideal choice for your household.

Puppy or Adult?

Next, you will need to address the question of whether to adopt a mature dog or a puppy.

Puppies are dealt with more fully in a later chapter, but the most obvious thing to point out is that a puppy will grow! The small bundle of fun that you bring home will increase in size, dramatically, over the course of the next six months. Owners also need to invest a considerable amount of time in house training their puppies, teaching them obedience, and socializing them. Many people regard this as part of the fun and challenge of being a dog owner; it helps them mold the puppy to their lifestyle and bond with their pet from an early age. Without adequate supervision, though, a puppy may destroy your furniture and chew your shoes.

An adult dog will be fully house trained (or not, as the case may be), with his character fully formed. It is essential to find out as much as possible about the dog's background before you take him home—and, if possible, to discover why the previous owners let him go. Rescue centers will furnish prospective owners with as much information as they can, but the background of some rescue dogs is obscure, and new owners can never really be sure what has happened in the past to affect their dog's character. Most—but not all—behavioral problems can be solved with patience and training, but the owner

must be prepared to devote time to this process. If you are a first-time owner, don't adopt a traumatized dog, because you lack the experience to provide the solutions to its problems and cope with the consequences.

If you decide on an adult dog, carry out a few simple tests to assess his or her character:

- *How does the dog react as you approach it? A relaxed animal will look up expectantly, or perhaps approach you, but an anxious one may bark or even cower.*
- *Watch its reaction as you put on a leash: does it accept the leash without fuss?*
- *Try to gauge its reaction to strangers, children, and other animals. Is it easily frightened? Does it appear dominant or aggressive?*
- *Leave it alone with a toy for a few minutes to see whether it accepts solitude. An insecure dog prone to separation anxiety will whine.*

Above all, if you are inexperienced with dogs, don't adopt one without obtaining reliable advice.

Male or Female?

In general, male dogs are more dominant and aggressive than females, especially those of dominant breeds. Males are larger and, if given the chance, more likely to roam. Females are generally easier to train, demand more affection, and are a little more placid. These temperamental differences are less marked in smaller breeds. It is important to know that females that have not been spayed will come into season twice a year, when they have a menstrual cycle and emit a bloody discharge. They must be isolated from males to avoid an unwanted pregnancy—and this can be extremely difficult to achieve! Spaying is strongly recommended unless you're sure you want to breed.

When you have decided on the dog you want to adopt, try to learn as much about her as possible, to assess what your new four-legged friend will need and to prepare yourself for the challenge of caring for her.

Finding a Dog

Once you have decided what type of dog you want, you must acquire one from a reliable source. Pet shops, regrettably, are not the best place. Animals kept in pet stores are not housed in ideal conditions and are often prone to behavioral problems because of their treatment during the formative months of their lives.

Good breeders are a reliable source for a pedigree animal. Breeders can be traced via your national kennel club, by asking a veterinarian, or searching the Internet. They can also be found at dog shows, and this will give you the opportunity to find out which breeders are likely to have puppies available. You will also be able to find out how much puppies cost. Again, pedigree dogs do not come cheap! Be prepared to wait for a puppy, too, as many of the most reputable breeders have waiting lists. You may be asked to pay a deposit, and the breeder may want to learn about your background, to check that you are prepared to offer the puppy a good home and to devote

enough time to its needs. Good breeders will proffer advice, help you with your selection, and guide you through the trials of house training and grooming.

Dogs can also be privately purchased from local advertisements, and such transactions are usually very simple. You should, however, ask to visit the pups with the mother, in order to see how they interact with her and with the rest of the litter, and to find out how they have been cared for. In the case of mutts, seeing the mother will also help gauge some idea of what the fully grown dog will look like—and perhaps the owner has details of the puppy's father. You should check that the puppies have had regular human contact from birth, as they will be more likely to be readily socialized.

Finally, pet-rescue or rehoming centers are often an excellent source for obtaining dogs and are committed to the welfare of the animals in their care. To their credit, they usually check that prospective owners have the resources to deal with their new dog by questioning new owners closely about their expectations of pet owner-

ship. They often carry out behavioral and medical assessments on their temporary charges and aim to supply new owners with as much information as possible about each dog's background. Remember that, although some dogs have been cast out by uncaring owners, there are many other reasons for a dog needing to be rehoused. These include long-distance relocation, the arrival of a new baby, or an owner becoming physically unfit to keep the dog. A dog from a good home should be well adjusted, responsive to training, and comfortable with strangers. There are many types of rescue centers: some dealing with all dogs, others that are breed-specific. The latter are best found by contacting breed clubs.

Choosing: Dos and Don'ts

- ✔ Do choose a dog that is interested in its surroundings.
- ✔ Do choose a dog that appears relaxed and responsive in human company.
- ✔ Do visit a puppy to see it with its mother and littermates.
- ✔ Don't select a dominant, snappy, or aggressive animal if you lack experience with dogs.
- ✔ Don't choose a puppy that appears unwell.
- ✔ Don't take home a puppy that is not weaned or ready to leave its mother. Pups should be at least six weeks old
- ✔ Don't choose a dog that is overly timid and shies away from human contact.

3

Dog Equipment

Having decided to acquire a dog, the next step is to prepare your house for the new arrival. New owners quickly discover that every one of their dog's needs (and many you didn't know he had) are catered for by a burgeoning industry of pet supplies. No longer is there simply a choice of two dog foods in the supermarket; whole aisles are now devoted to doggy treats. Small pet shops have been replaced by enormous superstores where canine retailers assault owners' checkbooks with a dizzying array of leads, collars, toys, and bedding. It is equally important to go around your house and make sure it is safe for a dog. Trailing electrical cords must be secured or removed, bottles of toxic household cleaners should be put out of reach, heavy and breakable objects stowed out of harm's way, and gates and fences secured.

Tempting though it is to buy a variety of items, it is more sensible to acquire a basic set of equipment for

Essentials

- ✔ Collar and identity tag
- ✔ Leash
- ✔ Food bowl
- ✔ Water bowl
- ✔ Food
- ✔ Toys
- ✔ Chew items: chew toys (or rawhide) are good for teeth, especially for teething puppies
- ✔ Toothbrush and toothpaste
- ✔ Brush for grooming
- ✔ Nail clippers
- ✔ Bed
- ✔ Crate (if you are training a puppy, or for travel)

your new dog so you can see what works best for both of you. Remember, you can always go shopping again later! On a more serious note, only buy what you can afford. A loving home is almost as important as shelter and food, and not even the most discerning dog will notice how much you have spent on him, so doggy "luxuries" aren't a priority.

As long as your new dog has a warm, draft-free sleeping area, feeding and water bowls, collars and leashes, a chew toy or two, and a couple of items of grooming equipment, he will be comfortable and well cared-for. Don't wait until you've brought your dog home to acquire these vital items; purchase them in advance of your new pet's arrival so that his bed, toys, and food are waiting for him and so you can concentrate on getting to know and settling in the newest member of your family.

🐾 *Once you have invested in the basic essentials, remember that providing a loving home is more important to your dog than buying him expensive equipment.*

Feeding Equipment

It is vital to dedicate a separate set of bowls and cutlery for your dog and to keep them apart from human utensils, for the sake of proper hygiene in your household. You will need a knife, fork, and spoon for decanting dog food, a can opener, and a couple of food and water bowls, which should be robust and reasonably heavy so that the dog cannot pick them up.

To an extent, the size of the food bowl should match the size of the dog.

Big dogs have big appetites and will require more food than smaller animals. Similarly, very small dogs may not be able to cope with large food or water bowls. The ears of long-eared dogs, such as Basset Hounds or Cocker Spaniels, will overhang a food bowl and become messy as a result, so try to find deep food bowls with a narrow opening to avoid this problem (the ears can then hang down either side of the bowl). Stainless-steel bowls are more expensive than plastic ones, but they last longer, are easier to clean, and can't be chewed by excitable young puppies.

Ceramic dishes are usually fairly heavy, but they may shatter if dropped and they must be replaced to ensure proper hygiene if they become cracked.

🐾 *There are many food bowls available, but stainless steel provides the best combination of durability and hygiene. A rubber rim makes it difficult for your dog to tip or slide his bowl.*

Larger dogs and older, arthritic pets will appreciate having their feeding bowl raised off the floor, so that they do not have to bend down too far to reach it. Raising the food and water bowls also makes digestion easier for them.

Wash up the food bowls in hot water after each meal and make sure that your dog has access to a constantly replenished bowl of fresh water at all times. It is sensible to place the feeding and water bowls on a mat, for easy clean-up of spills.

weatherproof building with a warm, comfortable bed raised off the floor, and indoor space should be provided for cold winter nights. The kennel should incorporate a window for adequate light and ventilation, but must be free from drafts. Kennels are not a sensible option for small lapdogs, or for those whose origins lie in warm parts of the globe—but for large, densely coated working animals, or northern breeds such as Spitz dogs, they are ideal.

Dog crates or carriers make ideal sleeping quarters and are also useful if you travel with your pet. Hard, molded-plastic containers are excellent, because they provide security and comfort for the dog, especially if fitted with a washable foam pad or blanket.

Beds and Bedding

All dogs will appreciate a corner of the house that they recognize as their own territory. This is most commonly in the kitchen, but it can be anywhere warm. The most important criterion for bedding is that it should be washable. Dogs like to feel the security of lying against a "wall" (which can simply be the side of its bed).

Larger, more hardy dogs can be kept outside in a kennel, but it must be a robust,

Wire crates are another option; they allow the dog to feel part of the family life around him, yet still allow him the security of his own space. They can be made more comfortable by the addition of a crate pad, a washable foam bed. Crates are also useful if you wish to confine your dog to a limited area when you are out, or if you are house training a puppy. Some designs are collapsible, so they can be easily cleaned or moved.

Many owners recoil from the idea of confining dogs in crates because they seem so similar to cages, but they are often an ideal solution. They provide security for a dog, especially if he has been accustomed to it since puppyhood. Once a dog is "crate trained" he'll retreat to his cozy home for a nap or whenever he feels like quiet time, and he'll happily go inside if told to do so. Don't banish your dog to his crate as a punishment or confine him there for long periods while you're out—it should be a place that he enjoys.

🐾 *There are endless choices of cozy beds for your dog, but remember that what looks most appealing to you might not be the most sensible choice for your pet. For a new puppy, a wire crate (shown on page 241) with an easily washable, quick-drying pad is probably the best option.*

You may prefer to provide a mature dog with a simple dog bed, and once again, there is a wide range to choose from. A molded-plastic dog bed lined with a doggy mattress or a washable fake fur will provide a snug bed. Beanbags are also comfortable, as they mold themselves to the dog's body shape and provide good insulation, and the covers are easily removed for cleaning. Wicker pet baskets look attractive and make an excellent bed for mature dogs, but they are eminently chewable and difficult to clean, so they're not a suitable choice for a new puppy or a sick or incontinent dog.

Collars and Leashes

Responsible dog owners provide their dogs with an identity tag noting the dog's name and address, so that he or she can easily be returned should he stray.

Dogs must always be taken for a walk on a leash, as this is the only safe way to control a dog near traffic and to prevent her from running off if she sees a cat across the street or she's startled by something. So, a collar and leash are vital pieces of equipment for any new dog. There are a wide variety of collars available, ranging from simple webbing to leather, and with thousands of ornate designs. The most important factors in your choice are that the collar is of a suitable design, that it fits properly, and that the dog cannot shrug it off. A puppy that isn't leash-trained will be likely to pull and may need a nonconventional collar. For a small,

energetic pup a body harness will provide enough restraint without putting excessive pressure on the windpipe, as a regular collar would. A large, powerful, or dominant dog would benefit from a head collar. He might recoil initially and try to remove the head collar until he's used to it, because the pressure on his muzzle feels to him as though you're challenging his dominance. However, he'll soon learn not to pull, and this is essential to prevent him from thinking he'll take *you* for a walk, rather than vice-versa—a problem that will magnify as he becomes bigger and stronger. Many experts recommend head collars over choke chains for leash training, because the latter can, if used incorrectly, damage a dog's throat. For a trained dog, a conventional collar should be adequate, with the strength and length

🐾 *A head collar (below, not to be confused with a muzzle) is a safe and effective training tool that gives you more control than a regular neck collar.*

chosen to suit the dog's size. To check a collar's fit, try to place two fingers between the dog's neck and the collar. As long as the gap is no larger than two fingers' width, the collar fits. A wider gap would allow the collar to slip off, and anything more narrow may constrict his throat. Nylon collars are useful for dogs that like swimming, as they dry quickly and will not rot. Rolled leather collars are a more expensive option, but are excellent for long-haired dogs, as they do not trap the hair on the neck.

Leashes vary in length according to their purpose; a short, strong leash is all that is necessary for walking a well-behaved dog, but for training purposes you will probably want to invest in a longer leash, and some owners use a long "house leash" to accustom young dogs to leashes indoors. See page 210 for advice on training your dog to walk to heel on a leash. Longer leashes are also a sensible option if your pet proves unreliable off the leash—for example, in a rural setting where she might chase wild animals or farm livestock if allowed to run free.

Toys

All dogs should be allocated a couple of toys that are theirs to enjoy when (and as) they wish. Owners who are working on controlling dominance may also keep a special bag of toys that are dispensed for short, well-defined play sessions. By removing these toys at the end of a play session, the owner exerts control over the dog, which serves to emphasize his or her position in the pack hierarchy.

Dogs have a natural desire to chew, tug, or "worry" things, and the best way to ensure that your favorite shoes do not

🐾 *Squeaky toys (above) are always a popular choice with frisky pups, if not necessarily with their owners! A variety of chewable, chase, and tug toys should keep your pup out of trouble.*

become the object of canine devotion is to provide more attractive doggy toys. Make sure that any toys you buy are tough and well-made, avoid anything that looks poorly constructed or that has parts that could become dislodged and then swallowed by your puppy. Replica bones, bouncy balls (of a suitable size, large enough for the dog to grip, but not small enough to swallow), Frisbees, and "tug toys" can all be incorporated into stimulating games.

Grooming

The amount of grooming required by particular coat types was probably among the deciding factors in your choice of dog. However, even short-haired animals need a daily brushing to keep their coats healthy and looking good. The various types of brushes and other grooming items are designed for the different needs of different coat types. Short-haired breeds like Bull Terriers need little more than a quick once-over with a rubber brush and a chamois leather, whereas long-haired dogs such as Lhasa Apsos will need the attentions of wide-toothed combs and soft-pinned brushes. Dogs with thick, dense coats like Labrador Retrievers must be groomed with a soft brush and then a firmer bristle brush to remove dirt. Periodically, dogs must be bathed—so get some canine shampoo, which will not irritate your dog's eyes or skin.

🐾 *A selection of grooming tools: nail clippers (left) and combs, mitts, strippers, and brushes suited to different coat types (see also page 181).*

All dogs should be groomed each day, and your routine should include checking and cleaning the teeth. Special toothpaste and toothbrushes are available, but buy a toothbrush in a size to fit your dog's jaws and never be tempted to use human toothpaste, which is unsuitable for dogs. Nails and claws must also be trimmed regularly with dedicated pet nail clippers. Consult Chapter 5 for more details.

Preparing Your Home for the New Arrival

The best way to prepare your home for the arrival of a new dog is to try to view the world from a canine perspective, both literally and figuratively. Dogs are intelligent and curious animals and will investigate items they are not familiar with; for a dog, a new home has endless possibilities, not all of them safe. If you get down on all fours you will see your home in a new light, noticing trailing

wires, unsteady table legs, attractively accessible ornaments, and chewable toys or household items—all of which pose a potential danger to your dog. Remove all these hazards and make sure that houseplants are moved out of reach, as some are poisonous for animals. Bathroom ointments and cleaning substances are especially toxic (as well as messy), and must be stored out of your dog's reach. If you organize your possessions as you would if you had a toddler in the house—putting anything dangerous or valuable on shelves or stored securely in cupboards—you will be able to relax and enjoy your new dog without worrying either about his safety or your favorite vases.

Check that your outer doors are secure and cannot be opened by the dog. Make sure the rest of the family are reminded to shut doors firmly behind them, which will prevent Fido from following them outside and straying onto the road.

Outside, check that your borders are secure; in other words, that your fence is sturdy, that a dog could not dig underneath it, and that it is high enough to contain a leaping dog. Puppies are especially drawn to holes and gaps and are often small enough to slip through apparently tiny holes. They also have a tendency to get stuck in unlikely nooks and crannies, so it may be necessary to position paving stones around the bottom of your fence to prevent this. Ensure that any gates can be firmly latched or locked and that a mischievous pup could not slide open the bolts or squeeze underneath.

Ponds and swimming pools are potential hazards for dogs, particularly for younger animals. It may be difficult for your dog to clamber out of the water after her unauthorized dip, so cover small ornamental ponds with a metal grille to prevent accidents. If you have a swimming pool, she must be trained never to walk on the cover, and you should avoid letting her play inside the fenced pool area, except when she's under proper supervision.

Some dogs just love to dig, so to preserve your flower beds, why not dedicate an area of your garden to the dog? Install a sandpit where he can bury toys and train him to use it by rewarding him when he does so, rather than punishing him when he digs elsewhere. See pages 225 and 238 for more on digging.

Extra Gear for Comfort

- ✔ For pet hair pickup, get some impregnated sponges or tacky rollers.
- ✔ Use deodorant to neutralize doggy smells and spills.
- ✔ Treats will help you make friends with your new dog—and train her more easily.
- ✔ Ear cleaner is useful for removing dirt in your dog's ears.
- ✔ Special canine shampoo will not irritate your dog's skin or eyes.

Cars and Travel

Most dogs will have to travel in a car at some point, whether it is for a short journey to the park or vet, or for longer journeys on vacation or to visit friends and relatives. Urban dogs, in particular, will quickly become accustomed to car journeys, but many dogs find car travel uncomfortable, and others become very excited by it. Younger dogs and puppies may be prone to carsickness, so go prepared with old rugs or sheets and wipes to clear up any unexpected spills.

Dogs react well to familiar things, so a dog that is crate trained will happily travel in his or her crate when it is installed in the car. Smaller dogs may benefit from a soft, flexible travel carrier, which has handles and a window to allow the animal to see out. Make sure that there is adequate room for the dog to stand up, lie down, and turn around in the carrier. If you are traveling by air with your dog accompanying you in the body of the aircraft, this is an ideal option. Some airlines do not allow this, in which case you should acquire a hard-shelled carrier, which can double as your dog's bed at home and can also be used on car journeys.

If this is not an option, your dog will have to sit on a passenger seat in the back and should be secured with a special canine seat belt to prevent him from moving around. Restraint is necessary both to prevent the dog making unexpected movements and to protect him in the event of an accident (when he is just as vulnerable as an unbelted human). Give your dog a familiar rug to sit on, as he will appreciate the smells of home.

One additional option is to install a wire barrier across the back of your vehicle, to keep your dog from climbing forward and causing a distraction while you are driving.

Don't feed your dog immediately before a car journey, and make sure he's well exercised before you set off. When traveling with your dog, remember to take frequent breaks to allow him to have a run, relieve himself, and have a drink. Car travel can be hot and

Leaving a dog in a stationary vehicle is never a good idea, but if it is unavoidable and can be kept brief, open all the windows slightly, and park the car in the shade. On a hot day, dogs should never be left in a parked car, as they overheat all too quickly (and many die of heat exhaustion every year). Leave your dog at home in hot weather—he will be safe there, happier, and more comfortable.

stuffy, and dogs have inefficient control of their body temperature, so make sure that your vehicle is well ventilated. Water is essential, so it is sensible to carry a large bottle of water and a bowl in your car; it is possible to obtain nonspill travel water bowls for use in cars, and these are ideal for dogs in travel crates if you are on a long journey.

🐾 *Dogs should soon get used to car travel if they start as puppies, and will settle easily. The plastic bed is ideal for calm passengers. Letting a wet, muddy, or shedding dog sit directly on the car seats will soon make your car uninhabitable by humans! For dogs that just can't keep still, the metal barrier or a travel carrier will make your journey safer and smoother.*

4

Puppy Love

No one can deny the appeal of a small, cuddly puppy. Puppies bring out the nurturing and cherishing side of just about everyone's character, even the most tough and unlikely of individuals. Children are even more susceptible and are usually twice as vocal in their appreciation of (and subsequent demands for) a puppy.

If you have ever watched a litter of puppies tumbling and playing together, you will probably have harbored secret thoughts about acquiring a faithful four-legged friend. You may have pondered upon the long-term companionship of a loyal pet, but, more likely, your thoughts were focused on cuddling a winsome, wriggling, twisting, trusting bundle of fur. Limpid eyes, slightly clumsy movements, helplessness, and a mischievous spirit are the characteristics of most young mammals, but the special appeal of young dogs is that they grow into devoted, steadfast companions—self-reliant, yet faithful to their human family.

Acquiring a puppy is a major decision. Everyone in the family must realize that the immediate future will be a little more chaotic, with a great deal of their time and effort being devoted to the puppy's needs. Young pups must be fed three or four times a day, and they must be housebroken and trained to behave in a way that suits family life. This can't be done if you are out all day.

Furthermore, over the next few months the puppy will teeth, and during the teething process the puppy will regard almost anything as suitable chewing material. It is also worth remembering that, in adopting a puppy, you are taking on a pet for at least a decade—possibly longer. The way you care for and train your puppy will affect the formation of the dog's character, so it is not a decision to be made lightly.

It is never sensible to present a friend or a relative (especially a young person) with a puppy, however adorable, as a surprise gift. Apart from the fact that acquiring a dog is a long-term commitment that cannot be made on someone else's behalf, puppies are very hard work in the early weeks of their life, and puppy owners must be adequately prepared for this. An animal-welfare charity coined the slogan "A dog is for life, not just for Christmas." As breeders and rescue centers have become aware of the large numbers of dogs that are abandoned or returned in the weeks after Christmas, many have stopped selling puppies in the pre-Christmas period, in the hope that potential owners will buy or adopt puppies only after careful thought and consideration.

Having said all that, remember that bringing up a puppy is extremely rewarding and a lot of fun, too—as long as you are prepared to devote time to it. Acquiring a puppy is the best way to develop a trusting bond with a dog, and your reward for all the hard work will be a loyal friend and devoted companion.

Choosing a Puppy

Consult the previous chapters and spend some time talking to other dog owners to help you decide which breed to choose or whether to look for a crossbreed or mutt. Don't make the decision on a whim arising from your friend's having told you her dog is expecting a litter soon. Once you have decided on the type of dog you want, you will need to research reputable breeders to arrange for the purchase of a puppy or check with your vet, local newspapers, and rescue centers if you are not looking for a purebred dog. Do not be surprised if a rescue center requires you to wait for the puppy you want, or if the breeder has a waiting list.

🐾 *Puppies are irresistible, lovable bundles of fun. Most people find the burden of their care and upbringing is amply rewarded by the benefits and joy they bring.*

Any reliable breeder or owner will let you see the litter with its mother to help you make your choice. If you are not an experienced dog owner, take someone knowledgeable with you to help you make your choice. A breeder should be able to furnish details of the father, even if it is only a picture and a few background details. (Remember that the stud dog probably belongs to someone other than the breeder from whom you are purchasing the puppy.) Knowing what the parents look like will give you some idea of your puppy's potential size and appearance as an adult. If you are buying a pedigree dog, the breeder will be able to provide certificates, registration papers, and all the relevant paperwork to certify that your puppy is purebred.

Once you have decided which puppy you want, check for obvious signs that it is healthy. The eyes should be clear and bright and the coat should be healthy.

There should not be any sores or scabs, the ears should be free from mites, and it should not have a cough or any discharge from the nose or mouth. If you are buying a purebred dog, check in advance of your visit for details of hereditary health problems associated with the breed, and ask the breeder to show you certificates or veterinary reports confirming the health of the mother and father.

Take your time. If you do not feel happy with any of the litter, walk away and look elsewhere. All puppies are adorable, so you may need to exercise self-restraint, especially if you're inexperienced in the care and training of dogs. You must live with your choice for many years, so make sure it is the right one. If you are paying a fee for the puppy, especially a large fee for a purebred dog, ask the breeder for a receipt that includes a written agreement that the sale is dependent on a satisfactory vet's examination within forty-eight hours of taking your puppy home.

Paws for Thought

🐾 Always visit the breeder or owner to see a puppy with its littermates and, most importantly, with its mother, to assess the health, appearance, and temperament of the puppies and mother. When visiting a litter, get down to the puppies' level to encourage them to come to you, so you can distinguish which ones are responsive to people and which are shy. Do not take pity on an excessively shy, nervous dog or pick out the most dominant puppy in the litter, unless you are an experienced owner and can confidently deal with the behavioral challenges presented by dominant or anxious, overly submissive dogs. If the owner or breeder has already promised all the puppies to other homes except one that is very dominant or submissive, wait for another opportunity.

The First Weeks

Newborns are completely dependent on their mother for food and warmth for the first two weeks of life. Born blind, their eyes open at about five days. And over the next two weeks, as their senses mature, they become gradually more independent. As their bodies become more efficient at regulating temperature, puppies become increasingly adventurous, moving away from their mother, wagging their tails, and learning to interact with their littermates. During this period, it is important that they become used to human contact, and they should be handled a couple of times a day. These early weeks are critical for puppies, as they absorb sights, sounds, and smells that will help them in later life. By the fourth week, additional food should be introduced gradually to the puppies to begin the weaning process. Puppies usually leave their mother between seven and twelve weeks of age, at which time they should be weaned and ready to be separated from their mother and littermates.

🐾 *Newborn puppies usually have their needs fulfilled by their mother without a great deal of intervention. However, they are at their most vulnerable during the first week of life and should be carefully monitored in case anything goes awry. The environment should be kept warm, as puppies can easily become chilled at this stage.*

🐾 *A newborn puppy typically loses a little weight during its first day, but weight should increase steadily thereafter, and the weight at ten days should be double the birth weight of the pup.*

🐾 *When the pups begin to move away from their littermates and mother they are at risk of becoming chilled until their bodies can regulate temperature more efficiently, at about three to four weeks old.*

🐾 *Puppies cannot see or hear at birth. The eyes begin to open at around ten days old, though this could happen as late as fifteen days. The ears begin to function around the same time.*

Bringing Your Puppy Home

Leaving its mother and its familiar surroundings will inevitably be a major adjustment for a young pup, and new owners should be prepared for this. To ease the puppy into his new home, ask the breeder or owner for an old blanket or sheet with the scent of the puppy's mother, and put this into his bed to help him sleep.

With the arrival of a new puppy, the human family members are usually excited—especially children, who will likely want to play with the puppy immediately. The transition from mother to new family is also exciting for the puppy, but the new sensations, smells, and people can often be overwhelming, so try to make sure that the puppy's transition is as gentle as possible and that a routine is established as soon as she arrives at her new home.

Try to arrange to bring your pet home at a time when the house is relatively peaceful—for example, when the children are at school. In this way, the puppy can meet the family gradually, after he has begun to become accustomed to his new surroundings. If possible, arrange for two people to pick up the dog—one to drive the car, the other to sit with the puppy in the back. Young puppies are often carsick, so protect the seats with old towels or blankets if he's not in a carrier.

Once you get home, take the puppy straight to his sleeping area. A puppy crate is ideal; it will give him security, help greatly with house training, keep him out of mischief, and provide the owner with peace of mind. Like small babies, puppies need a great deal of sleep, so try to find him a draft-free, relatively peaceful corner,

but don't isolate him too much from the hubbub of the household. If you have space, the kitchen or family room is often a good choice.

Providing a dog crate for your puppy is a good way to ensure he has his own territory. Until your puppy is comfortable in the crate and chooses to seek it out as his sanctuary, crates should only be used for sleep or rest times. Your puppy may need to be encouraged to use his crate at first. Do not force him in and clamp the door if he's reluctant! Put a blanket in the crate with the scent of his mother (or the one he slept on when you brought him home) and lure him inside with a treat, praising and reassuring him as you do so. Repeat this until his fear or reluctance disappears, leaving the door open until he is completely happy in the crate. Encourage your puppy to rest in his crate after he has been playing or exercising, but never leave him there for more than two hours during the day while he's young.

The first few nights in the home are not always peaceful, as the dog adjusts to its new way of life. Many experienced owners recommend putting a covered hot-water bottle (warm, but not too hot) and a ticking clock in the puppy's bed, to simulate the warmth and heartbeat of the mother. Wrapping the hot-water bottle in a blanket that smells of the mother will also soothe a young dog.

If the puppy wakes in the night, she will find a human presence very comforting. But if you wish to accustom your dog to sleeping alone, it is sensible to do so from the beginning. At first, you may have to get up in the night to comfort her. But the puppy should quickly learn when and where to sleep and to settle without company. Puppies have small bladders, so do not leave her for longer than six to eight hours without taking her to relieve herself, and avoid letting her eat or drink for the last two hours before bedtime until she has grown up a little.

If your puppy does not adjust to her bedtime routine and cries or howls for more than fifteen minutes, bring her crate or basket next to your bed for the first few nights. During the day, make sure she takes naps alone in her designated sleeping area, so that she gets used to it gradually. After a couple of weeks at most, she should be comfortable sleeping there at night.

The whole family must work together to provide the new puppy with security and a regular routine of feeding and sleeping. This means that it is sensible to plan where the dog is going to sleep, eat, and play before it arrives. If the puppy will have to spend time alone, once mature, accustom her to this by leaving her for a few minutes after waking from a sleep (even if she whines).

Paws for Thought

🐾 Small children and puppies should never be left unsupervised.

🐾 The first few days are important in establishing a routine and in laying down ground rules for playing with the new pup. To begin with, play with the dog gently and quietly—do not overexcite him with boisterous games. Puppies need naps during the day, so do not overwhelm him with lots of attention when he needs a snooze. Finally, puppies learn from their games, so playtime is a good time to begin basic training.

🐾 If you already have pets, remember that they may react with jealousy to the arrival of a new animal, which is likely to become the center of attention. Old dogs may enjoy the company of a younger animal, but must be allowed to assert their position as top dog in the household. Do not leave the two dogs alone until you are certain that they are used to each other and will treat each other with respect.

🐾 Cats are famously aloof and may simply ignore the new arrival in a disdainful manner until she realizes that the newcomer is a permanent addition to the household. To ensure domestic peace, it is prudent to put the cat in a carrier when the animals first meet. She will be secure, and the dog will be able to approach her, sniff her, satisfy his curiosity, and leave her alone. An unrestrained cat will likely zoom out of the room on first sight of the puppy and, even more likely, the puppy will chase her and will regard this as an excellent game. Your house will become a pet raceway at every opportunity, and if the dog frightens or corners your cat, she'll probably lash out at him. See page 202 for further advice on introductions.

Meeting the Family

With a bit of luck, your young puppy will prove to have an outgoing personality—being curious of the world around him and friendly toward new faces. It is too much to expect a new puppy to tolerate shocks, though, and the behavior of small children (however well intentioned) is often unpredictable and may provoke snappy or anxious behavior from a puppy. If you have children under the age of ten, spend plenty of time explaining to them that their new dog must be treated gently and with respect at all times. Explain that dogs communicate by barking and by facial expressions or body postures, and encourage them to watch their pet's body language for clues as to its feelings.

- Teach children to approach the dog from the front or side, and never from behind.
- Children should learn to keep their hands low and not to wave them around too much, in case the dog thinks they are playing and jumps up to them.
- Creeping up behind a dog and startling it is both dangerous and unkind, so make sure your children understand that "surprise" games are unacceptable.
- Teach children to stroke the dog on its flanks or back, but to avoid its head, ears, and paws.
- Make sure that children understand that tail pulling is forbidden and that dogs are not toys.

Children and puppies will soon become the best of friends, as long as the children respect the puppy and the pup's temperament is well suited to life with youngsters.

Puppy Training

Choosing a name for your new puppy is the first step in training her. Young dogs do not recognize many words, but once you've chosen a name, use it often when you call or address her. A short, simple name is best for the purposes of training; giving her a long name that is then abbreviated will only lead to confusion, as this kind of subtle distinction is completely lost on a dog. Before you begin training your puppy, read the section that discusses training more fully, on pages 198–200, for the general principles.

House Training

The most critical part of early training is teaching your pet where it is acceptable to relieve itself. Dogs are naturally clean animals and will not willingly soil their sleeping or eating areas, but small puppies have small bladders and are also prone to urinate with excitement or fear (common emotions in a young dog). House training can begin any time after five weeks of age.

Consistency, constant vigilance, and patience will speed up the process of house training, but there will undoubtedly be accidents. Take your dog outside last thing at

night, each time she wakes up (even after brief naps), a short time after meals or when she has drunk water, after great excitement, and when you see her circling around (sniffing out a good spot). The last is a clear signal that she needs to go, so act quickly! If you provide plenty of opportunities throughout the day and keep an eye on her at all times, ideally, for the first week or so, accidents should be few and far between.

Begin by teaching your dog where she can relieve herself. If you take her outside, take her repeatedly to the same spot in the yard, where the dog will recognize her own odor. It may be necessary to keep your young puppy inside until her immunization process is completed, in which case, take her to a newspaper-lined area or special purpose-designed puppy pad. Retain one piece of soiled paper and put it underneath the top sheet to encourage her to return to the same place until you can train her outside.

Give your puppy lots of praise (and a treat, if you like) immediately after she has eliminated in the correct place. Respond to accidents by saying, very firmly, "No," and then moving her to the right place. Do not punish or scold the puppy for making "mistakes" or for failing to perform when you've taken her outside, because she may become fearful. Do not put the puppy outside and then wait until she comes in to reward her, either, because she won't connect the reward with the elimination. When you clear up an indoor accident, try to remove the odor completely by using a strong enzymatic cleaner, as this will discourage a repeat performance in the same place.

You will soon learn the signs that your puppy needs to relieve herself, and she'll soon learn where you want her to go. Eventually, she will learn to alert you when she needs to go out, but it is up to you to remain vigilant and to take the lead in the house-training process until she reaches this stage.

Feeding

With small stomachs, puppies need to eat little and often—usually three or four times a day, depending on the size of the dog. They are usually weaned off their mother's milk at the age of five or six weeks, and breeders will often supply new owners with a diet sheet. Adjust your puppy's diet gradually, as sudden changes may result in an upset stomach. This is unpleasant for both of you and will interfere with your puppy's house training.

Choose a special puppy food suitable for the size of your pet, as these have carefully balanced combinations of vitamins, minerals, and calories designed to suit a growing dog. Ask your vet for a recommendation if the owner or breeder did not provide guidance. Let your puppy eat as much as he needs in fifteen or twenty minutes, and then remove the food bowl. Leaving food continually available encourages obesity and means that the dog will not look forward to mealtimes as a treat.

Feeding is another opportunity to implement behavioral training and to teach your dog lessons for life. Dogs can be possessive of their food, and feeding is one means by which they exercise dominance (or otherwise) within a pack. To show your pet that you are "top dog," teach him to wait for his meal until after you have had yours, and do not give him tidbits from the table (apart from anything else, they may not suit a puppy's delicate stomach). Watching a small puppy growl and defend its feeding bowl may seem comical, but as the dog becomes bigger, this snarling behavior is less amusing and can develop into a serious problem that is more difficult to correct. Dogs must be taught that they must not chase off anyone who comes near (especially their owner!). While your puppy is feeding, deliberately pat the bowl or move it slightly. If the puppy ignores you, reward his behavior; if he growls, say "No," but repeat your actions at the next mealtime. If he continues to behave possessively, take the food away when he growls and return it when he's stopped complaining. Continue to do this until he is fully accustomed to your handling his food whenever you choose.

Immunization

More general areas of canine health are dealt with in a later chapter, but it is important to note at this point that young puppies must undergo a course of vaccinations to protect them from a number of infectious and potentially fatal diseases. Before they are weaned, puppies absorb antibodies against infection from their mother's milk. But in that critical period between weaning and the age when they are mature enough to form their own antibodies (about three months), they are vulnerable to infection from other dogs and from germs brought inside on the soles of shoes or on clothes.

Some puppies begin their course of vaccinations as early as six weeks, but more often puppies are inoculated at eight, twelve, and sixteen weeks against distemper, hepatitis, canine parvovirus, and leptospirosis (administered as a one-combination shot). Kennel cough (or bordetella) vaccine may also be dispensed with the first shots. In the United States, the first rabies vaccinations are usually administered at sixteen weeks of age. Worming treatments are usually recommended for puppies at the same time as the initial vaccinations. Make sure your vet advises you on all the potential diseases your puppy may be exposed to in your area, and keep a record of your puppy's vaccinations, as you'll need this not just to remind yourself of booster dates, but also to present to kennels when you go on vacation.

While your puppy is vulnerable to infection, you'll need to keep him indoors and apart from other dogs, although you'll be able to take your puppy to visit another dog that you know has been properly immunized. The puppy can pick up infections on his paws anywhere outdoors that other dogs may have been (and, in the case of some infectious diseases, where other animals have been). Unless you have a secure, private yard, do not take chances by taking him outside, even if this means that you are forced to delay outdoor house training. If you are unsure whether or not your yard is suitable for your puppy in these first weeks, consult your veterinarian. Even if your new puppy had his first immunization shots before he left the breeder, it always advisable to take your pup to the vet for a complete checkup shortly after you bring him home.

5
Basic Care
and Grooming

Your dog's health is of paramount importance, and while it is unlikely that he will cruise through life without any health problems, many illnesses and afflictions can be prevented by a basic care routine. Daily grooming, providing a diet suitable for his age and size, and regular veterinary checkups all contribute to your dog's well-being. If you notice radical changes in his behavior or alterations in his bowel or urinary habits, or if he rejects his food, consult your vet, as these are symptoms of underlying health problems.

Identification

In most places, owners are obliged by law to attach some form of identification to their dog. Wherever you live, this should be a priority. Collars and engraved name tags should be worn in any case, but microchipping is an additional (and permanent) method of securing your pet. The vet can implant a tiny microchip in the loose fold of skin at the back of the dog's neck, a procedure that is no more painful than having a vaccination. The microchip carries an identification number that is unique to your dog. This number is stored in a national database, along with other information, such as the dog's age, vaccination history, owner, and address. If a scanner is passed over the microchip, the relevant details will appear on a computer—accessed by a vet or the police. The American Kennel Club runs a Companion Recovery Program that uses a database of microchipped animals. In some places you are required by law to display your dog's rabies vaccine tag on his collar in addition to his identity; check your local laws.

🐾 *A number tattooed on a dog's ear or inner thigh is one option for secure identification, but microchipping is becoming a popular alternative.*

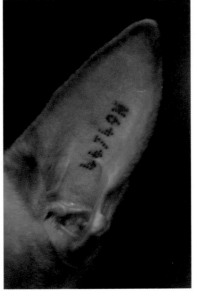

Diet and Feeding

Like humans, dogs need a well-balanced diet that is suitable to their size and calorific output—and this varies considerably from breed to breed. Furthermore, puppies have additional dietary needs, in terms of vitamins and minerals, as do nursing bitches, while older dogs will also benefit from a carefully formulated diet. Pet-food manufacturers present the consumer with a wide variety of choices, both in terms of special food for dogs of different sizes and ages, and types of regular food. It is worth taking the time to read dog-food packaging carefully to ensure that you are giving your dog a diet appropriate to her size and circumstances. A good diet will ensure that your dog reaches her full potential of growth and development.

Adult dogs usually require one meal each day (although it might be more convenient to divide this into two lighter meals) and they must have access to fresh water throughout the day—especially in hot weather and if their diet consists mainly of dry food.

Adult dogs usually need to defecate three to four hours after feeding, so do not give a large meal late at night, particularly when you are house training. Do not overfeed your dog and do not allow her to have table scraps unless you compensate for these in her meal sizes, as this can eventually lead to obesity, which puts additional strain on her heart and joints.

As in humans, obesity in dogs can derive directly from overfeeding and underexercising, and ultimately results in a shorter life span. A healthy dog should have an identifiable waist when seen from above, and the ribs should be palpable, if not visible. If you

The Menu

Dogs are naturally omnivorous, a characteristic inherited from their wild, scavenging ancestors. And, like us, dogs are what they eat. A dog that is poorly fed will appear skinny, his coat will be dull, and he will be more susceptible to digestive problems, sores, and parasites. All pets clearly thrive on a balanced diet containing the protein, carbohydrates, fatty acids, vitamins, and minerals necessary for

🐾 *Chew toys and rawhide "bones" (below) are helpful for your dog's dental health and are particularly important when your puppy is teething. Rawhide chews occasionally cause stomach upsets; check the packaging to avoid harmful chemicals.*

a fully functioning, healthy animal. Dogs do not need fruit and vegetables in the same way that humans do, as their bodies efficiently make plenty of vitamin C, although a regular daily amount of fruit and vegetables is good for them and is included in many foods.

are training your dog with treats or want to provide her with a more varied diet by allowing her to eat additional foods, adjust the meal size accordingly. Don't give in to a begging dog; you should stick to the quantities recommended by your veterinarian.

When deciding what sort of food to give your dog, take into account the amount of time you can devote to food preparation. Some owners enjoy preparing fresh food every day for their dog. But in general, a more balanced diet is provided by manufactured food, which combines convenience, palatability, and the right nutritional mix for your pet's age and activity level. There are two main types of food to choose from.

Canned foods (also known as moist or wet food) are widely available; some provide a complete diet, while others must be supplemented with dog meal or kibble. They are composed of meat, offal, fish, or poultry, mixed in with vitamin and mineral supplements. Canned foods are excellent for larger or more energetic dogs, as they have a high protein content. It is important that you feed your dog the correct amount of food for her size. Make sure that uneaten food is disposed of and that half-used cans are refrigerated between meals.

🐾 *If you feed your dog canned foods, make sure you provide her with chews to help remove plaque and maintain her general dental health. Pig ears (top right) can be given to adult dogs and older puppies.*

Complete dry meals are less costly, easier to use, and, for puppies, good for developing teeth. They are a mix of cereals, fats, protein, and mineral meals, and they are available as pellets or as shapes (often bone-style). They are sometimes coated with fat to improve flavor, and some brands must be rehydrated with water. Dry food is generally higher in calories than canned food, so smaller portions can be used. Dry food is a better choice than canned if your home is warm or humid and if your dog "grazes" rather than eating his food all at once.

In addition, doggy snacks in the form of meaty treats, bone-shaped biscuits, and even "doggy chocolates" are also available, which are useful as training aids or as occasional treats. Generally high in calories, these snacks should be taken into consideration when you work out your dog's daily caloric intake. Keep human sweets and chocolate well away from your pet, and remember: In sufficient quantities, chocolate is poisonous to dogs. If your dog veers toward obesity, try giving him low-fat dog treats. Grated carrots can be used to bulk out your dog's normal food. Dogs' appetites often decrease in hot or humid weather, so adjust their food intake accordingly in summer.

It is generally best to choose one method of feeding and to stick to it. But if you do decide to change your dog's diet, do so gradually, to allow

Remember to provide plenty of fresh water with meals and throughout the day, particularly if your dog's diet consists mainly of dry food.

Active working dogs, or those with constant access to space for running with other dogs, consume far more calories than pets whose activities are more limited. Do not overfeed your dog. You may think it's what she wants, but, ultimately, it's not kind to her.

your dog's digestive system to become accustomed to the new food. Mix in a little of the new food with the regular diet, gradually incorporating more of the new and less of the old over a week or so. During the transition, your dog may be susceptible to wind or diarrhea; always check with your vet if this is severe or persists for more than a few hours.

Grooming

Dogs are naturally clean animals and, left alone, will keep themselves comfortable by rolling on the ground, scratching, and licking matted fur or sore spots. However, after a swim in a murky pond or a hike across a muddy field, you may prefer to improve your dog's levels of personal

hygiene by intervening, simply for the sake of your home! But there is more to grooming than simple cleanliness. A regular grooming routine enables you to bond with your pet and to become familiar with his healthy body; so you will notice any changes in his health more quickly.

All dogs must be groomed and checked regularly, irrespective of their coats or lifestyles. Obviously, long-haired dogs need more care, and owners keen to show their dogs in competitions will follow a rather more rigorous grooming routine than, say, the owners of a working Collie. A basic grooming session should aim to clean the dog's face, teeth, and paws, brush the coat thoroughly, and check the dog all over for signs of parasitic invasion, abrasions, or other lumps and bumps. Ideally, this should be carried out every day. Some long-haired breeds must have their coats tended by professional dog groomers, who are trained to strip and clip coats. Follow the advice of your breeder or veterinarian for breeds with these specialized grooming requirements.

🐾 *Checking for signs of fleas, ticks, and skin abrasions, cuts, or irritations is a time-consuming process if your dog is long-haired.*

Well-trained dogs are easier to groom than more unruly animals, and it is sensible to groom your puppy from an early age so that she gets used to the routine and does not object to being touched. This practice also helps you establish dominance over your pet, so it is especially important for dominant puppies. Always speak softly to the dog during grooming, stroke her back, and then begin brushing as gently as possible to allow the dog to get used to the sensation. Grooming promotes the bond between a dog and her owner, and once the dog realizes that brushing is relaxing and pleasurable, it will become a relatively quick and easy process.

Brushes

The phrase "different strokes for different folks" seems strangely apt for the world of dog brushes, of which there are many choices, depending on the particular requirements of the coat type. In order to maintain your dog's coat in tip-top condition, you will have to brush it regularly. If you have more than one dog, allocate one set of brushes to each—don't share them between dogs, as this increases the risk of transferring parasites or skin diseases.

Dogs with long, glossy coats should be brushed daily to remove dead hair and to prevent the coat from tangling and matting. Short-haired dogs can escape with a quicker brush or rubdown every other day.

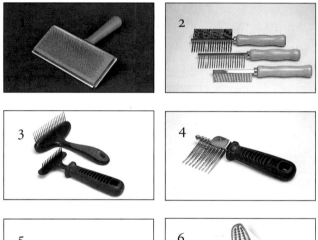

Daily Grooming

Short-haired dogs with low-maintenance grooming needs may not require a daily brushing, but should nonetheless be checked each day for scratches, irritations, and ticks or fleas, depending on the exercising environment. Before you begin, get your equipment ready. You will need a bowl of warm water, cotton balls, and brushes to suit your dog's coat. (Short-coated breeds benefit from brushing with a hound glove and chamois leather, while long-coated dogs will need a selection of brushes to cut through tangles. See left for more specifics.) Some coats need regular clipping, but before you purchase electric clippers, ask the advice of a professional groomer as to what type is the best for your dog. After trying it out, you may come to think that clipping is an art better left to the experts. Similarly, wire-haired breeds, like Schnauzers or Airedales, must have the dead hair stripped from their coats every three or four months, either by hand or with a stripping tool. It is entirely painless, but it can be a long job that is best tackled over the course of several days.

A quick-reference guide to brush types:

1 Slicker brushes can be used on all breeds to remove dead hair and help control shedding.
2 Fine-toothed flea combs can be used to check the coat for fleas and to groom the facial hairs of your dog.
3 Coarse double coats (such as those on a Collie or Golden Retriever) can be aerated with a rake comb.
4 Dematting combs are used for coarse or long coats.
5 A combination pin and bristle brush. A pin brush is excellent for long coats; the bristles are rounded and smooth to avoid scratching the skin. Bristle brushes are ideal for short coats and for giving the finishing touch to a long-haired dog's grooming session.
6 Rubber grooming mitts are used to shine a short-haired coat once the dead hair has been brushed away.

🐾 *Your dog's face should be cleaned carefully with moistened cotton balls.*

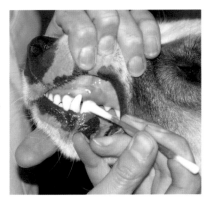

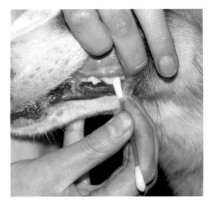

Begin by brushing the coat all over to remove the worst tangles, debris, and dried mud. Then moisten a couple of cotton balls with warm water and wash the face, paying particular attention to the eyes and nose. If your dog has a wrinkled face, clean the folds of skin carefully. Use more damp cotton balls to clean around the anus and tail. Check the ears for mites and for any buildup of wax. There should not be any redness, odor, or inflammation. Check your dog's mouth and teeth every day or so. Use a canine toothpaste and toothbrush (or cotton buds) to clean the teeth and check that the gums are not inflamed. Never use human toothpaste, as dogs dislike the flavor and the foaming sensation. Puppies and young dogs usually keep their teeth in good health simply by chewing rawhide or eating dry food, but they should become accustomed to

❧ You should begin brushing teeth (above) and checking the claws and dew claws (below) when your puppy is young, so he gets used to being handled.

you checking their teeth. Consult your vet if your dog develops bad breath, sore gums, or any bleeding or ulcers in his mouth (but remember that your puppy will start to lose his first teeth at four months or so, and you will see traces of blood at this stage.)

Toenails need clipping regularly. The nails of any dog that is walked on sidewalks or other hard surfaces will remain naturally short, but they must still be checked regularly. Dew claws do not wear down naturally, so must be trimmed regularly, too. It is best to ask your vet for guidance if you are unsure about clipping your dog's nails, as it is all too easy to accidentally cut the quick (or nerved part) of the nail, which is extremely painful for the dog. If your dog has dark toenails, the quick is difficult to see, and you may wish to have your vet or groomer perform this task rather doing it yourself.

Bathing

Your dog will need to be bathed occasionally. Different breeds have different requirements; those with harsh double coats should not be bathed more than three or four times a year, otherwise the natural protective oils will be stripped away. Aside from cleansing the skin

and fur, bathing can ameliorate skin conditions like the mange or an irritating infestation of fleas.

A dog accustomed to baths from puppyhood will enjoy them and will have learned not to be afraid. Owners of large dogs have little alternative but to use the bathtub, but smaller dogs can be washed in a table-top plastic bath or washbowl. The whole process is easier in the summer, when you can use the wading pool and a hose!

Tips for Hassle-free Bathing:

🐾 Always use a specially formulated canine shampoo—human shampoos are made for skins with different pH values than a dog's.

🐾 Make sure that your bathtub has a nonslip surface (use a rubber mat, if necessary). The water should be lukewarm and, if you are using a shower head, make sure the water jet is not too powerful.

🐾 Wash the dog by stroking shampoo into the coat and then massaging right through the fur. Make sure that it does not get in the eyes or up the nose. Leave the head until last, as a dog's natural reaction is to shake itself. Do not neglect the underbelly, under the tail, and the legs.

🐾 Always rinse off the shampoo thoroughly, working from the head, along the back, and down to the hindquarters.

🐾 Dry the dog by rubbing all over with an absorbent cloth, then wrap in a towel and lift out of the bath. Let him have a shake and, if necessary, dry the coat with a blow-dryer.

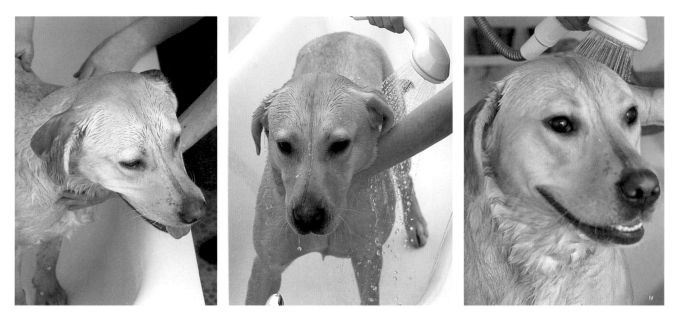

Breeding, Pregnancy, and Whelping

If you have a purebred animal, you may decide to breed from your dog. Breeders are required to maintain detailed records of litters, sires, and dams, and owners who choose to mate their animal with another of the same breed are advised to study the pedigree or family history of each dog to ensure that there are no genetic defects that may reappear. Breeding from a mixed-breed dog is a less certain prospect; the puppies will not necessarily look like the mother. But as long as you are confident of finding a good home for them, caring for a litter of pups is a rewarding experience. Be warned that it is irresponsible to allow your dog to become pregnant if you cannot take care of the puppies, for whatever reason, be it financial or circumstantial. Rescue centers operate with limited financial resources, so they cannot be regarded as a backup solution for your unwanted pups. Caring for puppies is a demanding commitment that should not be undertaken lightly.

Giving birth and looking after a litter of puppies puts a strain on the mother, so make sure you're aware of her special needs during this period. Her diet will need to be adapted to include sufficient calcium, which can be dissolved in egg yolk, to help when she's lactating.

The optimum age for bitches to whelp is between eighteen months and four years of age, and the upper limit is seven years. Vets are an excellent source of advice if you are seeking a mate for your dog, and they will, of course, be able to offer guidance on the care of your dog during pregnancy and after the birth.

Canine pregnancy lasts for sixty-three days (nine weeks), but there are no visible signs until the sixth week, when the abdomen is obviously fuller and the mammary glands become enlarged. The mother will need more food, probably about two-thirds more than her usual diet; and toward the end of the pregnancy, she may prefer small, more frequent meals.

Birth Checklist

- ✔ Make sure you have your vet's phone number at hand, as well as an emergency number for after hours.
- ✔ Prepare a birthing pack of old towels, disinfectant, and warm water.
- ✔ The first sign of action is that the mother begins to shiver and become restless. She will pant and her temperature will drop by two to three degrees—from a normal reading of 100–102°F (38–39°C).
- ✔ Once the first puppy arrives, the others should follow every ten to eighty minutes.

Call the Vet if:

- ✔ there is no sign of a puppy more than two hours after the start of contractions;
- ✔ more than two hours elapse between the delivery of individual puppies;
- ✔ labor appears unproductive and the mother becomes too weak or tired to manage strong enough contractions;
- ✔ the mother appears panicky, feverish, or is panting very heavily;
- ✔ the mother doesn't deliver a placenta for each puppy, because a retained placenta poses the danger of infection.

🐾 *From the moment of birth, when she licks the pup to remove the membrane and stimulate breathing, the mother takes care of her offspring's every need. Keep her in a quiet, calm environment and avoid disturbing her too much.*

If you are a first-time breeder, your vet may be able to arrange for you to view another whelping before your own dog gives birth. It is also possible to take a breeding class. In this way, you will have a better idea of what to expect and will feel more confident if you need to intervene during the birth. Some breeds need more help than others; some, for example, frequently need help to break the sac (the placental membrane) and to cut the umbilical cord, so ask other breeders for their advice. For safety, enlist the help of your vet or an experienced breeder for the birth unless you have hands-on experience.

Around eight weeks, but no later, introduce her to a specially prepared whelping box, which should be somewhere warm and quiet, with room for her to turn around. Whelping boxes are available from pet supply stores, but it is easy to construct one and line it with newspaper and washable synthetic fleece or old towels. Make sure that it has a guardrail that runs around the interior of all four sides of the box, to prevent the mother from accidentally crushing the puppies against the walls.

The mother will need more rest during the last couple of weeks, and should not undergo vigorous exercise. Take her temperature twice daily for the last week before the due date: When her temperature decreases (see opposite), delivery should follow within twenty-four hours. At this stage she may refuse or vomit a meal and display signs of restlessness. Most dogs whelp without difficulty, but it is a sensible precaution to notify your vet, in case a house call becomes necessary.

Newborn Care

The mother will lick each puppy as it emerges to remove the membranes and mucus and she will chew through the umbilical cord to separate it from the placenta. This also stimulates and warms the puppies. The puppies must suckle from the mother as soon as possible. Call the vet if any of the pups appear sick, if the mother ignores them or appears weak or anxious, or if a puppy will not feed straight away.

For the first two or three weeks, the mother attends to every need of the puppies—from feeding them to licking them to stimulate the elim-  ination of waste (which she will then consume). Make sure the box is kept clean and in a quiet, draft-free environ- ment. For the first three weeks of their life, puppies spend about 90 per- cent of the time sleeping. They are born with their eyes closed, and they generally open between day nine and day eleven, although they will not yet focus properly. Between

the thirteenth and seventeenth days, the ear canals open and the young dogs start to become more responsive to the world around them.

The mother must be kept warm, comfortable, and well-fed—her food intake will double, and possibly treble, as her body adjusts to feeding a litter of hungry pups. She will prefer small, frequent meals, and it is often a good idea to add powdered glucose to her drinking water, to give her additional energy. Calcium powder dissolved in an egg yolk (do not give the white) helps prevent eclampsia (a disease associated with low blood calcium levels in lactating bitches). As long as she appears settled and the pups are feeding properly, she does not need to see a vet immediately. If, however, she appears irritable or restless, or if there is a green discharge, contact the vet immediately, as she may have an infection. At any rate, the mother should be checked by the vet soon after the birth, to guard against problems such as eclampsia, metritis (infected uterus), or mastitis (infected mammary glands).

🐾 *No matter how adorable your children find the newborns, don't let them handle them. Only an adult should do this, gently and with respect for the mother.*

Veterinary Care

It is sensible to register your pet with a vet as soon as you bring him or her home. Young puppies, in particular, will need regular care in the form of vaccinations (see page 173), and even older dogs must be given a complete health check at least on an annual basis. Dogs can quickly develop an aversion to visiting the vet, which can become a serious problem if they are large and powerful! Make sure you accustom your dog to your vet at an early stage. Some veterinarians run puppy play sessions to help pups get used to the environment.

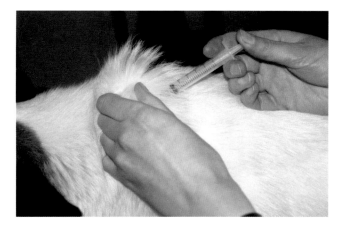

🐾 *Ask other dog owners and breeders for recommendations to find a reliable veterinarian you can trust to look after your dog throughout her lifetime.*

Spaying and Neutering

If you do not want to breed your dog, you should sterilize him or her. Dogs become sexually mature between six and twelve months of age, although they are not mentally mature until eighteen to twenty-four months. When male dogs are neutered they become less aggressive (as the testosterone levels are decreased), and sterilization reduces the number of unwanted puppies.

Spayed females (and their owners) are spared the problem of a surprise litter, as well as the twice-yearly "season" when the bitch is fertile. The idea that a bitch needs to have a litter for her own benefit is simply a myth; female dogs live full and happy lives without producing puppies. A bitch's season is between fifteen and twenty-one days long, when the dog will appear restless and moody and, for five days or so, will emit a bloody discharge. She also gives off a powerful hormonal message to male dogs that she is fertile, so during this time she must be kept away from potential mates. This can be very difficult to achieve unless you have a secure yard in which to exercise her.

Your vet will advise you on the best course of action, but dogs are usually neutered or spayed between nine and eighteen months of age (although, of course, these operations can be carried out at any age). These procedures are done under general anesthetic. Some vets prefer to spay after the dog's first season, while others will do it as early as three months of age. The timing depends partly on the breed, so make sure you check and plan for this as soon as you acquire your new puppy. The benefits clearly outweigh any disadvantages. Owners worry that their dogs will become fat, as neutered dogs have slightly lower calorific requirements than intact animals (about 15 percent less), but they will remain trim as long as their diet is appropriate.

Preventable Disease and Common Ailments

Some of the most common canine illnesses are easily preventable by making sure that your dog is regularly vaccinated. Puppies are given a course of inoculations to protect them from a group of diseases, which are listed opposite, and some of these require booster shots throughout the dog's life. This book provides a general guide, but in all cases your vet will be able to furnish more details and should be consulted for any additional recommendations that may apply where you live.

It is important that you are aware of any changes in your dog's behavior or appearance, so that you will be able to see if he or she is off-color. If you become concerned about your dog's health, make a note of all the symptoms, as the details will help the vet make an accurate diagnosis.

Eyes—are they bright and clear? They should not be red, nor should there be any discharge around the eyelids.

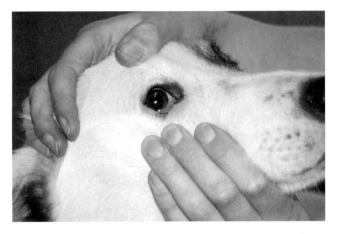

Ears—are the ears clean and free from discharge? There should be no excess wax or odor.

Nose—should be clean and slightly moist.

Mouth—check that the gums appear pink, moist and healthy (some breeds have mottled black gums), and that there are no blisters, ulcers, or inflamed spots.

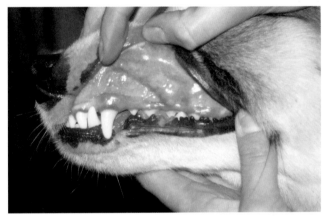

Temperature—the normal canine temperature is 100–102°F (38–39°C). *Caution*—get your vet to demonstrate the safe use of a thermometer.

General check—is your dog eating and drinking normally? Is he touching a particular part of his body, or does he appear lame?

The most common canine diseases are described below.

Infectious canine distemper (also known as "hard pad") is a highly contagious viral disease that attacks the brain and the spinal cord. Immunity can be maintained by getting your dog vaccinated every two years.

Infectious canine hepatitis is spread from dog to dog via contact with infected urine. As in humans, hepatitis damages the liver and can cause blindness.

Leptospirosis is a bacterial disease that is spread in a similar way to hepatitis, and which afflicts the kidneys and the liver. This disease is now very uncommon; dogs are immunized twice as a puppy, and they can have annual boosters thereafter.

Parainfluenza is an infectious respiratory virus that produces a severe form of kennel cough.

Canine parvovirus (CPV) is highly contagious and the most common fatal infectious canine disease. It attacks the bowel and, in young puppies, can damage the heart.

Bordetella is a serious, but rarely fatal, respiratory disease, and it is a common cause of kennel cough. It is an airborne infection that thrives in confined spaces, and most reputable boarding kennels advise their customers to vaccinate their dogs a couple of weeks before they arrive.

Rabies is spread through saliva, most commonly from animal bites, and it is always fatal. The British Isles are currently free of rabies, and inoculations are only given to animals traveling overseas. In the United States, however, the first rabies vaccination occurs at sixteen weeks, and a booster is administered a year later, with further shots between every one and three years thereafter. Immunization against rabies is legally required in many places; if your dog strays and is not wearing his rabies tag, he may be destroyed by public-health authorities, so it's important that you attach it securely to the collar.

Common Hereditary Problems

In the wild, only the fittest survive, but dogs are now the most domestic of animals and their genetic destiny has been so manipulated by humans that some breeds are prone to inherited disorders. Mixed-breed dogs can also inherit health problems, though they are less likely to suffer from genetic disorders than purebred dogs.

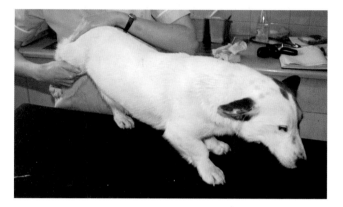

Hip dysplasia (deformed hip joints, which causes lameness at its most severe) is common among certain breeds of large dogs, such as German Shepherds, English Setters, American Cockers, Giant Schnauzers, Golden Retrievers, and Shetland Sheepdogs.

Deafness, which is hard to detect, can be a problem in American Foxhounds, Bull Terriers, Collies, Scottish Terriers, and Great Danes.

Progressive retinal atrophy is a degenerative disease of the eye that leads to blindness. It is first noticeable when a dog appears to have difficulty seeing at night. The breeds most at risk are: Border Collies, English Cocker Spaniels, English Springer Spaniels, Golden Retrievers, Gordon Setters, Labrador Retrievers, Pekingese, Pomeranian Poodles, Samoyeds, Shetland Sheepdogs, and Corgis.

There are many other common hereditary canine health problems. Reputable breeders will ensure that their dogs are checked for potential defects, and will try to breed with healthy animals in an effort to eliminate such disorders. Keep an eye on up-to-date sources for hereditary diseases that may affect your breed.

Parasites

Considerate dog owners clean up after their dog: Poop must be scooped and disposed of, whether or not this is a legal requirement where you live. At home, make sure your dog uses one particular corner of the yard, so that the transmission of zoonotic diseases (such as roundworm infection) is less likely—and so you are not continually worrying about what you might tread in.

Dog feces is unpleasant, and it is a source of disease for both dogs and humans. It can house roundworm eggs (*Toxcara canis*), which are able to survive for up to two years in the soil and are estimated to affect 15 percent of dogs in the United States, as well as being the most common parasitic worms in Britain. If swallowed by humans, the eggs become larvae, producing an allergic reaction, and in severe cases, blindness. Children playing in parks or gardens are more susceptible to toxocariasis than adults, and it is sensible to make them wash their hands when they come inside from playing or after they have been petting the dog.

🐾 *If your pet is sick or has parasites, keep her away from other dogs until she's clear.*

🐾 *For the sake of hygiene, make sure your children learn the importance of washing their hands after petting the dog—every time.*

There are few clinical signs of worms, unless the dog is very young, when he may appear potbellied and pass worms visibly in his stools. Infected puppies will also gain weight slowly. Checking your dog for worms should be a regular part of your grooming and hygiene routine. Worming treatments commence when puppies are just three or four weeks old, and treatments are administered every three to six months to adult dogs. Your vet will advise you on the best worming treatment and dosage, as this varies according to the parasite's prevalence where you live.

Dogs that live in poor and unsanitary conditions are also prey to intestinal worms, including hookworm or whipworm. These can cause diarrhea and more serious problems, such as bleeding or, in extreme cases, anemia. However, intestinal worms are rarely seen in pet dogs, but sheepdogs, dogs kept in outdoor kennels, and those exercised on grass are more susceptible.

Dogs that are allowed to eat animal carcasses or offal may catch tapeworms *(Dipylidium caninum)*. The life cycle of the tapeworm also depends partly on fleas, so this is another reason for rigorous flea prevention. The only visible sign of infection is small "rice grains" in the feces, but tapeworm infection is treated reasonably easily with medicine prescribed by the vet, in conjunction with insecticide to kill the fleas. The easiest way to avoid this unpleasant infection is to avoid feeding raw meat to your dog, and not to allow him near cat litter boxes (as some dogs will eat cat feces, which is also a host). Wash your hands thoroughly after handling meat and before and after petting your dog.

Fleas afflict many dogs at some point and it is very important to eradicate them as quickly as possible, as they are the host for roundworm and tapeworm larvae—and, of course, they are a serious nuisance if they infest your home. If you see your dog scratching, check his coat for telltale signs of reddish-brown flecks of dried blood that appear around flea bites. The fleas themselves are also reddish-brown. They can move quickly through a coat, sometimes leaping great distances, so it's not always easy to see them. The photograph above shows how tiny fleas are.

Fleas can be treated with a range of proprietary insecticides, but as they can live in carpets and bedding, it is not only your poor pooch that must be sprayed. Your house, soft furnishings, and your dog's bedding need thorough vacuuming and treatment with an insecticidal spray to kill both the fleas and the eggs. If you live in an area where fleas are widespread, consider using a flea-prevention treatment that is absorbed through the dog's skin. Ask your veterinarian for guidance.

Lice and mange mites can be caught from other dogs. Mange mites are invisible to the naked eye and burrow deep into the hair follicles, usually infecting puppies, or elderly or sick dogs, especially those with short coats. Demotic mange creates bald patches in the dog's coat and is unsightly, but not especially irritating unless it becomes infected, when the skin may thicken like elephant hide and develop pustules. A weekly bath in insecticidal solution usually removes the mites.

Other external parasites include "chiggers" or harvest mites, which look like tiny orange grains. They latch on to dogs' paws in the autumn, and occasionally the area above the eyes, and are extremely irritating to the dog. Insecticidal shampoo usually kills them off, although anti-inflammatory medicine may also be necessary.

Blood-sucking ticks are another irritant, afflicting dogs that live in the countryside around sheep or deer and in many suburban areas. They can be killed by smothering them in oil and carefully removing the whole parasite—but beware of leaving the head behind, which will irritate the skin further, possibly causing an abscess. If Lyme disease, which is spread by infected ticks, affects your area, again consider giving your dog a systemic tick-prevention treatment absorbed through the skin.

Sarcoptes mites inhabit the ear tips and elbows by burrowing into the skin, causing the area to develop sarcoptic mange, which makes the area itchy and scabby. Dogs can damage themselves further by constantly scratching, so this condition must not be left untreated. The mites may also infect humans with itchy, mosquito-like bites. Infected dogs must be bathed weekly for at least four weeks to kill the parasites.

Skin and coat disorders are usually limited to the appearance of fleas or other parasites, although incessant scratching can inflame the skin and cause further irritation. Localized hair loss may occur when mange mites or other parasites are present.

Paws for Thought

🐾 This book is not designed to supplant professional diagnosis and treatment of canine conditions and disorders. If you suspect your dog has a health problem, or if she's had an accident, always consult your veterinarian. Information given here may sometimes conflict with regional practices and recommendations. Let your veterinarian be your guide.

Other Common Health Problems

Your dog is susceptible to many other common health problems and accidental injuries. Not all of these require veterinary care, but if you are in doubt, always visit your veterinarian.

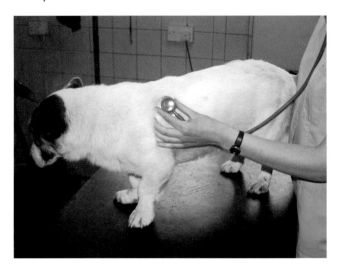

Anal glands: The anal sacs or glands produce the secretions dogs use for scent marking. If they become blocked this is both painful and irritating. If you notice your dog scooting or dragging his rear end along the ground, the anal glands may need emptying. Your vet can do this easily and can teach you how to do it.

Digestive problems: Persistent diarrhea accompanied by vomiting that lasts for longer than a few hours is a matter for the vet. Vomiting alone is not usually a cause for concern, as dogs are natural scavengers and occasionally throw up after eating something unsuitable. Some dogs are regular consumers of grass, which they eat to ease abdominal pain and which usually provokes

First Aid Kit

Prepare a canine first aid kit and never mix up the contents with those from the family kit. Make sure the vet's telephone number is prominent. The most useful items are:

- ✔ Cotton balls or cotton-wool pads
- ✔ Cotton-tipped buds or swabs
- ✔ Adhesive and gauze bandages in two widths (2 in. and 4 in.)
- ✔ Sharp-ended scissors
- ✔ Blunt forceps
- ✔ Thermometer
- ✔ Antiseptic cream and/or spray
- ✔ Eyewash and eyedropper
- ✔ Petroleum jelly

a bout of vomiting. If your dog becomes ill in this way, do not feed any solid food, and offer small drinks of water (preferably cooled boiled water, which can be mixed with soluble glucose powder) every one to two hours. Once the dog has recovered, feed only bland food for a day or so (boiled rice with chicken is usually ideal for this). If you notice blood or bile, or if the vomiting is repeated, you must consult your vet. Occasionally, vomiting may be a symptom of gastric torsion or bloating, or even canine parvovirus.

Diarrhea can be caused by a change of diet, or simply a cold. Do not give the dog solid food, but allow constant access to drinking water. Contact your vet if you notice blood, if your dog vomits as well, or if the diarrhea does not clear up within twenty-four hours.

Constipation can usually be cured by altering your dog's diet. Offer him soaked biscuits rather than dry food, as well as some lightly cooked green vegetables. If he won't eat these, look for specialized dog foods that have been formulated to ease constipation.

Gastric distension (also known as gastric torsion or bloating) usually afflicts larger dogs or those with deep chests, such as Great Danes, but any dog can suffer from it. It is a true emergency and is often fatal—so get help quickly! About two to four hours after a meal, the dog will show signs of discomfort and the abdomen will be hard and distended.

Lick granuloma usually occurs on the foreleg when a dog licks or touches a cut (or bandage) so much that the skin becomes raw, or the cut infected. Apart from treating an infected cut with a bandage and, if necessary, antibiotics, the best way of preventing the dog from licking it again is to fit him with an Elizabethan collar.

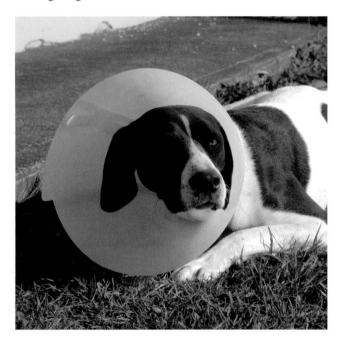

Ear problems: If you notice your dog shaking her head a great deal or scratching her ears, and especially if there is aural discharge of any sort, it is likely that she has an ear problem. Ears are prone to occasional invasion by ear mites, which spread easily between dogs. If you notice a large buildup of wax, be suspicious. Mites can be treated with insecticidal ear drops. If an ear appears inflamed, it may have a foreign body lodged inside. Your dog will probably shake his head excessively in an attempt to dislodge it. The vet will be able to remove it and may administer anti-inflammatory ear drops. A dog that appears unsteady on her feet or cocks her head to one side may have an inner-ear infection. The vet will probably prescribe antibiotics to treat it.

Eye problems: Conjunctivitis is a common infectious condition that causes inflammation of the eyelid and eye membrane, usually accompanied by reddening and a discharge. Your vet will prescribe eye drops. If your dog's eyes are irritated, dry, or clouded, always consult your veterinarian.

Heat exhaustion can be fatal, and it is usually the fault of careless owners. Dogs should never be left in cars, even with the windows open, unless parked in the shade on a cool day. The signs of heat exhaustion are distress, panting, and shallow breathing; the tongue may appear swollen or blue, and sometimes the dog vomits or even collapses. Revive the dog by pouring cold water over him. This is a critical emergency, so once he's breathing more easily, take him to the nearest vet.

Paw problems: If your dog's paw is bleeding profusely, she may have stepped on a sharp object and may need to have the pad stitched. Do not try to remove any embedded object; take her immediately to the vet or emergency center. If she is licking her paw constantly or appears lame, again, visit your vet, as her paw may be damaged, even if there is no obvious cut or bleeding.

How to Give a Pill

1. Grasp the upper jaw firmly.

2. Open the lower jaw while holding the upper jaw securely.

3. Slip the pill onto the base of the tongue.

4. Close the mouth gently, but firmly.

5. Hold the jaws shut.

6. Tilt the head back and stroke the throat to encourage the dog to swallow.

Caution—only attempt this if you know the dog is not aggressive.

Nursing a Sick Dog

If your dog needs to be kept warm, make sure that her room is warm and draft-free. Only use a hot-water bottle or heater if your vet advises it. In this case, a covered hot-water bottle can be placed in the dog's bed—but make certain that it's not too hot and the dog will not be able to burn herself, especially if she is not able to move easily.

If necessary, the easiest way to administer pills is to crush them into the dog's food. However, if the tablets must be given at other than meal-times, or if this puts your dog off his food so that he refuses to eat it, the key to success is to place the pill as far back in the mouth as possible. It is possible to buy special pill dispensers from pet-supply shops, but if you do not have one, follow the step-by-step instructions left.

It is very tricky to administer liquid medicine to a dog with a spoon, so get a syringe. You can fill it with the precise amount of medication, slip the syringe into the dog's mouth from the side, and trickle the medicine in slowly so that the dog does not choke. Ask your vet to demonstrate.

Older Dogs

Dogs are considered to be in their senior years from the age of about seven, although this varies considerably from breed to breed. Large dogs generally do not live as long as smaller animals: Great Danes and Boxers, for example, usually manage nine or ten years, whereas small terriers can live for up to fifteen years. The signs of advancing age appear gradually, but are easy to spot: Your dog will slow down, will generally be less excitable, may even appear irritable sometimes, and the hairs around the muzzle may begin to turn gray.

Older dogs tend to gain weight, so alter your older dog's diet gradually to accommodate a less active lifestyle, and provide food that is easy to digest, high in fiber, but contains fewer calories. Overweight dogs have a strain on the muscles, joints, and the heart, and they are more at risk from other medical problems such as tumors and diabetes. Dogs over the age of seven should be checked by a veterinarian every six months.

As in aging humans, dogs suffer from declining vision and hearing, stiffening of the joints, and may prefer a quieter life than they did when young. The arrival of a younger dog

sometimes enlivens an older dog, which will enjoy the company of another animal and the status of being "top dog." Older dogs sleep a little more and enjoy midday naps. They may bark more frequently, perhaps because their hearing is declining or because something else is troubling them. Owners need to be flexible and understanding to accommodate their dog's changing needs, and they need to understand that their dog may become frustrated at her inability to do things. Try to avoid putting your dog in stressful situations and stick to a familiar routine. Older dogs still need exercise, however, but they will not run around as energetically as younger animals. Gentle exercise helps to keep the joints mobile, will ease bowel problems, and will stimulate him—so introduce a regime of short but frequent walks, which are more suited to an older animal.

If it becomes clear that your older dog is in constant pain, has little independence, and has a poor quality of life, you may decide that it is time to end his or her distress through peaceful euthanasia. Though it is naturally upsetting for a family that has loved a pet for several years, for a dog weakened by old age and disease, this is sometimes the kindest thing an owner can do. Your vet will advise you when this decision becomes appropriate.

6

Socialization and Training

DOGS: AN OWNER'S GUIDE

Dogs are intelligent creatures and, over the centuries, they have been trained and bred by their human owners to perform all manner of tasks—ranging from retrieving game, warding off intruders, herding sheep, and pulling sleds to more arcane tasks like providing circus entertainment. The natural aggression of some breeds has been exploited to turn them into fighting dogs and, even today, the fastest dogs, Greyhounds, are used for human entertainment at dog tracks around the world. Many

dogs thrive on the intellectual stimulation and close personal bond that trained work provides. Labrador Retrievers, for example, are trained to work with blind and deaf people, acting as their eyes and ears in everyday situations. Collies and sheepdogs make reliable and intelligent herders, performing complex tasks across long distances with remarkable speed, focus, and accuracy.

All dogs—from untiring working animals to small, pampered lapdogs—should be trained to behave properly, even if it is only to sit, to stay on command, to relieve themselves in the correct places, and not to howl, whine, or become overexcited in the face of strangers, other dogs, or new experiences. For their own safety and yours, dogs must be taught to walk properly on a leash. If you cannot rely on your dog to come when called or to walk on a leash, life outside of your home is going to be stressful for both of you. As an owner, you are liable for your dog's bad behavior, and no one is exempt from the laws governing pet restraint (as Britain's Princess Anne found out when she was fined in court in 2002 after her Bull Terrier attacked two children). It is an offense in Britain to own an animal deemed to be a dangerous dog, and in the United States, laws vary from place to place. Most

cities, for example, require that dogs are kept on a leash in all public places except in designated areas, and most towns have stringent antilitter laws (requiring that you must pick up your dog's poop). It is sensible to acquaint yourself with local laws before you acquire a dog.

Not everyone loves dogs, but well-trained animals are infinitely more pleasant than poorly trained ones. As a responsible owner, you should ensure that your dog is under control at all times. It should not jump up at strangers or bark madly at new faces, other dogs, or new experiences. You must also ensure that your dog cannot escape from home, roam, and cause trouble—or even get hurt. Equally, if you own a female dog that is not spayed, make sure that she is especially secure during her season. You should always clean up after your dog: and dispose of the poop hygienically.

The main reasons for training a dog are to ensure the safety of the dog and all who come into contact with it, to teach it to behave as you want it to, to establish its position in the family hierarchy, and to provide the animal with structure and mental stimulation. Training covers three main categories. Behavioral training teaches basic good manners, such as how to behave around people, house training, and walking on a leash. Obedience training teaches a dog to perform specific actions, such as sitting, walking to heel, or lying down on command. Activity training is excellent for working breeds, who thrive on the stimulation of being trained to retrieve, herd, or to perform agility sequences.

There is some truth in the saying, "you can't teach an old dog new tricks," as training is best begun at an early age so that a dog learns to cope with new experiences and to recognize his place in the family "pack." Mature dogs can be trained, but the process is much more difficult and time consuming. One of the first lessons that young dogs must learn is where to relieve themselves (see page 171). Next, every dog must recognize his status and learn to coexist with his family through play and in everyday situations. Then, young dogs must learn to cope with the world around them, which is referred to as "socialization" (the process by which puppies acquire social skills and learn to view the world with curiosity, not fear or aggression). All the while, your puppy should be learning basic obedience, and his lessons must be constantly and consistently reinforced.

Golden Rules of Training

🐾 Be aware of your dog's instinctive behavior and work with, not against, her instincts.

🐾 Use simple, one-word commands consistently. For example, say "Sit!" or "Down!" but not "Sit down!" or "Lie down!" Communicate these commands to everyone in your household to prevent confusion.

🐾 Reward good behavior frequently and lavishly with praise; use treats as well as praise when training for obedience.

🐾 Do not punish your dog by hitting her. For instructions on correcting behavioral problems, see pages 232–41.

🐾 Repeat training frequently and consistently.

🐾 Do not let her forget commands because of insufficient practice. To avoid boredom, vary the routine and follow with playtime.

🐾 Remember that your dog is eager to please you. Be firm and clear so that she understands what you want her to do.

🐾 Establish your dog's trust by positive reinforcement so that she knows when you are pleased with her. Ignore or correct her when she misbehaves or demands attention, but do not scold excessively or hit her or do anything else that might make her fearful.

Establishing a Position in the Family Hierarchy

When training your dog, remember that his instinct is to behave as a member of a pack, where there is a definite hierarchy; and you, the owner, should be the dominant partner, or "top dog." Within packs of wild animals, the dominant dog, or alpha male (usually the largest and strongest) exercises his right to eat first, to choose where to sleep, and to initiate contact with other animals. In return for these privileges, the alpha male defends the pack and always leads from the front (going through narrow openings first, for example). The other members of the pack respect this and, although they compete among themselves for food, they rarely challenge the alpha male. Despite thousands of years of domestication, these instincts are still what drive the behavior of your pet. The human family is his pack, and the dog must learn that the owner is the dominant animal, through training that is best started as soon as he is weaned and reinforced during the first eighteen months of a dog's life.

If you lay down the rules for behavior and stick to them, you will be rewarded by an affectionate relationship with your dog. The dog must learn that he is inferior to all members of the human family, even (and especially!) small children. If he does not accept this, he will try to challenge family members for position by snarling aggressively over toys or by growling when told to leave the room or to get off furniture. As long as you treat your dog kindly and firmly and make it clear that you are in charge, he will respect you and accept his place in life. Dogs do not mind being told how to behave; they are more comfortable with structure and consistent rules, without which they may become confused.

How to Establish Dominance Over Your Dog

🐾 Always feed your dog at a time that suits you, not when the dog demands food—and, preferably, after you have eaten.

🐾 Do not share your food with him or feed him near the dining table.

🐾 When you play, do not let the dog win all the games, especially games of tug or of speed.

🐾 Never let your dog assume a position of physical dominance over you or your children (standing on top of your prone body during play, for example).

🐾 Groom your dog regularly so that he submits to your attentions, and reward him during and after each session with praise and treats.

🐾 Do not let your dog sit on the furniture or on your bed. Occasionally go and sit in his bed.

🐾 Play with your dog—but if he is being very demanding, ignore him.

🐾 Teach him to let you go through doors and corridors first—do not let the dog run ahead of you.

Exercise and Games

Dogs adore playing, and they do so from their days in the litter with their siblings. When puppies play, they learn how to interact with other dogs and to improve their coordination and hunting skills. All dogs need play to provide mental stimulation as well as physical exercise. Dogs deprived of games become bored, and they may find an outlet for their energies in destructive behavior.

Different breeds enjoy different types of games. Intelligent dogs like Collies and German Shepherds particularly enjoy games of hide-and-seek, whereas terriers like chasing and "shake" games, as these imitate their behavior when they hunt small game, which is what they were bred to do. (Do not encourage these activities if your puppy shows dominant tendencies or if there are small children or babies in the family.) All active dogs enjoy running and chasing, and herding and retrieving dogs especially enjoy games of fetch. Puppies should not be exercised too vigorously during their first ten months, as experts believe stress and trauma to the young joints and bones can cause lasting damage (consult your vet for detailed advice on this). Bigger breeds require more exercise than smaller dogs. As your dog gets older, remember that he may not be as vigorous or as tolerant as in his youth.

Some experts now frown on the old favorite of throwing a stick for your dog to chase, as the wood may splinter and hurt your pet. Fortunately, substitutes are available with an enormous variety of toys, from Frisbees and tug toys to balls and thick ropes. Make sure that anything you buy is of robust construction so that it cannot become a choking hazard and that balls are small enough to bite, while being too big to swallow.

Chasing balls or Frisbees reflects a dog's natural instincts to chase prey, and retrieving breeds will usu-

ally return the toy to their owner. Never throw balls directly at dogs, in case they are hit—always throw a ball away from a dog so she can jump for it.

Many dogs enjoy games of tug-of-war, using thick rope or a strong tug toy, although more dominant breeds like Bull Terriers or Rottweilers may regard this as a trial of strength. Don't play tug with dominant dogs. In any case, it is always sensible to end a play session with a human victory, to emphasize the dog's submissive position.

At the end of a play session, gather up the toys and put them somewhere out of the dog's reach. This shows that they are your toys rather than the dog's, and it also separates these toys from the dog's chew toys, thereby making playtime more interesting for the dog.

Playing with Other Dogs

Dogs are curious about other dogs, and they often enjoy playing with animals they meet while out for a walk in an area they regard as neutral territory. At a first meeting, keep the animals on their leashes while they sniff each other and assess the other dog. Fighting is less likely between members of the opposite sex, but watch out for signs of aggression by observing their body language— if staring eye contact begins, divert your dog's attention.

When your dog meets another of the same size and sex, make sure she does not pull on the leash, as this is an aggressive act. Praise her for her calm behavior and quiet investigation of the other animal.

Dogs that know each other may indulge in play fighting, and they will have learned as puppies how to use their whole bodies (including their mouths) when they indulge in romps. When playing, dogs mouth their partner with a special inhibited bite, but if a human joins in, dogs often become so excited that this can evolve into hard biting. Show your dog that hard biting is unacceptable by making him walk away.

Socialization

The world outside your home is strange, exciting, and possibly frightening for a small young dog, so it is important to introduce a puppy to as many new situations as possible while it is young. A dog that accepts that the unknown is not necessarily overwhelming, and that reacts with curiosity rather than fear, will be well equipped to cope with unusual experiences as an adult. So, take her out in the car, arrange for friends and children to meet your dog, and take her around the neighborhood to get her used to the area you live in (be it urban, suburban, or rural). Many socialization activities can be undertaken while your dog is undergoing puppy immunization. Take the chance to introduce him to people and healthy, vaccinated dogs while he is very young.

Meeting New People

As part of a puppy's socialization, it is sensible to accustom him to different faces, so that he can learn to accept strangers without showing suspicion or fear. So, invite a selection of friends to meet your new dog, and try to ensure that they are a broad mix of short, tall, large, thin, bearded, long-haired, curly-haired, hat-wearing, dark, and fair! Don't overwhelm the dog with several visitors at once, and arrange the meetings for both indoors and outdoors (once your puppy's immunization is completed) so that the dog realizes that visitors' faces can appear anywhere. Allow the dog to sniff the new person, and encourage the person to bend down to the dog's eye level so that the dog gets used to the approach of strangers.

If you live in a city, it's particularly important that your dog gets accustomed to meeting strangers and other dogs. You will not be able to walk him if he's not adequately socialized and, therefore, displays anxious or aggressive behavior.

Meeting Other Animals

It is reasonably easy to train a puppy to accept other animals, but with an older dog that is unused to other pets, the training process will probably take longer. Remember that dogs are natural predators and that they are inclined to chase anything they regard as prey, be it rabbit-, cat-, or even toddler-sized!

Snowball was furious when Fred first moved in, but they are now devoted companions.

Before introducing a cat to a puppy, make sure the young dog has been exercised and is reasonably calm. Keep it on your lap or on a leash while the cat watches from its basket, carrier, or a place of safety across the room. Talk gently to your puppy, and praise it for sitting quietly while the cat is in the room. Repeat this exercise every day, and after a few days the cat's nervousness should begin to abate and the puppy will be less excitable with the cat. The length of time this takes depends partly on whether the cat is accustomed to dogs.

An older dog, especially one from hunting or chasing stock, may find it harder to conquer its instincts to pursue a smaller animal. Before you introduce the animals, let them sniff each other's bedding. Persevere with the same quiet introduction routine as above. Keep the dog on a short leash and stroke it calmly while the cat is in the room, while praising it in a gentle voice if it shows no sign of chasing.

Don't forget that terriers and hounds (and other dogs bred to pursue rats, rabbits, and small animals) have a natural inclination to chase, and that they will not distinguish between beloved household pets and wild creatures. Puppies can be trained to live peacefully with small caged pets, but older dogs will find it more difficult. It is a sensible precaution to banish your dog from the room if you are handling caged pets such as mice, gerbils, or hamsters.

If you live in the country, take your pet for walks past fields of cows and sheep to acclimate him to them. Keep him on a leash and allow him to sniff around the field and to investigate as closely as the cattle or sheep will allow, but do not let him bark, growl, or lunge at the animals. Similarly, if hens or ducks are part of your everyday landscape, make sure your dog becomes used to them while on a leash. (A dog that worries sheep, cattle, or other farm animals is a menace to farmers and, in many places, laws allow farmers to shoot on sight dogs that could pose a threat to their livestock.)

Dogs and Small Children

A dog accustomed to family life since puppyhood is usually relaxed around children (though some breeds are not well-suited to playing with children). Train your puppy to accept children as friendly beings by letting the children gently stroke the puppy from an early age. Make sure that the children do not threaten the dog by crowding around it, and encourage them to be gentle at all times (and, especially while the dog is very young, do not let the children become too boisterous).

Involve the children in the puppy's training so that they can learn the basic commands used to control the dog. Close supervision is critical—never leave small children alone with a dog, however reliable the animal seems, for the safety and well-being of all parties.

If you acquire an older animal from a rescue center, it is vital to check its background. A snappy or nervous animal will find it hard to relax in a boisterous family atmosphere. If you have children, it is kinder and safer all around to ensure that an older dog new to your household is good with kids *before* you take the plunge. Do not take chances with your children's welfare. If the dog's behavior concerns you, return him to the rescue center.

Introductions

When you introduce a dog to its new family, put it on a leash and let a child approach it. Warn the child not to stare at the dog, as the dog may regard this as aggressive behavior. Let the child stroke the dog gently along its side, but do not let him pat the dog's head. Praise and reward the dog if it remains still and quiet. Discourage overly boisterous play, especially if your puppy is likely to grow to a large size.

New Babies

Preparing your dog for the arrival of a baby is a sensitive matter. The dog may feel displaced and jealous of a new arrival that takes up all of the owner's time and attention, so advanced planning is vital. A few weeks before the birth, harden your heart and adopt a more aloof attitude toward your dog by ignoring him more than usual and withholding some of his usual treats. If he sleeps in your room, change this habit before the arrival of the baby. Once the baby has arrived, restore your affection so that the dog associates the baby's presence with love and attention.

When your dog meets the baby for the first time, enlist the help of your partner or a friend. Babies make sudden noises and movements that may alarm the dog, so it is sensible for one of you to hold the baby and the other to have the dog on a short leash. Let the dog look at the baby and sniff it, but do not let it touch the child. If possible, feed the dog while the baby is present, as this is another way of reinforcing your affection for your pet. On no account should a dog be left alone with a baby.

🐾 *Don't expect your new puppy to be as laid back with children as this Labrador Retriever, who's learned to love and trust his human family and accept the rough and tumble of boisterous games. Children must learn how to behave with dogs before you introduce your new pet to them, and your dog may need time to adjust to children.*

Basic Obedience

When you acquire a dog, it is sensible to initiate a regime of basic training immediately. Older dogs must learn how your pack household operates, and puppies must be taught the rudiments of good behavior (which, at its most basic, means learning how to interact with people). If the dog is a puppy, any training must be in short sessions, which will seem like games—the very fact that you and your dog are interacting is part of the puppy's socialization.

The most effective method of training your pet is by positive reinforcement—that is, praising or rewarding her when she behaves well, and ignoring or correcting

🐾 *Involve older children with training exercises, but, for consistency, make sure they use the same commands and techniques as you do.*

More Training Tips

🐾 Keep training sessions reasonably short—ten to fifteen minutes to start with—so that the dog does not become bored.

🐾 Choose a quiet area, away from distractions, until the command is reinforced. It is usually best to work indoors each time a new command is introduced.

🐾 Do not become angry with your dog if she seems a little slow to master a task.

🐾 Reward your dog with praise and give her a treat or a toy immediately after she has accomplished a task.

🐾 Be consistent: If you decide to reinforce commands with hand signals, you must use them every time you practice the command.

🐾 Keep it fun and always end practices on a positive note, with a treat if you are using them as part of your training.

bad behavior. Patience and consistency are vital, and physical or verbal punishment are not options. Most professional trainers agree that food rewards help to concentrate the dog's mind in the early stages of training. It may be best to reward your dog the first few times she completes a new command successfully, and then to reward her more randomly—this will encourage her to work harder to earn the reward.

Use clear, one-word commands for each maneuver and try to ensure that the words for different commands sound dissimilar, so that the dog does not become confused. Some trainers advocate the use of a "clicker," a small device that produces a consistent clicking sound. See the box on page 211 for instructions. If there are children in your household, you'll need to explain to them that your pet must be trained with a clear and consistent set of commands in a disciplined atmosphere. It's unfair on the puppy if the primary elements of obedience training are treated by the children as part of puppy playtime.

Step-by-Step: Sit

1. Make sure your dog is not overexcited before you begin. Show him a treat in your hand so that he approaches you.

2. As he reaches you, draw the treat slowly above his head, until he tilts his head back to follow the treat.

3. As he bends his hind legs and sits down, give the command: "Sit!" Praise the dog and give him the treat.

Repeat this sequence several times during each training session. Before long, he'll sit on command without the incentive of a treat. Continue to praise him lavishly each time he sits on command.

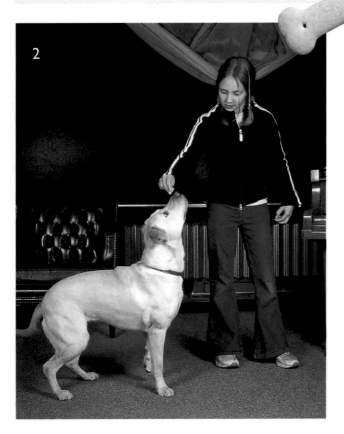

Most dogs will learn the "sit" command readily, and many puppies get the message within just a few minutes during their first training session. It is vital that you teach your dog this simple command at an early stage, rewarding him with liberal praise and repeating sessions frequently to reinforce his obedience, as this command is the foundation for more difficult training excercises that will follow.

Step-by-Step: Down

The "down" command requires more concentration from your dog and will need greater patience to teach and frequent repetition to reinforce. If your dog is reluctant to lie down, lift her into a begging position and, with one palm under each of the dog's forelegs, lower her down and praise her. As your dog progresses, train her to lie down even while distracting activity is going on around her. Once you have taught your dog to obey this command, you will be able to exert greater control over her in many situations.

1. Tell your dog to sit and let her see a treat you have concealed in your hand.

2. Move the hand with the treat toward the floor while saying "Down!"

3. Make sure the dog sees the treat in your hand; she will lower herself toward it.

4. When she has reached the "down" position, reward her and praise her.

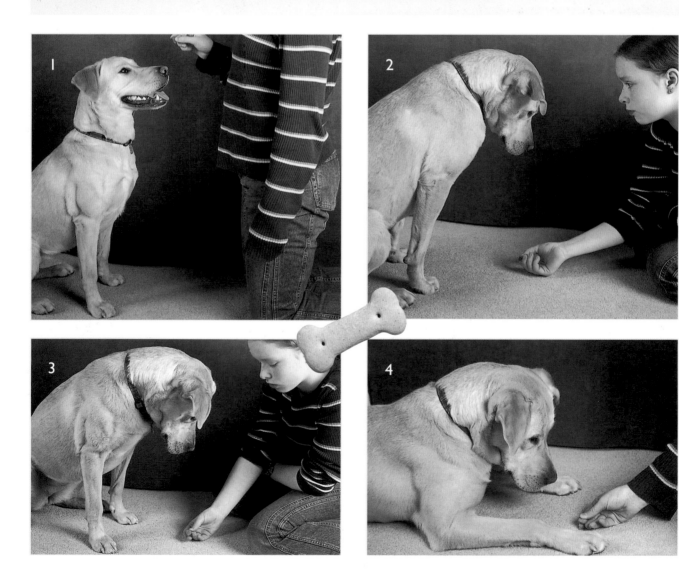

Watch Me

This command teaches your dog to make eye contact with you, which will ensure that he stays under your control.

1. Stand in front of your dog, holding a treat in one hand.

2. Draw your hand toward your face.

3. When the treat is at eye level and the dog is looking at you, say "Watch me!"

4. After the dog has maintained eye contact for a few moments, give him the treat.

5. Repeat frequently, gradually maintaining the eye contact for longer periods.

Stay

Once your dog has mastered the sit command, she can learn to stay. This is a more difficult exercise for a young dog, whose natural instinct is to return to or follow her owner.

1. Put a leash on the dog.

2. Hold the leash loosely and tell the dog to sit or lie down, then step away from her (but don't turn your back on her).

3. Command her to stay and, if you wish, reinforce this with a hand signal—hold your palm out in front of the dog.

4. Walk slowly away from the dog, maintaining eye contact with her. If she gets up, make her sit or lie down again.

5. If she stays for the count of five, go back to her, praise her, and give her a treat.

Repeat the exercise, gradually walking farther away and turning from her. Once she has mastered these steps, repeat them without the leash.

Recall Training

Recall training, or getting your dog to come on command, should also be introduced from the puppy's earliest weeks. Begin by saying "come" every time she runs over to you, and she will begin to associate the word with the action. This is one of the most basic and important commands, and you should never let your dog off the leash in an open space if you are unsure whether or not she will return on command. Be aware too, that a young puppy may be quite timid and come back to you whenever you call her, but, if you don't train her rigorously while she's young, she may begin to gain in confidence and choose to ignore your calls when she becomes a more adventurous adolescent. Therefore, you must go on reinforcing this command even when you think your dog has mastered it.

1. Stand a short distance from your dog with a treat in one hand.

2. Let the dog see the treat and say "Come!"

3. As the dog comes to you, open your arms and bend down to welcome her.

4. Once the dog has reached you, praise her and give her the treat.

When you have repeated this exercise frequently so that your dog knows the command, this should be practiced outdoors in a secure area. Let your dog burn off some energy by running around off the leash first, and make sure that there are no other distractions. Repeat the exercise several times each day while you are outdoors and reward lavishly each time. The importance of recall training cannot be overemphasized. If your dog ignores you and continues playing, you can't punish him when he returns or simply snap the leash on and end his playtime, because he'll soon learn that it's no fun to do as he's told. The only reliable way to train him effectively is to repeat the exercise constantly, gradually calling more often when other distractions are present, and use liberal positive enforcement. It is sensible to carry tasty treats with you on every walk for the first year or so, to help you teach him to come every time he's called.

Walking to Heel on a Leash

Allowing your dog to take you for a walk, instead of vice versa, is both tiring and potentially dangerous. Before you can try this outside with a new puppy, you'll need to practice indoors so that he becomes accustomed to his collar and leash. Dogs should never be allowed to pull on their leashes. They should, ideally, walk at your pace with their head positioned near your left leg. If you are right-handed, hold the leash in your right hand and take up the slack with your left hand—left-handers may feel more comfortable with the leash in their left hand. As with recall training, leash training must be practiced frequently.

1. Attach a leash to the dog's collar.

2. With the dog close to you and on your left, tell him to sit.

3. Walk forward with the leash held loosely while saying "Heel!" in an upbeat tone.

4. If the dog pulls ahead of you, jerk the leash and say "No!"

5. Tell him to sit whenever you stop. Reward him when he walks correctly to heel and each time he sits when you've stopped.

Training Classes

Training classes are useful for first-time dog owners and their pets, as well as for owners of strong-willed dogs. Owners will learn to understand canine behavior and will learn effective training techniques that they can implement at home. Classes are available for dog of all ages and cover everything from basic behavioral training to preparation for advanced competitive training.

Try to find a class with a maximum of twelve dogs, and, if you have a puppy, join one specifically for puppies when the dog is about fourteen weeks old. Visit the class first, without your dog, to check that you like it. Make sure you  approve of the methods of the teacher (who may have particular views about the use of choke collars or snack rewards, for example). Puppy classes are fun for the dog and owner—if sometimes chaotic—and they provide an excellent opportunity for socializing your pup.

If your puppy or adult dog does not respond well to training, then both of you may benefit from the attentions of a personal trainer. Although this is a more expensive option, your investment will prevent many problems later. Contact your breed association, veterinarian, or look on the Internet or in local newspapers for a list of local obedience classes and trainers.

🐾 *These highly trained dogs represent the very pinnacle of doggy obedience. With the help of their owner/trainer, they are demonstrating their skills to an admiring audience at the Crufts dog show.*

"Clicker" Training

In training, dogs learn by conditioning to repeat actions that bring positive reinforcement and to avoid those actions that lead to negative consequences. In recent years the "clicker" has become an increasingly popular device with dog trainers, whether amateur or professional. The clicker is a plastic box that contains a metal strip; when this is pushed and released, a sharp clicking sound is produced. The clicker is an excellent tool for training by conditioning.

To use the clicker, teach your dog to associate the click with good behavior by clicking and rewarding with a treat simultaneously whenever you are in training sessions and he performs the command correctly. The sound is unique and will quickly become a more distinctive signal than your words, and, thus, a more effective training tool (by prompting a "conditioned response") than simple verbal praise. Beginning with the "sit" command, follow the training instructions on page 206, using the clicker and treats as rewards as soon as the dog sits. Gradually allow more time in the sit position before clicking and rewarding. This teaches him to sit until he hears the click.

Once he has learned that the click means he's doing the right thing to please you, he'll look forward to obedience lessons as soon as he sees you pick up the clicker. Bring the clicker when you're out exercising at the park and reinforce recall training this way. Your dog will learn to come on demand whenever you're out if he thinks you have the clicker and treats in your pocket!

7

Why Does My Dog
Do That?

Dogs are descended from wolves, animals that live in packs of at least two, and usually more, creatures. Like wolves, dogs are sociable animals and they prefer the company of other dogs (and humans) to living alone, principally for reasons of survival. Canine logic, like that of most animals, is governed by a strong survival instinct, so behavior centers on actions needed to ensure protection, food, and warmth. Every one of your dog's behavioral traits can be traced back to this basic equation.

In a wolf pack, there is a strict hierarchy of animals and a sophisticated set of rules that allow a number of animals to coexist successfully. Wolves are the world's most successful predators (after human beings) and they pool their resources by hunting collectively, sharing their food, and huddling together for warmth, thus increasing their chances of survival. There are separate ranks of males and females, each sex being led by the strongest and most dominant animal, sometimes referred to as the "alpha" male or female. Subordinate wolves defer to the pack leader, who will always eat first, reproduce first, choose the pack's sleeping area, and exercise the right to initiate contact or grooming. In return for these privileges, the alpha male or female will lead the pack in defense. The social hierarchy within the pack is strict, yet it helps encourage cooperation among

individual members, who will fight to defend the pack and its territory, rather than simply themselves. Individuals know by instinct that they must work to maintain the pack unit in return for the benefits of protection, food, and the chance to reproduce. As long as the pack leader is strong enough to maintain its position as superior to the rest of its pack, the squabbles over food and sleeping areas are left to the lesser animals (though the alpha wolf or dog will eventually be challenged for its position by a younger, stronger animal).

🐾 *Your family dog regards the human members of your household as its pack. By providing discipline, shelter, security, and a regular supply of food, your family members teach the dog to be the subordinate in your "pack hierarchy"— an instinctive role for him.*

Nature ensures that both wolves and dogs learn, from birth, to live in packs—as they are born into litters of several animals and must compete for attention, warmth, and food from their leader, the mother. This is the first natural pack, and for three weeks the puppies are entirely dependent on their mother for survival. Then they acquire the sensory devices and the strength necessary to experiment with physical contact and to absorb the practical and social skills vital for survival. Wolf cubs and puppies learn about pack behavior and hierarchy through play with their siblings in the litter, and once a dog is strong enough to leave its mother, it transfers its allegiance to the new source of food and warmth, its owner.

Like wolves, dogs naturally want to live in a pack, and most are content to follow a dominant leader. For most domestic dogs, the pack is now the human family. The dog will work to defend the pack territory— the house and yard—and will follow and obey the pack leader, the dog's owner. More importantly, his behavior can be adapted by

🐾 *This well-trained dog knows who's boss and is happy and always eager to please her young "leaders."*

🐾 *Sibling puppies learn about their role in the pack from their early days as littermates. They can develop pronounced dominant or submissive tendencies by the age of just twelve weeks.*

training, so that dogs will follow human behavioral cues rather than just canine ones. So, for example, dogs can be taught to approach strangers with curiosity, rather than in fear and with loud barking.

Although canine behavior has been altered over the centuries by domestication and the needs of humans, the roots of your dog's behavior still lie in his descent from wild wolves— so try to remember this when you are communicating with him, and you will probably understand each other more clearly.

Canine Body Language

Perhaps one of the reasons that dogs are so highly regarded by humans is that communication between the species is reasonably successful, despite the fact that dogs cannot verbalize their feelings. Both humans and dogs are highly social creatures who do not simply confine their interaction to the bare minimum needed for survival—they enjoy the company of others and they interact for the purposes of play and entertainment. Both species also demonstrate the ability to share more complex emotions, such as sorrow.

Dogs communicate through a complex range of nonverbal messages based upon body language and scent, sometimes enhanced by yelps, whining, or barks. Their posture, tail position, and facial expression all contribute to conveying a dog's message regarding his status and needs, and much of this is learned at a very early age from the mother. Eye contact is another important factor; an aggressive dog stares hard at his "enemy," while a submissive one avoids eye contact and will display dilated pupils. The mouth is often a good indicator of mood; there is no mistaking the meaning behind aggressively bared teeth, while the "submissive grin," when the mouth is pulled tautly over the teeth, is the sign of a subservient, possibly fearful animal. Look at your dog's ears for further clues as to his mood. An alert, confident animal will display erect ears (if he can!), whereas a frightened dog will position his ears flattened against his head. The tail of a submissive dog often hangs down between his legs, while that of a dominant animal is held erect and still; if the dog is simply alert and friendly it will usually wag its tail in excitement.

The posture of a dog is also important in understanding body language. An aggressive animal will try to make itself look as big as possible, by raising the hackles on the back of its neck and by standing in a forward stance with its ears raised. A frightened or submissive dog leans back, lowering the front legs and pushing the tail down and, if really overwhelmed, will lie on its back with the vulnerable underbelly exposed.

🐾 *Flattened ears can signify relaxation or fear. The snarl is a well-understood signal!*

🐾 *French Bulldogs (above) have batlike, erect ears that distinguish them from other bulldogs. They usually have good hearing and make excellent watchdogs.*

🐾 *This Springer Spaniel has low-set, floppy ears. When he's alert, the ears are higher and held forward (below) but if he's nervous they will move lower and farther back on his head (above).*

Why Do Dogs Prick Up Their Ears?

Selective breeding has radically altered the shape of many breeds of dogs' ears from the original, erect shape of wolves' ears. In fact, over the generations, the ears have changed more than any other part of the dog's body. The long, pendulous ears of a Bloodhound could not be more different from the batlike ears of a French Bulldog or the triangular pricked ears of a Siberian Husky. All dogs have acute hearing, but those with pricked ears are able to swivel them in the direction of the noise they are focusing on. The movements of dogs' ears are also a vital part of their body language: Pricked or erect ears indicate a state of alertness, while flattened or lowered ears demonstrate submission or fear.

Canine hearing is far more acute than that of humans; dogs are able to hear sounds outside the human range, often from a great distance (possibly up to four times further away than humans can hear!). Scientists have shown that dogs are able to locate the source of the sound in milliseconds.

So, when a dog pricks up her ears or cocks her head intently to one side, she can probably hear someone approaching long before the noises become audible to her owner.

Barking, Howling, Whining, and Growling

The second method of canine communication is by howling and barking, and as canine hearing is exceptional, this is most useful to dogs over long distances, although it is a less subtle method of interaction than body language. Dogs make four distinct kinds of noises with very different meanings. Barking in different tones usually demonstrates alertness and excitement, warning of the approach of visitors, perhaps greeting them, or demanding attention. Pack animals howl to summon the rest of the pack for hunting—and although this is a less common noise for a domestic dog, hounds in particular may howl when left alone, in the hope that the rest of the pack (or, in this case, the human family) will return when they hear them. Growling is an aggressive or defensive noise, while whimpering or whining is a cry for attention or a sign of pain.

The setter (opposite) is protecting his territory as a stranger approaches. He begins with a warning growl and becomes more agitated as the visitor comes closer. The two watchdogs (opposite below) have spotted a passerby close to their territory.

The mother dog immediately pays attention to a puppy's whimper as a genuine sign of distress, but adult dogs only make this noise to provoke sympathy, and interestingly, they never do it in front of other dogs.

Dogs have firm ideas about the area that constitutes their territory and they are not happy when strangers invade their space. They regard it as their duty to alert other members of the pack when someone new approaches, hence the welcoming or warning bark. Dogs often begin barking long before a visitor comes into sight, but this is probably because your dog can hear or smell them from a greater distance than you can.

Some breeds have strong territorial instincts, which prompt them to protect their space or their owner, or both. While many people acquire dogs for this very reason, protective behavior must be kept under control to avoid danger to others—and possibly even to members of your own household. Your dog should not be allowed to bark constantly or to display aggression to anyone. If your dog develops signs of aggression or nuisance barking, refer to pages 234–36 and 239. It may be best to find a behavior specialist if you need help correcting either problem.

This Springer Spaniel is howling because he's noticed other dogs nearby. He is not responding fearfully or aggressively; he simply wants to summon his fellow pack members to come play with him.

Scenting

Dogs have an acute, highly developed sense of smell, far more efficient than that of humans, which enables them to track prey and (more often today) to ascertain which dogs have been walked along their route. Animal behaviorists also suggest that a keen sense of smell also makes animals, and dogs in particular, more sensitive to changes in the health of their human companions and to environmental changes. This may explain why there are reports of dogs behaving "oddly" before the onset of natural disasters, like

earthquakes, and why it is said that some dogs can predict when their owner is about to have an epileptic seizure. Dogs produce odors and secretions from a number of sites and glands in their body—in saliva, urine, and sexual discharges, which provide information for other dogs about the sexual status of the animal. The anal sac glands deposit a drop of pheromone-enriched liquid on top of the dog's feces, which is as individual and distinct as a human fingerprint. Wolves urinate around the boundaries of their

🐾 *This dog has a healthy, moist nose, which he uses to gather information about other dogs nearby (or that have recently passed by) and people. All dogs have a highly developed sense of smell and can be trained to use their scenting abilities for a variety of useful purposes.*

🐾 *Beagles (left and above) are among the most popular breeds of household pets, but they begin to show their scenting instincts as young puppies. Make sure you work hard on recall training while your puppy is young and can adapt her behavior.*

territory to ward off other animals, and unneutered male dogs often demonstrate this habit for the same reason. A female that is in season may also do this, with a powerful scent to indicate to any passing males that she is ready for mating.

Why Does My Dog Lick?

Humans regard licks from their dogs as a sign of affection and, indeed, in some ways they are right. Actually, however, the dog has a variety of messages to convey. Licking is an important part of how a dam cares for her pups: She must lick away the amniotic sac surrounding each pup upon birth, and lick each pup to stimulate the elimination of waste for the first few weeks of life. Licking is also part of the grooming routine. Apart from keeping themselves clean, they reduce their own odor by doing this, which, in the wild, helps protect them from keen-nosed predators. Dogs also lick their wounds instinctively (this can sometimes be excessive, as described on page 193). In the wild, as wolf cubs (or wild dogs) grow larger to the stage where they need weaning, their first solid food is that regurgitated by the mother. When they are hungry, cubs or pups will lick their mother's face and throat to stimulate her reflux action, and thereby encourage her to feed them.

As dogs grow older, the licking becomes a form of greeting and of bonding between pack members, as well as an important means of sharing information about where each dog has been. Dogs lick their owners as an extension of this bonding process. They probably learn, too, that their owner regards the licking with affection, and that this fondness may result in a snack for the dog.

Paws for Thought

Dogs lick people as a sign of affection, for the reasons described here. However, don't forget that your dog will also lick things that smell good to her—and you must *never* let her share human food. Watch out for toddlers when they've been snacking, as their hands and faces may look tasty and are within a dog's reach. Make sure you wash your toddler's face and hands after he's been in contact with a dog.

Why Does My Dog Jump Up?

Dogs jump up to assert themselves and to demonstrate their dominance over other pack members. Young dogs often jump up while playing with each other and, in doing so, they are learning the natural behavior of predators, who need to make themselves look aggressively large to scare off the opposition. When dogs are playing, the more dominant animal will often brace himself against the other dog in order to gain a higher and therefore more advantageous position. In a pack, the alpha male may pass out food to the other members, and the animal that jumps highest will probably be fed first.

If you allow your dog to get higher than you by resting his paws on you or by leaning on a chair, he will come to think that he is the dominant partner. Similarly, discourage your dog's tendency to jump up at you or visitors, because it sends out the signal that you are submitting to his leadership, and this will make for an animal that is hard to discipline.

🐾 *Puppies jump to greet people as an expression of natural exuberance. They should be firmly discouraged from jumping up at people from an early age to prevent this leading to troublesome dominant behavior.*

Why Does My Dog Roll Over?

Any animal that rolls over and exposes its belly is exposing the most vulnerable part of her body to attack. An animal will only do this if she trusts her companion or if she is demonstrating submission. In dogs, this behavior is usually a sign of submission to the pack leader, although human owners interpret it as a sign of affection and a signal that their pet wants a romp or a tickle. It is a request from the dog to initiate contact or grooming and is often accompanied by a relaxed facial expression with a lolling tongue.

Dogs strike another attitude when initiating play, either with humans or other dogs. They will sometimes adopt the "play bow," by lowering the front paws and leaning back to raise the hindquarters.

Dogs rely on their sense of smell to assess situations and other animals, and interdog communication relies directly on scent and smells. Dogs have scent glands located around the head and tail area, which they use to leave their scent mark everywhere they have been. Their whole body is imbued with an individual odor made up of pheromones and the visible and invisible remnants of where they have been. These important scent markers are removed by washing, so a freshly laundered dog with a beautifully scented glossy coat does not feel quite comfortable until he has reestablished some of the aromas that make him recognizable. He does this by rolling around his territory.

Although most dogs are nowhere near as fastidious as cats about their personal hygiene, in the wild, they roll around partly for the purpose of grooming—to scratch themselves, to remove parasites, and to clean off dried mud and twigs from their coats. Many breeds have thick double coats that are covered in natural insulating and waterproofing oils, and frequent bathing removes them and ruins the condition of the coat. "Dry cleaning" the coat by rolling on the ground, therefore, makes good sense.

Rolling around on the ground is natural canine behavior (as is a vigorous shake when wet), so resign yourself to the fact that your newly washed pooch will not remain pristine for long!

🐾 Daisy, the Labrador, submits to Bruce to show him that she's not challenging his dominance. Dogs establish mutually "who's boss" each time they meet.

Why Does My Dog Sniff?

The canine olfactory system is a great deal more efficient than that of humans, and it is a dog's most acute sense. Sniffing the ground when out walking reveals much about who's been past and what has happened in the hours before you and your dog arrived. Scenting is also a vital part of hunting prey.

The moisture of dogs' famously damp noses helps to capture scents and transmit them to the nasal membranes, which form convoluted folds and house some 200 million scent receptors (compared to the 5 million possessed by humans). Information received here is transmitted to the area of the brain devoted to scent, which is proportionally larger than its human equivalent.

Some breeds have more efficient scenting systems than others. The most successful dogs bred to pursue quarry by scent, Bloodhounds and Basset Hounds, have folds of skin around the nose that trap aromas, and long-nosed German Shepherds are almost as sensitive. These breeds are used by security services and drug agencies around the world to sniff out drugs and to follow the trails of missing persons. Short-nosed breeds, such as Pugs, are physiologically disadvantaged and are not so sensitive to smell.

🐾 *City dogs that visit a dog park every day sniff their friends enthusiastically, but this pair (right) are leashed as they cautiously greet one another.*

When dogs sniff each other, they are communicating at a fundamental level and discovering important factors about their companion, such as the status of the dog within a pack, the animal's sexual condition, and possibly even the health of the dog. The anal sac glands (small, grape-sized glands located inside either side of the anus) and the perineal glands that surround them secrete powerful pheromones that are probably sex-related.

Why Do Dogs Scent Mark?

Dogs urinate against vertical objects to leave a kind of scented calling card at nose level, to indicate to other dogs that this is their territory. Pheromones secreted in their urine or feces convey information to other dogs about the animal's status and sexual condition. Behaviorists have noted that a male dog may mark as many as eighty different spots within a four-hour period, and urban dogs, who share their territory with many others, scent mark more frequently than rural animals. Females scent mark less frequently than males, but a female in heat contains especially powerful pheromones that can be detected by males over long distances.

Why Do Dogs Dig?

Wild animals dig for several reasons: to bury food or waste, to pursue prey, or to dig out a shelter for sleeping. Dogs are no different, and a dog that excavates its owner's garden may be bored or may have sniffed an interesting scent that seems to lie underground. Some animals like to bury bones so that they can dig them up at a later date. If your dog is a digger, bury a toy or a treat in one area of the garden that you are prepared to surrender to your dog's games, and teach her to stick to that sector when she's digging or burying treasures.

Some dogs dig instinctively—especially terriers, which were bred to dig small animals out of their holes, while others are following the natural instincts of their ancient ancestors, who dug shallow holes in the earth to keep cool or to provide some sort of den while they slept. Digging is also part of a bitch's instinctive nesting behavior, shortly before she whelps.

Why Does My Dog Rush Ahead of Me?

In packs of wild dogs or wolves, the alpha male always leads from the front, leading his subordinates through narrow openings and coordinating the rest of the pack in defense or attack. There is an element of protection inherent in this behavior, as the dog wants to secure the boundaries of his territory, but it is actually a very dominant action—and if your dog habitually pushes ahead of you through doorways or corridors, he is probably confused about his status in the household. As the dominant partner, the owner should always make sure that she goes first, and she should reinforce the dog's obedience training to make sure he does not try to challenge her for position as "top dog."

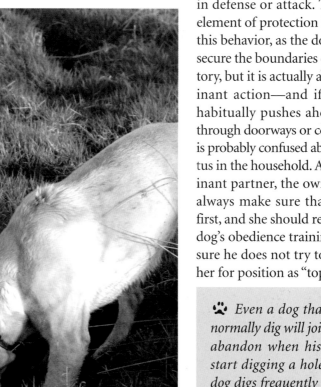

Even a dog that doesn't normally dig will join in with abandon when his buddies start digging a hole. If your dog digs frequently or obsessively, she might not be getting enough exercise or attention, or this could be a sign of underlying health problems.

Why Do Dogs Leap into Rivers and Ponds?

Some dogs are incapable of seeing a body of water without jumping in for a dip—much to their owner's distress! This behavior is most common in dogs bred for retrieving, especially those bred to work with waterfowl. All sorts of retrievers, Springer Spaniels, or any dogs with "water" in the breed name, find it impossible to resist swimming. Indeed, it is a shame to deny them the pleasure now and then. Newfoundlands are among the keenest of swimmers. Well adapted for swimming, with slightly webbed feet, a thick tail that acts as a rudder, and prodigious stamina, Newfoundlands are also capable of rescuing swimmers in trouble.

Most dogs don't need to be taught how to swim—they will either swim by instinct or resist the water altogether. However, it is sensible to watch your dog carefully to make sure that he can swim before you let him go too far from you. Never let him enter water with a current or swim in heavy surf, because he could drown all too easily in such conditions. In safe waters, though, swimming is an effective form of exercise for dogs that are naturally inclined to take a dip.

Dogs also plunge into water as a (possibly misplaced) means of keeping clean, to cool down, or (except in salt water) to have a refreshing drink.

🐾 These dogs all have something in common: a love of swimming. They are drawn toward the water instinctively, whether to cool themselves, take a drink, or simply splash around and have fun.

Why Does My Dog Chase Moving Objects?

The physiological construction of dogs shows that they are built to be predators that chase their prey. Hounds, in particular, have long legs and deep chests that house efficient cardiovascular systems, enabling them to run quickly and successfully over long distances. The hunting instinct remains very strong in many domestic dog breeds, which have inherited (albeit in a diluted form) the wolf habit of stalking, observing, chasing, and grabbing prey. Selective breeding has produced dogs with auditory and visual senses that are finely attuned to the movement of small prey, such as rabbits and game birds, and with the physical capacity to catch them.

Whenever a dog sees something moving quickly—whether it is a cat, rabbit, ball, or stick—his natural reaction is to chase it. Selective breeding has enhanced this trait in a number of breeds, such as Greyhounds—which is why Greyhound racing (when the dogs chase a small, scented, stuffed "rabbit" around a circular track) is such a successful and popular sport. Chasing is usually harmless fun and it provides an excellent physical outlet for your pet's energies.

In some cases, though, chasing can be dangerous, as when a dog with dominant tendencies or highly developed hunting instincts mistakes a small child or a family pet as being "fair game." Similarly, cyclists, joggers, or farm animals may also provoke your dog's predatory instincts. It is the owner's responsibility to prevent his or her dog from chasing people or animals and causing distress or, worse, physical harm. Do not allow your dog to roam too far from you when you're out walking, and call him back at frequent intervals when he is off investigating scents and unknown territory. Reinforce the dog's recall training to make certain that he remains under your control whenever he's off the leash. If you cannot completely rely on keeping him from chasing, you will need to keep him leashed for safety's sake.

🐾 *As long as your dog isn't aggressive, fetch is a great game. As well as providing hours of fun, the dog will get lots of exercise without exhausting you!*

🐾 *Don't be caught out leaving your dog in a fenced or walled area that isn't secure enough. Some dogs are capable of escapes that would impress Houdini himself!*

Why Do Dogs Stray?

Although dogs prefer to live in packs, they are also independent creatures that love to explore. It seems likely that most dogs that roam intend to return to the pack, but somehow get lost, or perhaps become adopted by another pack or family. Sadly, some dogs stray because they are mistreated by their owners.

Dogs exhibit great curiosity about the world beyond their immediate confines, probably because they can sniff a range of exciting scents from over the yard fence and can hear tantalizing noises from down the street. Unneutered male dogs most commonly stray when they can smell a female in heat, and they will roam great distances in search of a mate. Other dogs roam when they become caught up in tracking an enticing scent and simply zoom off, out of sight and earshot of their owner.

Prevention is the best solution for these matters, so make sure that your house and yard are adequately reinforced with a fence that is high enough to contain your leaping dog and strong enough to resist her attempts to dig her way out. Stray dogs can be a danger to themselves and others when roaming busy streets. Do not let your dog roam too far from you when you're out walking, and call her back at frequent intervals.

🐾 *Every year, thousands of stray dogs end up in rescue centers. Stray dogs can be a danger to themselves and others, can spread disease, and many will meet an unhappy fate.*

8
Bad Dog!

It is often said that there is no such thing as a "bad" dog, only bad owners. Some dogs are considerably more responsive to obedience training than others, but all dogs require consistent, firm discipline, exercise, and plenty of attention, and if these are not provided, behavioral problems will result.

🐾 *Some breeds, like the American Staffordshire Terrier, have a reputation for aggression and/or willfulness. Early obedience training is essential in these breeds, and they are not suitable for inexperienced owners. With proper training, though, they can make good pets.*

🐾 *The best cure for everything is prevention. Teach your puppy who's boss and how she's allowed to behave while she's young. You should be firm (right) but reward her with your affection (above).*

Paws for Thought

🐾 Most behavioral problems can be corrected, but not all. Aggression may suddenly occur when a well-behaved, docile dog suffers from epileptic seizures or other medical conditions. If your dog becomes aggressive—especially with people—and you do not have sufficient experience in handling problem dog behavior, seek help immediately from your veterinarian or a professional behavior specialist. Your safety, and others', could be at risk.

🐾 *Training is a lifetime process, not just a few lessons during puppyhood. Adult dogs, too, need their obedience reinforced and rewarded.*

🐾 *Regular repetition of lessons in good behavior, rewarded with lots of affection and occasional treats, keeps most dogs out of trouble.*

A dog that has been well socialized and adequately trained from puppyhood is unlikely to exhibit inappropriate behavior patterns. These problems are more likely to arise with challenging breeds and with adopted dogs, especially those that have not been well treated during their formative months. A great deal of "bad" canine behavior arises from fear—either of people, of other dogs, or of the unknown—and most of it can be overcome with patient training, perseverance, and care. It is important to understand why your dog is behaving in a certain way. Some "bad" behavior (such as chasing or chewing) has its roots in ingrained, instinctive canine behavioral traits, while other actions (such as incessant barking) are often learned from other dogs or because they result in attention from the owner. If your dog develops signs of antisocial behavior, first make sure that it understands what is and is not acceptable by repeating obedience training.

When addressing problem behaviors, the same principles apply as those given for basic training (see Chapter 6). Work with your dog's instinctive behavior, be consistent, reward good behavior, and do not hit your dog as punishment or you will probably induce fear-related aggression and undermine his trust in you. If you need to "punish" bad behaviors, try using a toy water pistol or houseplant sprayer immediately each time he transgresses. Once you have sprayed him a few times, he'll likely behave as soon as he sees you reach for the sprayer. Dogs do not remember what they did twenty minutes previously, so you must react to the problem straight away in order to avoid deepening your pet's confusion about what is and is not acceptable behavior. It is even more important to reward good behavior with treats and lavish praise if you are embarking on a program of correction for a problem behavior.

It is useful to remind yourself that your dog does not think like a human or understand most of what you say to her. She will respond to your tone of voice, but will not be able to follow your sentences. She will understand single-word commands if they are constantly repeated and reinforced, just as she learns other, non-verbal prompts (for example, she quickly learns that you are about to go out when you put on your coat or pick up your car keys). Concentrate on keeping your instructions clear, simple, and consistent.

Aggression

Aggressive dogs are not popular animals—they irritate and frighten many people and, in extreme cases, harm them. Behaviors such as growling, snarling, and biting people stem from a serious misunderstanding between the dog and the people around it. Canine aggression toward humans has a number of causes: It may be based on fear, or it may be a manifestation of dominant aggression on the part of the dog. Occasionally, your pet may be sick or in pain and may show this by growling or baring its teeth when you approach it. Unspayed females may become aggressive during their twice-yearly menstrual seasons. At this time, some bitches become possessive of toys and bones, or of their sleeping area.

Dominant Aggression

Dogs have different personalities, and some breeds are more strong-willed than others: Rottweilers, Doberman Pinschers, German Shepherds, and even smaller breeds like Jack Russells and Yorkshire Terriers are all self-confident types that require firm handling and good basic training to ensure that

🐾 *Even a naturally docile dog can develop dominant aggression. Always muzzle an aggressive dog until this behavior is successfully corrected.*

they accept their place in the hierarchy. Dominant dogs will stare down strangers, push through doorways ahead of their owners, and expect an immediate response to demands for attention.

If your dog threatens you by snarling or even biting you, it is challenging your position as "top dog," a sign that it is confused about its place in the family pack.

🐾 *Without an experienced, responsible owner, a Doberman (above) is likely to show aggression—after all, these dogs were bred specifically for their watchdog abilities. Don't let children groom your dog unless you are sure that she's reliably gentle and submissive, like Gemma (right).*

Methods for Reestablishing Dominance Over Your Dog

🐾 Reduce the dog's mobility by fitting a house-line (a medium-length leash for use indoors) so that you can control its movements.

🐾 Do not allow the dog to sit on any furniture or to sit in "dominant" places including doorways and at the top of staircases.

🐾 Do not respond to the dog's demands for attention, and leave him alone for short periods when he exhibits attention-seeking behavior.

🐾 Feed the dog only after you have eaten and do not give any scraps from the table or if he pesters for snacks or attention.

🐾 Occasionally, take your dog's food away when he is eating and return it to him in your own time. **Caution**—he may snarl or even try to bite you when you approach his food.

🐾 Groom your dog at least once a day. Your dog should learn to accept your handling his paws, scruff of the neck, and head.

🐾 Avoid dominance games like tug-of-war. Introduce retrieving exercises at playtime, as this will further emphasize who is in control.

This can be remedied in two ways. First, to protect the human household (especially if there are children around) the dog should be muzzled so that it cannot harm anyone, and it should wear the muzzle when out for a walk. Second, begin a program to reestablish your dominance and force the dog to accept its subordinate status. This must be done gradually by adults, not by children.

Fearful Aggression

Dogs usually exhibit fearful aggression when they are unsure or frightened of a situation. A dog that has been mistreated or poorly socialized as a puppy is likely to bark and snarl at strangers, and although this behavior will deter unwelcome intruders, it will also make life difficult (at the very least!) for your visitors. Some dogs are naturally anxious or timid and will demonstrate this by cowering or adopting a fearfully submissive pose in the face of strangers. However, they may suddenly lunge forward aggressively, possibly even biting whoever is within reach. This fear biting is the action of a dog with low self-esteem, and the problem usually stems from poor socialization as a puppy (although it sometimes

appears as an inherited trait in certain breeds). It is important to recognize the signs of fearful aggression, because any attempt to remedy the problem by reasserting your dominance over the dog is likely to make the problem worse.

If your puppy is timid around strangers, you need to increase its confidence. Do this by asking visitors to ignore it until it is brave enough to approach the visitor and investigate it. The visitor should let it sniff the back of their hand and perhaps give it a treat, while the owner praises the dog.

Older dogs that mistrust humans may need help from a professional trainer, as solving this problem and rebuilding the dog's confidence in humans can take a great deal of patience, time, and effort.

🐾 *Angus (above) is timid around people and other dogs. Here, his owner encourages him to meet other dogs, helping to bring him out of his shell.*

Aggression Toward Other Dogs

Dogs that are aggressive toward other dogs may be expressing territorial dominance, or they may simply be trying to chase off an animal that they perceive as a threat to their status. Alternatively, a poorly socialized dog may demonstrate fearful aggression because it is simply not used to other animals and is afraid of them because they are unknown. Male dogs are more likely to behave in this way than females, especially around the age of two. Neutering sometimes reduces the problem. Dogs can learn this type of aggressive conduct by copying their mother's reactions to other animals, and it is difficult to eradicate such deep-seated behavior.

Prevention is often the only way to address the problem. Watch your dog closely when you are out with it: Look out for such telltale signs as staring at another animal and pulling on the leash. If necessary, physically turn your dog's head away. Take a toy along with you, to divert his attention. If you think there is any danger that your dog might attack another animal, then muzzle him before you leave the home. Reward your dog when he ignores other animals.

Nervousness and Timidity

Nervous dogs do not always mask their fear with aggressive behavior. Some animals, especially small breeds, are nervous of loud noises, unusual objects, or even hands, and will cower behind their owner when confronted by them.

If your dog reacts badly to loud noises such as thunder or fireworks, resist the urge to comfort her too much, and certainly do not offer a treat, as she will associate this nervousness with rewards. Instead, make a tape recording of the noise and play it quietly to your dog (make sure she is on a lead), rewarding her if she is not nervous. Gradually increase the volume over the course of a couple of weeks until it is as loud as the original noise, and by then your dog should be able to cope with it without fear. Objects as diverse as baby carriages, a

🐾 *This Shih Tzu is timid and always hides when visitors arrive. She needs patient coaxing to help overcome her fear of strangers.*

person on crutches, wheelchairs, scooters, vacuum cleaners, bikes, or skateboards may provoke nervousness in a dog that is not used to them. The only way to conquer this is to introduce your dog to the offending object in quiet, controlled circumstances. Place a treat on the ground near the problem object, so your dog will have to approach it to get the treat. Over several sessions, place the snack gradually nearer to the offending item, until eventually the treat is underneath it or even on it. If it is a wheeled vehicle, make sure you move it occasionally to show the dog that it will not harm her.

A poorly socialized dog, or one that has been abused, may show a fear of human hands and cower every time someone approaches to pet her. The following procedure should help fix the problem, as long as you are sure the dog will not react with fear biting. Put a treat in the palm of your hand and place your hand on the ground so the dog can easily access it and can see that nothing else is concealed. Lured by the snack, the dog will probably eat from your hand. Once it has accomplished this, gradually move closer to the dog's side. The dog should let you stroke her without complaint, and she can then be rewarded with lots of praise and another treat.

Separation Anxiety

Separation anxiety is another common behavioral problem, characterized by a number of activities, ranging from whining when left alone, destructive chewing, hyperactivity, soiling, and extreme excitement, to clingy behavior upon the owner's return. Do check that your puppy is completely healthy before attributing his bad behavior to separation anxiety—it may be that he has a minor physical illness. However, if the problems only occur when the owner is absent, separation anxiety is the most likely cause.

Owners value loyal and faithful dogs, but animals that are exceptionally attached to their owners naturally miss them

🐾 *If your dog becomes overly excited as you prepare to leave the house, remain calm and ignore him so you don't indavertently reward him with attention.*

when they leave and want them to realize this—hence the whining or destructive behavior, which is simply a nonverbal means of communication. These dogs are likely to follow their owners everywhere and to become excited as the owner prepares to leave the house. If a dog is particularly fond of one member of the family, try to make sure that everyone else takes time to care for it, to lessen the animal's emotional dependence on one person. As a puppy, the dog may have been used to sleeping in the owner's room, and the dog may therefore feel insecure without the owner nearby. Elderly or sick dogs may react in a similar way. Owners that make a great fuss of their dogs may also find themselves with a dog that frets when they leave the house. With patience, you should find the right balance.

Behaviorists recommend several means of dealing with separation anxiety. The first is to slowly accustom your dog to your absences by leaving him alone for short periods and gradually increasing the time apart. Puppies should certainly get used to time alone.

The second is to introduce a calm routine before you go out. Make sure your dog has been well exercised, recently fed, and has had a chance to relieve himself. When you go out, leave a radio or TV on low, to simulate the noise of the household, and leave an old T-shirt or other item of clothing in the dog's basket (as he will find your scent comforting). Leave him with a couple of toys to divert him.

Ignore your dog for about fifteen minutes before your departure and, on your return, do not greet him until he has calmed down. Enter and leave the room quietly, without making a fuss, and avoid eye contact with your pet until his excitement has died down.

If your dog has trashed the house in your absence, do not react, as this is simply one way of giving him attention (nor will he understand if you punish him for something he did hours ago). Take the dog away from the scene of the crime before greeting him, calmly, and leave him in another room while you clean up the mess. The only sure way of preventing your dog from

🐾 *This dog is a faithful companion. She knows that when her owner goes out, he'll soon be back.*

🐾 *A much-loved dog should be secure enough to cope with your absences from home.*

chewing the furniture or ripping up the cushions is to leave him in a room where he can do no damage when you are out. With a patient and steady approach, however, you will be able to build up your dog's confidence about being left alone, so such incidents should cease. Your home is protected when your dog is crated, but it's unfair to leave him confined for long periods.

While you are working on this problem, another solution may be to ask a friend or neighbor to sit with your pet while you are out for longer periods until he settles down.

Digging

Dogs love to dig, especially those with terrier blood (which were bred to dig small animals out of their underground lairs). Other breeds, such as Huskies and Malamutes, occasionally excavate cooling holes for themselves in hot weather, and some dogs instinctively want to hollow out a pit to lie in or to hide food in. Sadly, dogs do not respect flower beds and plants, and compulsive diggers will drive a keen gardener to distraction.

One method of dealing with this problem is to surrender part of your garden to your pet. Bury a bone and encourage her to dig it up and, once she has done this a few times, hide some treats in the same area for her to find. Digging in this lucrative area should quickly become a habit for her.

Destructive Behavior

Destructive behavior is often the result of separation anxiety, but it is usually carried out by a bored dog, or in the case of puppies, by one that is teething and doesn't know any better. Chewing or scratching at the carpet, ripping bits of wallpaper, and taking large chunks out of the furniture or soft furnishings are not activities to be encouraged—quite apart from the sheer mess and destruction of valuable possessions, the dog may swallow something harmful. Remove all tempting items from your dog's reach.

Puppies chew between the ages of three to seven months (when they are teething), and although their jaws have not yet reached their full potential, their teeth are certainly sharp enough to leave marks. They must be given plenty of hard chews, such as rawhide and firm rubber toys. And keep shoes and slippers well out of the way! A puppy that is allowed to chew household items will think that this is acceptable behavior as an adult dog.

Adolescent or adult dogs that persist in destructive chewing probably need more stimulation, both physical and mental. As predatory animals, dogs are genetically predisposed to use their intelligence to search out food, and in doing so, will burn up their energy. The great majority of domestic dogs are not challenged in this way, but hide-and-seek games and the opportunity to sniff out new environments, as well as plenty of exercise, will keep most dogs happy and occupied.

🐾 *Puppies need to chew to develop their teeth. Make sure you provide plenty of tasty chew toys, or your puppy will probably be tempted by your shoes.*

Most dogs benefit from exercise sessions that last at least half an hour (at least twice a day) and incorporate some training or games. Dogs that are left alone for long periods inevitably become bored (see pages 237–38 for ways to alleviate this problem). So, if you are out at work all day, hire a dog walker or arrange for a friend or neighbor to walk your dog in your absence. If this is not possible, a dog is not the right pet for your present circumstances.

Frustrated animals also cause damage that may be focused in one particular area, near a door or window, for example. It may be that the dog can see or sense something outside that she is desperate to reach, such as a cat. Again, make sure the dog has plenty of distractions in her room, or remove her to another room if you cannot fix the source of her frustration!

🐾 *Most destructive behavior is exacerbated by inadequate exercise and attention. If you live in a city, take your dog out with you as often as you can so she doesn't become too lonely.*

Nuisance Barking

All dogs bark, and they do so in a variety of circumstances—the excited yapping of a dog when a visitor approaches, the warning barks from a dog on guard duty, or the endless whines from a dog that craves attention. To an extent, barking endlessly may be a learned behavior, copied from its mother, and sometimes dogs pick up this habit after a stay in kennels.

Dogs that bark as part of guarding behavior usually stop once the "threat" to their territory has passed by. Any dog that persistently barks every time a stranger approaches is trying to warn them away, and may simply be wary of new faces because she was insufficiently socialized as a puppy. Dominant dogs sometimes guard the house because they believe they should control the arrival of visitors; this is the behavior of a dog confused about its position in the pack hierarchy. In this situation, the dog should be made aware that the owner is in charge by reinforcing its obedience training.

Other dogs bark or howl to get attention, and this is usually behavior they learned as a puppy, when their newly devoted owner gave in to every cute little yelp. An older dog that barks every time she sees the owner get out the food bowl or the leash in preparation for a walk is less sweet, and should be trained to calm down. Cure the problem by ignoring the dog's method of attention-seeking by telling her to sit, and only then stroking her. Ignore the dog if she begins barking again, and withdraw your attention until she is silent. Give her your undivided attention when you are playing with her, and incorporate some training routines into your play sessions to emphasize your dominance.

Dogs that yowl when left alone are suffering from separation anxiety, which was discussed earlier in this chapter. Animals with strong pack instincts, such as Beagles, may benefit from the company of another dog to keep them from feeling lonely.

It is unnecessary to use an electric-shock antibarking collar. Barking is an instinctive behavior for a dog and punishment of this sort is cruel.

Chasing

Dogs that cannot be controlled and that persistently chase people or vehicles are both dangerous and annoying. They not only endanger themselves, but they provide a serious distraction to car drivers. As predators, dogs are natural chasers, and as the vehicles they pursue rarely stop, the dog thinks he has "won" by seeing off the perceived threat. The only real answer to dogs that chase motor vehicles is to ensure that they don't get the chance—make sure that your animal is secure within the house or yard, and on a tight leash when out on the street. Some breeds are genetically predisposed to chasing; long-limbed sight hounds such as Greyhounds are natural runners, and terriers love to chase, but they often have short legs so they cannot run very fast. Large dogs such as Huskies and Spitz breeds have a great deal of stamina and are capable of chasing for long distances.

If your dog harasses cyclists, the problem can be tackled by asking a friend to cycle past the dog while the dog is on a leash. When the dog tries to chase, the cyclist should firmly say "No," then stop and spray the dog with a water pistol before continuing. The cycle training exercise below may also prove useful.

Dogs that chase other animals, especially farm livestock, must be kept on a leash. In Britain and many other places, farmers are within their rights to shoot animals that disturb their cattle or sheep.

Train a young dog to become accustomed to farm animals if you live in or visit the country, and if he seems tempted, divert his attention with a toy and a chasing game. If your dog cannot be trusted absolutely, never let him off the leash near livestock.

🐾 *Hounds and terriers are likely to run in pursuit of small animals outdoors. Make sure your yard is secure. Herding dogs won't be able to resist chasing sheep; they should always be leashed near livestock.*

Cycle Training

1. Ask a cyclist to ride past your dog, which should be secure on a leash. As the bicycle passes, tell your dog to sit. Hold the leash securely and do not give him the opportunity to chase.

2. Reward the dog for sitting on command, and repeat the exercise until the dog sits every time without being tempted to chase the cyclist.

Mounting

The sexual behavior of a pet is something many owners would prefer to ignore, but occasionally a small dog's raging hormones become a mounting problem that must be addressed. Young dogs that mount table legs, cushions, or, more embarrassingly, human legs often

seem comical, but this behavior must be stopped early on or it may become an entrenched adult habit. In male dogs, neutering often stops it, but dominant female dogs often "practice mount," and spaying has little effect.

Old-fashioned remedies are the answer to what is, after all, a very old problem. Plenty of exercise, fresh air, and mental stimulation will help reduce the recurrence. If your dog persistently mounts inappropriate objects, use a water pistol to spray him mid-thrust—it will certainly put him off and should discourage him from repeating the behavior.

Mounting is not always sexual; in some cases, it is the action of a dog trying to exert its dominance. In this case, use the methods detailed on pages 199–200 to reduce the dog's status. Be careful when you correct a dog that is mounting, as you are likely to meet an aggressive reaction. If your dog seems oversexed, make it wear a houseline and say "No" very firmly if it tries to mount anything. Remove it to another room for a few minutes and, once it has returned, ignore it for a short while.

Fouling the Home

Most dogs are successfully housebroken as puppies, but dominant young males may sometimes urinate indoors. This is another sexual behavior, as they are marking their territory. Male dogs mark their territory outside by urinating on trees, bushes, and posts, to send out a message to other dogs that they are in the area, and they will repeat this behavior in the home if they are feeling insecure, or alternatively if they are aggressively confident dogs. The problem may be solved by reinforcing housebreaking training, by hormone therapy, or by neutering. It is usually a problem that appears in adolescent dogs (around eighteen months), and it must be stamped out early because it is harder to alter the habits of adult dogs.

More serious fouling problems are unpleasant, but usually result from a breakdown in communication with your dog. Some dogs foul when left alone and, if this is habitual, make sure you have given your pet the opportunity to relieve himself before you go out. Otherwise, try confining your dog to a small area. Dogs rarely foul their sleeping area, so if you fit a short houseline to his collar that prevents him from moving far from his sleeping area, he is unlikely to mess. You can confine him to his crate while you are out, but this method should only be temporary and is certainly not acceptable for a dog that is left for more than a couple of hours. If your dog fouls his sleeping area, he must be seen by a veterinarian.

9
Introduction to Showing Dogs

Dog shows not only offer owners the opportunity to show off their prized pooches, but are also a fantastic source of information for all dog lovers, whether they own dogs or not. In fact, prospective dog owners are advised to attend a couple of shows if they need help in picking a breed. Owners and breeders are usually delighted to share their knowledge with others. If you are in search of a particular breed of puppy, this is a good way to make contact with breeders.

To find out about dog shows in your locality, consult local newspapers, use the Internet, or check the telephone directory for local breeders or other canine organizations. National bodies like the American Kennel Club and the Kennel Club of Great Britain offer huge resources both on the Web and via traditional routes.

Dog Shows

Dogs have been organized as a source of entertainment for thousands of years. But until the nineteenth century, they were usually staged as a kind of sideshow, sometimes engaging in cruel practices like dog fights or bearbaiting. The first dog shows in which dogs were exhibited for their looks and for adherence to what has become known as a "breed standard" were held at the end of the eighteenth century, when selective breeding of dogs for particular characteristics began to grow popular.

In the early and mid-nineteenth century, dog shows were small, local affairs that took place informally in taverns and were entirely the preserve of male owners and a very limited number of dogs. In 1834, for example, a silver cream jug was the prize in a show for "9 lb. spaniels." But with the advent of cheaper and more efficient public transport, dog fanciers could travel, and a dog show in Islington, London, in 1862 attracted 803 entrants. Owners of different breeds of dogs formed clubs in order to breed their animals, and they began to maintain stud books. Joining breed clubs and showing off

🐾 *The Pekingese at left won the ultimate accolade of Best in Show at Crufts 2003, while the Foxhound at top won Best of Breed. The Great Dane above demonstrates his excellent conformation.*

their dogs was a natural progression and a means of attracting other dog fanciers and, ultimately, of improving the breeds by the introduction of new blood. Dog clubs and shows became an increasingly popular pastime, with clubs springing up in most major cities.

The most famous American dog club was founded more than 120 years ago in New York: the Westminster Kennel Club, so called because the few first meetings took place in the Westminster Hotel. In 1876, members noted the great success of dog shows in England (which, by now, even attracted entrants owned by royalty) and they decided to hold a show in New York. The First Annual New York Bench Show of Dogs was held in May 1877 and was a resounding success; the Westminster Dog Show, as it has become known, has been held annually ever since and is the most prestigious dog show in the United States.

In Britain, the founding of the Kennel Club in 1874 ensured that British dog shows became regulated. As the sport of showing

dogs became more widespread, the Kennel Club worked to move the shows from pubs and bars into more fashionable and accommodating exhibition halls, such as the Crystal Palace and the Ranelagh Pleasure Gardens in London. In 1880, all entrants to shows held under the Kennel Club rules had to be registered with the club.

Britain's most famous dog show began in 1886 when Charles Cruft, a young, ambitious promoter and former dog-food salesman, launched the First Great Terrier Show in the Royal Aquarium Music Hall in Westminster, London. Cruft worked with the Kennel Club to ensure that the show was perfectly organized, with outstanding facilities for the dogs and their owners, and the show was given considerable coverage by *The Times* of London. Cruft was an entrepreneur and, in 1891, a show held in the Royal Agricultural Hall, Islington, was entitled "Cruft's Greatest Dog Show" and was open to all breeds. Approximately 2,000 dogs were entered, and Cruft continued to run the annual show until his death in 1938. The following year, his widow asked the Kennel Club to take it over, and in 1948, the first Kennel Club Crufts was held at Olympia in London. Today, Crufts is held every March at the National Exhibition Center in Birmingham.

🐾 *The champion Kerry Blue Terrier shown above took the coveted Best in Show title at Westminster's 2003 event. Below, a prize Ibizan Hound demonstrates what it takes to win Best of Breed—and become the champion of its group, too.*

Entering Dog Shows

Owners can competitively exhibit their dogs in three main areas today: agility trials, obedience trials, and conformity shows—the beauty pageants of the dog-show world!

Dog shows range from the great formality and prestige of Crufts or Westminster to rather more relaxed outdoor affairs, but if you are serious about the potential of your pooch, make sure you enter shows held under the auspices of your national kennel club. Each

country has a differing set of rules that lay out the path of achievement necessary to become a champion dog; entrants to Crufts, for example, must already have won certain championship titles before they can be considered. Championship shows are the highest level of national competition, and dogs can work up to this level by winning challenge certificates and junior warrants (prizes for dogs up to eighteen months old) at other shows. Open shows in Britain are also held according to Kennel Club rules and, although they are smaller, often local events, they are an excellent training ground for dogs at the start of their showing career.

🐾 *Entering your dog into whimsical categories at competitions can be good practice and extremely amusing—especially if you spot an owner who resembles this handsome fellow on the right!*

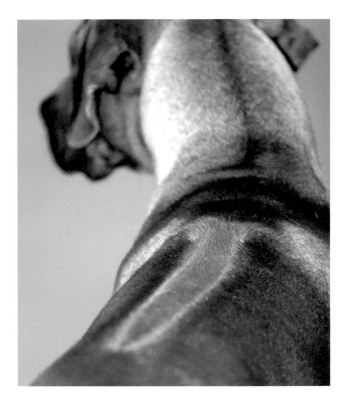

🐾 *No matter how attractive you think your dog is, there are rigorous breed standards that apply when showing a dog. This Rhodesian Ridgeback's strong, muscular body and conforming "ridged" back will be scrutinized by the judges.*

Exemption shows are less formal affairs (with less than 1,000 entrants) that lack the serious competitive element of championship and open shows, while providing a great deal of fun for all. They often include

kennel club) and compare your dog to the ideal form laid down for your breed. If you are still keen, visit a few dog shows to check out the competition; if your dog looks nothing like the winning members of his breed, perhaps you should think again, or consider whether you want to enter agility or obedience shows instead. Remember that your dog's temperament is important, too: Will he be happy and relaxed or find the rigors of a dog show too much? And do you have the time and resources to prepare your dog and attend shows? A few visits to shows will help you find out what's involved.

🐾 *This Border Collie is taking a well-deserved nap behind the scenes after performing in agility trials. Between the action, there's plenty of waiting around at dog shows. Does your dog have the right temperament to enjoy the total experience?*

🐾 *For your dog to look this immaculately groomed and at its best takes a lot of hard work and dedication. If you want to enter your dog in shows, bear in mind the many hours of serious preparation that are involved—and the travel back and forth.*

mixed-pedigree classes, as well as awards for totally frivolous categories such as "fancy dress" and "dogs that most resemble their owners."

Many owners believe that their dogs are prize-winning material, but they are unsure of what to expect in the competitive show world. Even if you are convinced that your dog is the most gorgeous in the world, the only person whose opinion really counts is that of the judge in the show ring. The quickest way to get an impartial opinion about your dog's chances is to ask the advice and opinion of an experienced breeder. In addition, check the breed standard for your dog (which is easily available from the national

Conformity Shows

Conformity shows judge a dog on its looks, movement, and personality, in accordance with the national breed standard. At most shows, one dog and one bitch of each breed win the points, and the rest leave with nothing. Popular breeds obviously attract far larger numbers of entrants than less popular ones, so your dog will stand a better chance if it is in a smaller breed class facing less competition. Dogs are generally ready and eligible to enter these shows from the age of six months, and you can prepare for them by joining a dog-showing class.

Preparation for a show depends largely on the breed of dog (long-haired dogs have more complex grooming requirements than short-haired animals, for example), but all show dogs must learn about discipline in the show ring. Dog-showing classes, which provide instruction about what to expect at a dog show, are useful to both dogs and their owners. The animals must learn to stand still while under scrutiny, and their owners must master the art of show-ring etiquette and behavior. Some breeds must undergo an examination of their bite and an assessment of their flews or tongue—so, before entering a show, it is vital to train your dog to accept this kind of inspection. Smaller dogs must become accustomed to standing on a table, while larger breeds are examined on the floor. Interestingly, the show ring is the one area of the canine world where owners are expected to adapt their behavior to suit their dog, trotting beside their animals at a speed that matches the dog's, for example.

🐾 *This charming Lhasa Apso will be judged against the recognized breed standards for both its physical and temperamental attributes.*

Once in the show ring, dogs are posed in front of the judges, who will examine them both from a distance and close-up. This is followed by a trot around the ring, so that the dogs' movement can be examined. In the final test, dogs walk directly to and from the judges. The dogs can be handled either by their owner or by a professional dog handler who is hired for the show—his or her services add considerably to the cost of showing a dog, but some animals behave better for a professional handler, so the cost may well be justified.

Championship dogs are the product of many months of hard work, and dogs may only qualify to enter championship shows when they have won several lesser shows. The point system is complex, but the "best of breed" accolade is not a title that is awarded lightly. The best-of-breed winners are then entered for the prestigious group award, and the ultimate champion, the "best in show," is chosen from these winners.

🐾 *A Pharaoh Hound should embody alertness, grace, and nobility as well as conforming to exacting standards of all aspects of appearance if he's to impress the judges in competition.*

Obedience Trials

Perhaps you feel that your dog is blessed with brains rather than beauty, or you have noticed that he learns new obedience skills unusually quickly. If you would like to utilize these skills, consider entering obedience trials, which demonstrate a dog's ability to obey his handler and to behave properly at all times. The AKC states that "the basic objective of obedience trials is to produce dogs that have been trained and conditioned always to behave in the home, in public places, and around other dogs." Dogs are trained to sit, stay, lie down, wait, and retrieve at various levels of ability, and the most successful are those animals and owners who share a close understanding.

Obedience competitions are also adapted to another genre of trial, "Heelwork to Music," in which dogs and owners perform obedience routines in time to music. These demonstrations make fantastic viewing, but, clearly, involve many hours of preparation and concentration. In order to enter, you dog must have mastered a high level of obedience training already.

Less musically inclined animals may prefer to demonstrate their nosing skills and enter a tracking contest, which tests a dog's natural ability (enhanced by rigorous training) to recognize and follow a human scent across different terrains and distances.

Entering Obedience Trials

To participate in obedience trials, specialized training classes are essential. The AKC recognize three levels of obedience trials, as follows:

🐾 *Novice Level* Exercises at this level include walking to heel with and without a leash, standing still, and staying or coming on command.

🐾 *Open Level* More complex and demanding exercises include retrieving and performing tasks in which the handler is at a distance from the dog when giving the command.

🐾 *Utility Level* Advanced obedience trials include scent discrimination and "directed" retrieving.

Agility Trials and Other Contests

Some dogs revel in the chance to demonstrate their intelligence and skills in a variety of agility trials. The American Kennel Club runs a comprehensive array of trials with the intention of allowing dogs to show off their willingness to work with their handlers under different conditions. Both handlers and dogs need to be fit to follow the obstacle course (which is up to 200 yards long) and to navigate hoops, hurdles, slaloms, seesaws, and tunnels—all in the quickest time possible. Owners can usually walk the course before the contest, but the dog does not see it until the starting whistle. The course is different each time, which provides a major challenge, and the owner's skill lies in telling the dog to tackle the obstacles in the right order.

Agility training is great fun for both dogs and owners. A great spectator sport, it is the fastest-growing canine sport in the United States and elsewhere.

Gundogs and retrievers are also eligible for the great many contests in field dog trials that test traditional country skills of working animals, such as flushing, pointing, and retrieving. Retrievers, pointers, and spaniels compete in separate events, and variations in the United States include water events and nighttime contests. Field trials are so popular that there is a burgeoning market for dogs bred specifically to compete in such contests. Sheepdog trials offer herding animals the chance to demonstrate their natural skills of finding and herding sheep along a designated route, with points gained for silence, speed, and concentration.

You can find out more about all these contests by contacting your national kennel club, by searching the Internet, or by talking to other owners and breeders. Local dog clubs are an excellent way to become involved, too. Contests sponsored by national kennel clubs are generally open only to purebred dogs, but other organizations also run contests for mixed breeds.

Finally, if you cannot travel to a dog show in person, you can enter a virtual dog show, via the Internet, by emailing photos of your pet to a website such as www2.dogshow.com.

🐾 *To excel in agility trials, a dog must have brains as well as brawn—and, of course, lots of practice. The dog and owner work closely together, so the dog learns signals that help it approach upcoming obstacles at an appropriate speed, for example.*

Further Reading and Sources

Books

Alderton, David, *The Dog Care Manual*, Quarto, 1986.

Bleby, John and Bishop, Gerald, *The Dog's Health from A to Z*, David & Charles, 1986.

Bower, John & Caroline, *The Dog Owner's Problem Solver*, Reader's Digest, 2001.

Cree, John, *Your Dog—A Guide to Solving Behaviour Problems*, Crowood Press, 1996.

Cunliffe, Juliette, *The Encyclopedia of Dog Breeds*, Parragon, 1999.

Fogle, Dr. Bruce, *RSCPCA Complete Dog Care Manual*, DK, 1993.

——, *RSCPA Complete Dog Training Manual*, DK, 1994.

——, *The New Encyclopedia of the Dog*, DK, 2000.

Gerstenfeld, Sheldon, L. with Schultz, Jacque Lynn, *ASPCA Complete Guide to Dogs*, Chronicle Books, 1999.

Hamlyn Encyclopedia of the Dog, Octopus Publishing, 2000.

Hearne, Tina, *The Official RSPCA Pet Guide: Care for Your Dog* Collins, 1990.

Johnson, Frank (ed.), *The Mammoth Book of Dogs*, Robinson Publishing, 1997.

Larkin, Dr Peter, *The Complete Guide to Dog Care*, Lorenz Books, 1999.

Macdonald, David W. (Ed.), *The Complete Book of the Dog*, Pelham Books, 1985.

Meadows, Graham and Flint, Elsa, *The Dog Owner's Handbook* Caxton Editions, 2001.

Morris, Desmond, *Illustrated Dogwatching*, Ebury Press, 1996.

Palmer, Joan, *The Illustrated Encyclopedia of Dog Breeds* Quarto, 1995.

Stockman, Mike, *The New Guide to Dog Breeds*, Hermes House, 1998.

Whitehead, Sarah, *The Dog: A Complete Guide*, Silverdale Books, 2001.

Woodhouse, Barbara, *Dog Training My Way*, Berkley Publishing Group, 1997.

Articles

Drozdick, Ron, *Showing Your Dog In Conformation—A Beginners Guide* (hometown.aol.com/rjdroz/dogsh1.htm).

Moore, Cindy Tittle, *Training your Dog* www.k9web.com

Addresses

The American Kennel Club (AKC)
www.akc.org
The AKC is the national canine authority in the United States, and its Web site provides a wealth of information.

www.akccar.com
The American Kennel Club Companion Animal Recovery program, with details of how to get your dog microchipped.

Westminster Kennel Club
www.westminsterkennelclub.org
With details of America's most prestigious dog show.

The Kennel Club
1-5 Clarges St Piccadilly
London
W1Y 8AB
www.the-kennel-club.org.uk

The National Canine Defence League

www.ncdl.org.uk

THE NCDL campaigns on issues of dog welfare and runs a national network of rehoming centers in Britain. This Web site is highly informative, with a series of links to other canine organizations.

Fédération Cynologique Internationale (FCI)

Place Albert 1er, 13

B-6530 Thuin

Belgium

www.fci.be

The FCI recognizes 330 breeds, and aims to promote purebred dogs. More than eighty national dog institutions are part of this umbrella organization, which also conducts international shows and trials.

Battersea Dogs Home

www.doghome.co.uk

The most famous rehoming center in the U.K. (probably, in the world) has a wide-ranging Web site.

Pets as Therapy

www.petsastherapy.com

Find out how to volunteer your dog in a complementary-care program, for example visiting sick or elderly people in hospital, or to request a visit.

Other Web Sites

These are useful sources of information on everything from choosing a dog, through training, feeding, grooming, and accessorizing.

www.aht.org.uk
www.animalsinmind.org.uk
www.caninebehaviour.co.uk
www.canine-behavior.com
www.canismajor.com
www.k9web.com
www.insideout.co.uk
www.padsonline.org
www.pawsacrossamerica.com
www.thepoop.com
www.un-reel.co.uk

List of Low-shedding Breeds

The following breeds generally shed minimally and are popular choices for households that include allergy sufferers. Note that the allergy sufferer should spend time with dogs of the selected breed before assuming that a dog of that breed will not provoke an allergic reaction.

Basenji, Bedlington Terrier, Bichon Frise, Border Terrier, Cairn Terrier, Chinese Crested, Irish Water Spaniel, Italian Greyhound, Kerry Blue Terrier, Löwchen, Maltese, Poodles (all sizes), Poodle mixes (e.g. Labradoodle), Portuguese Water Dog, Schnauzers (all sizes), Soft-coated Wheaten Terrier.

List of Family-friendly Breeds

The following breeds are among the most popular family dogs and are usually reliable with children. If you have children in your household, it is very important that you choose a reputable breeder and that your puppy is well socialized with children from an early age.

Airedale Terrier, American Cocker Spaniel, Australian Shepherd Dog, Bearded Collie, Bichon Frise, Boston Terrier, Boxer, Bulldog, Cavalier King Charles Spaniel, Collie, Golden Retriever, Keeshond, Labrador Retriever, Pointer, Poodle (Standard), Pug, Newfoundland, Shih Tzu, St. Bernard, Weimaraner.

INDEX

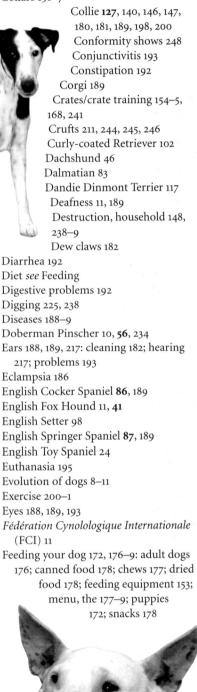

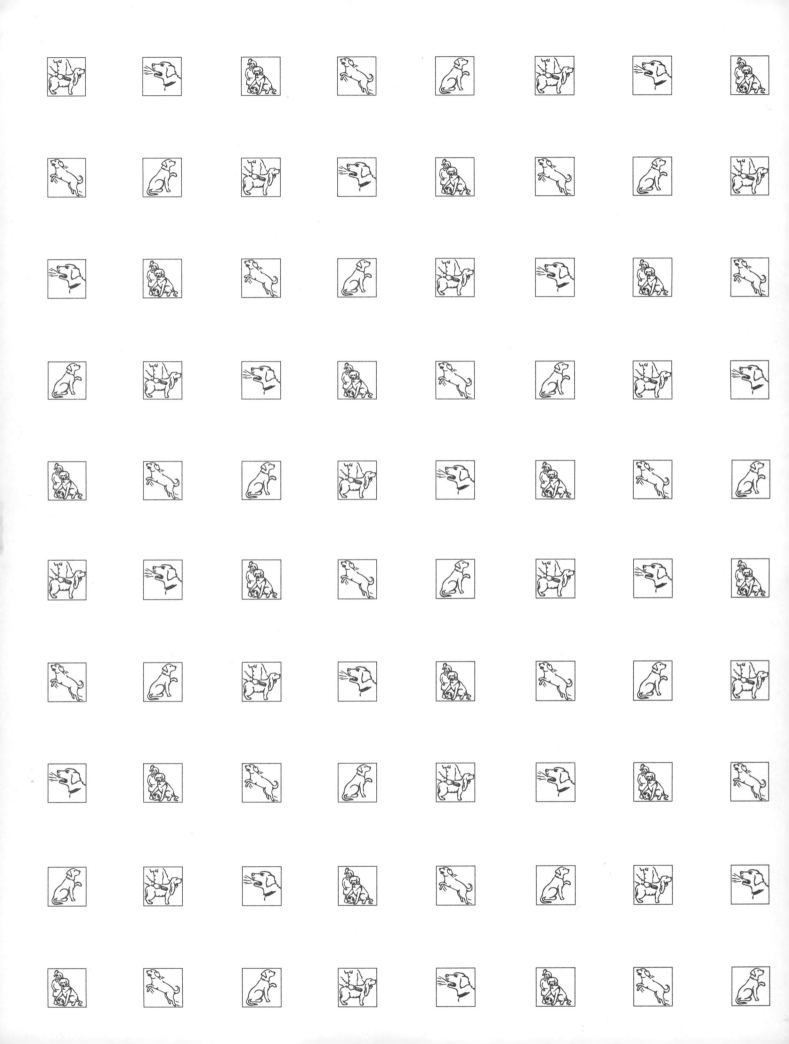